# MAURICE HERZOG

# Annapurna

### Conquest of the First 8,000-metre Peak

*Translated from the French by Nea Morin and
Janel Adam Smith*

**With an Introduction by Chris Boningtor**

D0583232

**TRIAD PALADIN**
**GRAFTON BOOKS**

LONDON GLASGOW
TORONTO SYDNEY AUCKLAND

Triad/paladin
Grafton Books
8 Grafton Street, London W1X 3LA

Published by Triad/Paladin Books 1986

Triad Paperbacks Ltd is an imprint of
Chatto, Bodley Head & Jonathan Cape Ltd and
Grafton Books, a Division of the Collins Publishing Group

First published in Great Britain by
Jonathan Cape 1952

Introduction copyright © Chris Bonington 1986

ISBN 0-586-08512-2

Printed and bound in Great Britain by
Collins, Glasgow

Set in Baskerville

To
Lucien Devies
who  was one of us

# Contents

# List of Maps

*All photographs courtesy M. Ìchac except Camp Iva, courtesy G. Rébuffat*

# Glossary

| | |
|---|---|
| anorak | wind-proof jacket with hood attached. |
| arête | ridge, generally one of the main ridges of a mountain. |
| belay | to secure the climber to a projection with the rope; the projection itself. |
| bergschrund | a large crevasse separating the upper slopes of a glacier from the steeper ice or rock above. |
| cagoule | long anorak descending below the knees. |
| chimney | a narrow vertical gully in rock or ice. |
| chorten | a Buddhist religious monument. |
| col | pass. |
| cornice | overhanging mass of snow or ice along a ridge, shaped like the curling crest of a wave and generally formed by the prevailing wind. |
| couloir | gully or furrow in a mountain side; may be of rock, ice or snow. |
| crampons | metal frame with spikes, fitting the soles of the boots, for use on hard snow or ice. |
| crevasse | a fissure in a glacier, often of great depth. |
| gendarme | rock tower or tooth on a ridge. |
| glissade | to slide down a snow slope, either sitting or standing, using the ice-axe to control speed and direction. |
| ice-fall | a much torn and crevassed portion of a glacier caused by a change of angle or direction in the slope. |

| | |
|---|---|
| line | a thin rope used for rappel or roping down (q.v.). |
| moraine | group of mountains. |
| massif | accumulation of stones and débris brought down by a glacier, which forms ridges. |
| névé | patches of snow, usually above the permanent snow line. |
| pitch | section of difficult ice or rock, anything from 10 to 120 feet in height. |
| piton | metal spike with a ring in the head, which can be driven into rock or ice. |
| rappel or roping down | system of descending steep pitches by means of a rope doubled round a projection. Usually the thin rope known as *line* is used. |
| rope | attaches members of a party together; a party may be referred to as 'a rope'. |
| scree | slope of small loose stones. |
| serac | tower or pinnacle of ice, found mainly in ice-falls. |
| slalom | zigzag descent on skis. |
| snap-link | large metal spring-loaded clip, which can be fixed to the rope or piton. |
| snow-bridge | a layer of snow bridging a crevasse. |
| spur | a rib of rock; sometimes used for an arête (q.v.). |
| traverse | to cross a mountain slope horizontally. |
| tsampa | roasted and ground barley or other grain. |
| verglas | thin coating of ice on rock. |

# Introduction

## by
## *Chris Bonington*

Maurice Herzog's *Annapurna* is as fresh and exciting to read today as it was in 1952 when it was first published in Britain. It marked one of the greatest breakthroughs in the history of mountaineering, for Annapurna was the first peak over that magic height of 8000 metres to be climbed. Before the Second World War greater heights had been attained on Everest and K2, but it's the reaching of a summit that captures the imagination of the public, and in all the attempts on 8000-metre peaks before the War each Expedition had been defeated, though some had come very close to success.

But Maurice Herzog's book is memorable for much more than the scale of the achievement. It captures the very essence of adventure. There is a Gallic élan about the team, only one of whom had been to the Himalayas before. They approached the giants of that range as if they had been peaks of the Mont Blanc massif, with the same enthusiastic naïveté as was seen in the very first Himalayan pioneers of the late nineteenth century. They were undoubtedly going into the unknown, for they were the first mountaineering expedition to be allowed into central Nepal. Their maps were inaccurate and they had the greatest difficulty even in finding Annapurna. Once on the mountain they found themselves in a race against the monsoon and only just snatched the summit in time. They were then caught in an epic descent that led to Herzog losing most of his fingers and toes through frostbite. It is this combination of glorious success and near-disaster that makes the story such a memorable one. But it is the vivid quality of Herzog's writing that makes this book such a great Himalayan classic.

To appreciate fully what the French expedition achieved it is worth setting it in the context of the development of Himalayan climbing prior to the start of the Second World War. The first serious attempt on an 8000-metre peak was made in 1895 by the famous British alpinist, A.F. Mummery. Strangely enough, his attempt demonstrates the way Himalayan climbing has gone full circle, for the drive in climbing development today is towards an alpine style of climbing on the highest mountains. In 1895, however, they were not ready for it.

There were just three in the team, together with two Gurkha porters, and they were attempting Nanga Parbat, at that time the most accessible of all the 8000-metre peaks. They first looked at the huge Rupal Face of the mountain but dismissed it as too difficult, and subsequently crossed the Mazeno Pass to reach the Diamir Glacier. The team tackled a rock spur on the face which, over eighty years later, the famous Austrian climber, Reinhold Messner, was to descend after making the first ascent of the Rupal Face. Mummery, however, was discovering from direct experience the problems of altitude and the colossal scale of the Himalayas. He retreated, but didn't give up and, with the two Gurkha porters, crossed the Diamir Col to explore the northern side. This was the last time he was ever seen and the cause of his death is as great a mystery as that of Mallory and Irvine on Everest in 1924.

The next attempt on a major peak was in 1902 with another small British expedition led by Oscar Eckenstein. This time their target was K2, the second highest mountain in the world. Once again they didn't really know what they were taking on, and it is not surprising that they only reached a height of around 6600 metres. An interesting aside on the expedition is that one of the members was Alesteir Crowley, who achieved considerable notoriety as a Satanist. On this expedition he threatened one of the members with a loaded pistol when the unfortunate man talked of retreat.

The two world wars marked very definite stages in the development of mountaineering, as of so many other aspects of human evolution and history. The post-First World War expeditions saw the beginning of the use of systematic siege tactics on Himalayan peaks, started on the north side of Everest by British expeditions and pursued, particularly by the Germans, on Kangchenjunga and Nanga Parbat.

The tactics involved the setting up of a series of camps, the use of fixed ropes in places, and the development of a corps of specialist high-altitude porters. On Everest oxygen was used for the first time in 1922. There were, in all, seven British expeditions to Everest between the two wars. Their approach was through Tibet, since Nepal was closed to foreigners. On first reconnaissance they discovered that the most obvious route was by the North Col and all subsequent expeditions attempted this route. They were beaten by a combination of altitude, snow conditions, and the rock structure of the upper part of the North East Ridge. Of these seven British expeditions, three reached a height of over 8000 metres. In 1924 Mallory and Irvine, using oxygen, achieved at least 8600 metres, where Noel Odell last saw them. It seems unlikely that they made it to the top, but this can never be totally discounted. On the same expedition Norton, without oxygen, climbed to 8350 metres, and in 1933 three climbers reached around the same height. But there seemed to be an invisible barrier stopping any of these pre-War expeditions getting all the way to the top. It was probably a combination of factors: the poor equipment of the time, bad luck with the weather and snow conditions, and the fact that not enough was known about high-altitude climbing in this period.

Everest was very much a British preserve, and so climbers of other countries had to look elsewhere. Only three 8000-metre peaks were attempted: K2, Kangchenjunga, the third highest mountain in the world, and Nanga Parbat. German and Austrian expeditions were the most active, which is not surprising since during this period climbers from these two countries were making technical advances well ahead of those of almost any other nationality, except perhaps the Italians.

There were two German expeditions to Kangchenjunga, reaching a height of 7700 metres on the North East Spur, and three expeditions to Nanga Parbat. On the 1934 expedition to the latter, led by Willi Merkl, he, Welzenbach and Wieland reached the base of the summit pyramid at 7848 metres. They were only 2 J metres below the top but dropped back to where the other two Germans and eleven Sherpas had pitched the top camp. The following day a fierce storm broke, and in the desperate struggle to retreat over the subsequent days Merkl, Wieland, Welzenbach and six Sherpas died from cold and exhaustion. It was the worst ever accident in the Himalayas, and emphasized the hidden dangers of these technically easy but very long and complex routes from which it is almost impossible to retreat during severe storms. Herzog's team were to have a similar experience in 1950. There was another German expedition led by Paul Bauer in 1938, but they had consistent bad weather and made little impression on the mountain.

Perhaps the boldest, and certainly the most elegant, pre-Second World War expeditions were on K2. Since Eckenstein's first visit the Italians had made three reconnaissance expeditions up the Baltoro but, in 1938, it was the Americans who made the first serious attempt, with a compact expedition of only five climbers led by Charles Houston accompanied by six Sherpa high-altitude porters. Houston had been on Nanda Devi in 1936 when Bill Tilman and Noel Odell reached its 7816-metre summit. It was the highest peak to be climbed before the War, and in many ways the attempt was in the idiom of the modern compact expedition.

Houston, unaffected by the traditions and state of mind that inevitably influenced expeditioners from the Alpine-based countries, was inspired to tackle K2 by Bill Tilman's approach to climbing. His team was very nearly successful as their high point was 7924 metres, just near the foot of the summit pyramid, on a climb that was undoubtedly the most difficult technically that had been achieved in the Himalayas up to that date. (Forty-two years later, Peter Boardman, one of Britain's most outstanding modern climbers, was to be most impressed by the difficulty of a section that has been named 'Houston's Chimney'. His 1980 expedition was able to get only a little higher than that first attempt.)

A second American assault was made in 1939 by a completely different expedition led by the German-born Fritz Wiessner. He was probably the most talented of all the pre-War mountaineers, having pioneered extremely hard rock climbs in Saxony and the Eastern Alps, and having been a member of the 1932 Nanga Parbat Expedition. Unfortunately, however, his team members were comparatively inexperienced. In spite of this, climbing with his Sherpas he pushed the route up to the base of the pyramid and very nearly managed to reach the reasonably easy ground that would have taken him to the summit, but the climbing had proved too difficult for his Sherpa companio Pasang Kikuli, who insisted on retreating.

The only other climber on the mountain at this stage was Dudley Wolfe, a rich American who had, in part, funded the expedition. He was one of the least experienced members of the team and probably should never have been allowed to get up to the penultimate camp (VII). When Wiessner and Kikuli staggered down to his camp, frostbitten and exhausted, he elected to stay there by himself to await their return for another attempt. It was a lunatic and, in the event, disastrous decision, since, unknown to Wiessner, Jack Durrance, another member of the team, had ordered the Sherpas to strip all the camps below Camp VI.

Wiessner and Kikuli only just managed to reach base camp. They sent Sherpas back up to bring Wolfe down but by this time he was too weak to move. The weather now broke and Wolfe and three of the Sherpas, including Pasang Kikuli, who had returned to the mountain in this desperate rescue bid, lost their lives. Inevitably there were recriminations, with Durrance, who had made a series of very controversial decisions, blaming Fritz Wiessner for the disaster. It is only in comparatively recent times that Wiessner has been fully exonerated.

This was the last pre-War expedition to the 8000-metre peaks. It demonstrated, as did several other of these expeditions, just how dangerous Himalayan-climbing can be. It certainly has become no safer over the years. In my own experience of 8000-metre peaks, someone has been killed on every single expedition. It's a frightening toll which throws into perspective the achievement of all the members of the French Annapurna expedition who, after Maurice Herzog and Louis Lachenal reached the summit, managed to get them back down despite their state of exhaustion and a raging storm.

Climbing on the Himalayan giants is like walking a shaking tight-rope with the potential of disaster constantly with you. So why do it? For the allure of danger, the mystery of the unknown, the sheer beauty of the mountains around you, and the drive of ego. All of this is captured by Maurice Herzog in *Annapurna*. It is what makes the book one of the great classics of expedition literature.

# Foreword

The whole of this book has been dictated at the American Hospital at Neuilly where I am still having rather a bad time.

The basis of the narrative is, of course, my memory of all that happened. In so far as the record is comprehensive and exact, that is due to the Expedition's log which Marcel Ichac so faithfully kept—an essential document, sometimes written up at the very moment of action. Louis Lachenal's private journal, and the details supplied by all my friends, have been of the greatest possible use. So this book is the work of the whole party.

The text, often colloquial in style, has been revised and put into shape by my brother Gerard Herzog, the sharer of my earliest mountain pleasures, as indeed of my earliest experiences of life. If it had not been for the confidence I had in his rendering, and for the encouragement he gave me day by day, I doubt if I should ever have been able to finish my task.

The name of Robert Boyer, who did so much for our Expedition, does not figure in this record and yet his understanding friendship was a tonic in my darkest hours.

This is the first time I have written a book; I never realized before what a long business it was. Sometimes the job was almost too much for me, but I have undertaken it because I wanted to set down, on behalf of all those who went with me, the story of a terrible adventure which we survived only by what still seems to me an incredible series of miracles.

The following pages record the actions of men at grips with Nature at her most pitiless, and tell of their sufferings, hopes and joys.

As I conceived to be my duty, I have given a plain truthful account of what happened, and have tried—so far as lay within my powers—to bring out its human aspect, and convey the extraordinary psychological atmosphere in which everything took place.

All the nine members of the Expedition will have more than one reason for cherishing this record. Together we knew toil, joy and pain. My fervent wish is that the nine of us who were united in face of death should remain fraternally united for life.

In overstepping our limitations, in touching the extreme boundaries of man's world, we have come to know something of its true splendour. In my worst moments of anguish I seemed to discover the deep significance of existence of which till then I had been unaware. I saw that it was better to be true than to be strong. The marks of the ordeal are apparent on my body. I was saved and I had won my freedom. This freedom, which I shall never lose, has given me the assurance and serenity of a man who has fulfilled himself. It has given me the rare joy of loving that which I used to despise. A new and splendid life has opened out before me.

In this narrative we do more than record our adventures, we bear witness: events that seem to make no sense may sometimes have a deep significance of their own. There is no other justification for an *acte gratuit*.

Hôpital Américan de Paris
*June 1951*

# Preface

The conquest of Annapurna has stirred up general interest which is still increasing. It was, beyond all question, one of the greatest adventures of our times, and most nobly carried out.

Maurice Herzog and his companions have crowned a long series of attempts and successes, by climbing not only the highest summit yet attained by man, but also the first summit of over 8000 metres, the first to be climbed of the very highest mountains of the world.

With this victory, achieved at a first attempt and in an unknown region, they have succeeded in an enterprise which the most experienced Himalayan travellers had considered impossible. That outstanding English climber, the late Frank Smythe, who had been on five Himalayan expeditions, had conquered Mount Kamet and had attained the highest point (8500 metres) reached on Everest, had declared that 'Mountaineering in the Himalaya presents such difficulties that, as far as one can see, no expedition will ever succeed in climbing one of the twelve highest peaks at a first attempt.'

This, however, is exactly what the Annapurna Expedition of 1950 achieved.

Victory in the Himalaya is a collective victory, for the party as a whole. Every member of the expedition, each in his place, whether more or less favoured by circumstances, has been worthy of the trust placed in him; one and all carried out with unswerving devotion their duty of bringing the two injured climbers safely down. We give them in full measure the gratitude they have so richly earned; but at the same time we realize that the victory of the whole party was also, and above all, the victory of its leader.

The other members of the party have been the first to confirm the wisdom of our choice of a leader by the affection, and even reverence, in which they hold him. But it was not the Himalaya that revealed Maurice Herzog to us, for his past record had convinced us that we had entrusted the Expedition to the most valiant of them all. The Himalaya did, however, provide him with the opportunity—ultimately, alas, in the most appalling circumstances—to be the very soul of a great adventure, and this he accomplished in the most moving and magnificent way.

What a range of gifts he has shown! His intelligence and character opened many fields of activity to him. His grasp of the practical side of life debarred him neither from the poetry of Mallarmé nor from the Pensées of Pascal. He was as much at home in a city office as on one of the great Italian ridges of Mont Blanc. His great goodness of heart, which won him so many friends, did not prevent him from taking firm decisions, when necessary, or forming a clear-sighted judgment of people. A level head controlled the natural exuberance of an abounding vitality.

The facts speak for themselves. His remarkable physical fitness throughout the Expedition, which surpassed even that of Lionel Terray and Louis Lachenal, 'the two steam-engines', considered by all to be in a class by themselves, was the reflection of his will and of the faith in victory which ne inspired in everybody, even in all of us at home, so many thousands of miles away.

Spending himself to the limit, reserving for himself the hardest tasks, deriving his authority from the example he set, always in the vanguard, he made victory possible. That last long stage to the top bears the stamp of his judgment and determination. The natural thing would have been to establish a sixth camp, but Maurice had the vision to realize that one more day spent on the climb might cost them the summit, and so he decided to make an all-out dash.

All France knows the price that had to be paid. And Maurice faced his ordeal with a resolution and courage perhaps even more admirable than that he displayed on the climb. He showed an utter disregard of self. It was typical of him that, as they emerged from the crevasse where they had bivouacked, his first thought should be for the others, and his first words a request that they should leave him behind, and increase their own chances of safety.

The endless return march in the monsoon rains, the succession of amputations, the long months of immobility and their accompaniment of pain—from all these he has emerged at last, standing on his own feet again, with a heightened simplicity and moral sensibility, as though purified by fire. It is with a sense of wonder and fulfilment that we see him turning again towards life as towards renewal, seeing more good in it because he himself is a better man.

And this book which we now hold in our hands is a triumph without parallel, a triumph of the heart and of the creative understanding. It is not like any other book. It reads like a novel, but it is truth itself, truth almost too elusive to grasp or to express. Its easy familiar tone, its straight-forward presentation of people and events, give it a striking authenticity. For the first time, we are all members of a Himalayan expedition, we are all present beside the leader and the rest of the party. You are taking us with you, too, my dear Maurice, to the very end—to the end of the ordeal, to the end of an almost unbelievable experience.

It is impossible to read these pages without being overwhelmed by the sensitive awareness, and the kindliness, that went with so much courage and such dogged determination.

Thank you for being so well aware that one can put aside modesty without becoming vain. If it were not so, then every advance of the spirit would go unrecorded. It takes courage to draw the veil from those moments when the individual approaches most nearly to the universal.

That wonderful world of high mountains, dazzling in their rock and ice, acts as a catalyst. It suggests the infinite, but it is not the infinite. The heights only give us what we ourselves bring to them. Climbing is a means of self-expression. Its justification lies in the men it develops, its heroes and its saints. This was the essential truth which a whole nation grasped when it offered its praise and admiration to the conquerors of Annapurna. Man overcomes himself, affirms himself, and realizes himself in the struggle towards the summit, towards the absolute. In the extreme tension of the struggle, on the frontier of death, the universe disappears and drops away beneath us. Space, time, fear, suffering, no longer exist. Everything then becomes quite simple. As on the crest of a wave, or in the heart of a cyclone, we are strangely calm—not the calm of emptiness, but the heart of action itself. Then we know with absolute certainty that there is something indestructible in us, against which nothing shall prevail.

A flame so kindled can never be extinguished. When we have lost everything it is then we find ourselves most rich. Was it this certainty that all was well that gave Maurice Herzog the steady courage to endure his ordeal?

The summit is at our feet. Above the sea of golden clouds other summits pierce the blue and the horizon extends to infinity.

The summit we have reached is no longer the Summit. The fulfilment of oneself—is that the true end, the final answer?

LUCIEN DEVIES
*Président du Comité de l'Himalaya*
*et de la Fédération Française de la Montagne*

# 1

## *Preparations*

The day fixed for our departure was close at hand. Should we ever manage to get everything done? The entire personnel of the French Alpine Club was mobilized. The lights burned late into the night at No 7 rue La Boétie; there was a tremendous sense of excitement, and the Himalayan Committee sat nearly every evening. At nine o'clock, punctual to the minute, these people, upon whom at this stage the fate of the Expedition depended, would arrive, and vital decisions were taken at their secret councils: it is the Committee which settles the budget, foresees contingencies, weighs up the risk and, finally, chooses the members of the expedition.

The names of the members of the party had been known for a few days. I was to have a splendid team. The youngest member was the tall and aristocratic Jean Couzy, aged 27; he had been a brilliant student at the École Polytechnique and was now an aeronautical engineer. He had not long been married but had not hesitated to leave his young wife, Lise. A quiet man, with a far-away look in his eyes, he always seemed to be turning over in his mind the latest problems of electronics.

Couzy's usual climbing partner, Marcel Schatz, was going with us too. He was two years older than his friend, of a heavier build, and always well turned out, for the very good reason that he was manager of one of his father's prosperous tailoring establishments. He liked efficient organization, order and method. Whenever a bivouac was needed on a climb he was always the one to set to and get it ready. As he was unmarried, and an ardent climber, there was nothing to prevent him from spending all his holidays in the mountains; although he lived in Paris, and so at some distance from his paradise, he was rarely to be found in town at week-ends,

Louis Lachenal had been an amateur, climbing for his own pleasure, until he became, a few years ago, an instructor at the National School of Ski-ing and Mountaineering. To the inhabitants of Chamonix he ranked as a 'foreigner', which means that he was not a native of the valley—he came from Annecy. In spite of this dubious origin, as it seemed to the local people, who are jealous of their mountains, he had succeeded, along with Gaston Rébuffat and Lionel Terray, in being admitted to the Company of Guides of Chamonix, a body unique both for the quality and number of its members. He was of medium height, with a piercing eye, and in conversation could administer a very pretty repartee. He loved exaggeration in everything, and his judgments could be devastating. Absolutely honest with himself, he was perfectly ready, if occasion arose, to own himself in the wrong. As often as they could manage it he and Lionel Terray would go off together, as amateurs, to enjoy themselves on the finest climbs in the Alps.

Lionel Terray, although a native of Grenoble, was also a Chamonix guide, and he and Lachenal formed a crack partnership: they were a couple of regular steam-engines. Like his friend, Terray had a weakness for dogmatic and exaggerated statements, and there was continuous rivalry between them to see who could go one better than the other. Terray was unbeatable and would never give in. Although the son of a doctor, and a highly cultured man, he liked to be thought a well-meaning tough, all brawn and nothing more. It was pure love of the mountains that brought him to climbing, and he was entirely happy as a guide. During the war he farmed a holding at Les Houches; anyone who came to help him there had to be fond of mountains and of hard work—and he measured their capacities by his own. He went over to Canada last year to teach the new French method of ski-ing, and brought back some notable additions to his repertory of curses. 'Just now,' he wrote to me, 'I am ski-ing *en tabernacle*'—ski-ing like hell. He was in Canada at the moment and would get back only a week before we sailed. Until then everything had to be done by letter.

Gaston Rébuffat had a scandalous origin for a mountaineer, and even worse for a guide. He was born at the seaside! It would take the Company of Guides many years to live this down. All the same, it was on the cliffs of the Calanques, between Marseilles and Cassis, that he did his first climbs. He was the tallest man of the party, towering over the rest of us by nearly a head. He had done all the finest expeditions in the Alps, and thought nothing of going straight on from one big climb to another without a rest between. His young wife, Françoise, and his daughter seldom saw him during the season's round of Chamonix, Cortina d'Ampezzo, Zermatt and so on. He was away in Italy giving a series of lectures, but I had asked him to return at once.

These men formed the assault parties, and no better men could be found in France. No one disputed this—not even secretly. If a vote had been taken among climbers, the same names would have been put forward.

Nor was there any question about our camera-man: Marcel Ichac indeed was one of our trump cards. He had already been to the Himalaya, in 1936, and had taken part in a great many expeditions. As soon as he arrived I should have the benefit of his advice, but just now he was in Greenland with Paul-Emile Victor, and immediately afterwards he would be off to the USA to film the world ski championships, at Aspen, arriving back only a few days before we left for India. He would have several jobs to do. Not only would he film the expedition, he would be responsible for everything connected with photography. We should each have a camera, but the maintenance, supply and care of all the films would be his business. Collecting and documenting our scientific observations would be another responsibility of this intelligent, enterprising and lively-minded man. Ichac had managed to solve one of the climber's biggest problems—a wife is always a risk!—by marrying another climber.

We hoped Jacques Oudot would be our MO. He was a first-class surgeon, and we should all be able to treat ourselves to the luxury of a fracture. But he was up to his eyes in work, and had very prudently given orders that he must not be disturbed at the Salpêtrière hospital where he performed vascular surgical operations under the direction of his chief, Mondor. The things he dared to do appeared so incredible to me that I was always asking him, 'And d'you mean to say he didn't die?' Simplicity of ignorance! Anyway, my questions about surgery always seemed to cause him great amusement. There are not many surgeons who climb, and I knew from personal experience how invaluable Oudot would be to us.

'Oudot, have you made up your mind?'

'Just now I am very busy.' His shrewd little eyes blinked cagily. 'I'll tell you tomorrow,' he would promise.

This performance had been going on for a week; Devies and I were on tenterhooks. Two days before our departure we finally dragged from him the longed-for 'yes'. His job would be to keep us all in good health, to deal with emergency ailments and accidents, and also to keep me constantly informed about the physical condition of the party and their degree of acclimatization. In addition he would exercise his skill upon the local populations.

There was the thorny question: the liaison officer. Our preference was for a Frenchman whom we should be likely to get on with and to understand. Robert Tézenas du Montcel had spoken to us, a few days previously, of a young diplomat at the Embassy in New Delhi. A lot would be required of him: as well as English he must know and speak Hindustani and the principal local languages—Gurkhali and Tibetan. He would have to arrange all the transport and would also be responsible for good diplomatic relations with the Nepalese authorities in the capital of Katmandu as well as in the regions through which we should be travelling. Francis de Noyelle seemed the ideal person. Furthermore he was entirely at home in the mountains, being himself an ardent climber—an indispensable requirement in our party.

Noyelle was the only one I did not know, but his parents and his sister gave me such a clear picture of him that I had the feeling I was dealing with a friend. He was a well-built, self-reliant, keen-eyed young man, accustomed to dealing with the local high-ups. Not long ago he made a trip to Katmandu with Monsieur Daniel Lévi, our Ambassador to India and Nepal, who enjoys considerable prestige in these countries. He took part in the negotiations which succeeded in obtaining the rarely granted permission to penetrate far into Nepalese territory. In India, Professor Rahaul, who had himself already taken part in several Himalayan Expeditions, would help Noyelle in Darjeeling to recruit the Sherpas[1] whom for the most part he knew personally.

That was our party—all tough chaps, all men of marked individuality and striking character. All of them ardently wished to go to the Himalaya which we had talked about for so many years. Lachenal put it in a nutshell: 'We'd go if we had to crawl there.'

Let me put it clearly on record that their zeal for the adventure was entirely disinterested. From the start every one of them knew that nothing belonged to him and that he must expect nothing on his return.[2] Their only motive was pure idealism; this was what linked together mountaineers so unlike in character and of such widely dissimilar origins.

In the days remaining before our departure Schatz and I went round to hustle up all the firms supplying our equipment. Our arms were sore from all the injections we had to undergo: yellow fever, cholera, smallpox. But who cared?

---

[1] Sherpas are Buddhists from a high valley in the east of Nepal. They are mountaineers and are semi-professionals on Himalayan expeditions. They are engaged by contract.

[2] Every source of income, without exception, will go to form a fund for subsequent expeditions.

4

On the evening of March 28th the Himalayan Committee met for the last time with all the members of the Expedition present. Lucien Devies, the President and chief promoter of the Expedition, outlined a history of Himalayan achievement and specified just what he expected of us:

'The Himalaya, by their size,[3] fully merit the title of "the third pole". Twenty-two expeditions of different nationalities have tried to conquer an "eight-thousander". Not one has succeeded.'

Then he defined our objectives:

'Dhaulagiri, 8167 metres [26,795 feet], or Annapurna 8075 metres [26,493 feet] in the very heart of Nepal. Should these prove impossible—and that would be no disgrace—"consolation" summits ought to be attained. With its six tons of equipment and provisions the Expedition must cross the Indian frontier and penetrate into hitherto forbidden Nepalese territory. After a march of three weeks up into the high valleys, the party will arrive at Tukucha, the Chamonix of Nepal, which enjoys a remarkable geographical situation. It lies between Dhaulagiri and Annapurna. Until now Himalayan expeditions have picked objectives in regions already known and explored. But we have absolutely no information about our two "eight-thousanders". We know nothing about the approach routes, and the maps at the Expedition's disposal are sketchy, and practically useless above a certain height. So that as soon as the party reach Tukucha, their headquarters, they must begin by reconnoitring the two massifs. Only after they have become familiar with the lie of the land, and have drawn up a plan of attack, will they be able to launch the attempt. . .'

Devies went on to say that investigations must be carried out—medical, geological, ethnographical, meteorological and geographical.[4]

Clearly it was a tremendous undertaking; but I had complete faith in my colleagues. Our party was the best that could be assembled, and we all appreciated each other's individual qualities. Our stores and equipment further increased our confidence. French industry had made an exceptional effort, and in very few months had produced equipment which combined the maximum of strength, lightness and convenience.

[3]The chain of the Himalaya extends for about 1800 miles. It includes something like 200 summits of over 7000 metres (23,000 feet), and 14 over 8000 metres (26,000 feet).

[4]The geological investigations of the Expedition have been communicated to the Académie des Sciences (meeting of April 23rd, 1951). With the aid of the information collected the general lines of structure of the Central Himalaya have been traced.

The dull and dreary office in which we were meeting took on that evening an imposing and solemn air. There was nothing to add. After this silence we should be launched upon extraordinary adventures which we could not as yet picture but of which as mountaineers we could form an idea. The bridges were now down between those grave, judicious persons on the one side, and, on the other, the bronzed and vigorous members of the expedition.

Then suddenly Lucien Devies stood up. After a moment, and carefully enunciating each syllable, he said:

'This, gentleman, is the oath which, like your predecessors in 1936, you must take: "I swear upon my honour to obey the leader of the Expedition in everything in which he may command me regarding the Expedition." '

Mountaineers don't much care for ceremonial. My colleagues stood up, feeling both awkward and impressed. What were they supposed to do?

'Now gentlemen . . . your turn Matha, since you are the senior'— and he turned towards Marcel Ichac.

Henry de Ségogne, who had led the 1936 expedition, and had spared neither pains nor advice to help the next one get started, was equal to the occasion. 'Come on, Matha,' said Ségogne. Terray's almost timid answer could be heard at the same time as Ichac's. In turn my colleagues swore to obey the leader of the Expedition in all circumstances, especially at moments of crisis. They were pledging their lives, possibly, and they knew it. They all put themselves completely in my hands. I should have liked to say a few words, but I just couldn't do it. There is no feeling to equal this complete confidence of one man in another, because it is the sum of so many other feelings put together. In that moment our partnership was born. It was for me to keep it alive.

The Committee acted in princely fashion—if they gave me all the responsibility, they also gave me an entirely free hand. As this memorable session drew to a close I felt very sad about one matter: Pierre Allain, that great figure of French mountaineering, who had done so much for us, would not be coming. His health, which had been undermined during the war, no longer allowed him to undertake long expeditions. I knew, better than anyone, just how much the Himalaya meant to him, and tonight was for him a Paradise Lost. But his face showed no hint of it. He even smiled, for he was delighted to see us set off. Far away in Asia we should often think of the friend who was fated to stay behind.

6

# 2

## The Himalaya

•

The moment we took off, Oudot, who was dead tired, fell asleep. He hardly woke until we reached Delhi, though from time to time he would open an eye to grumble: 'Damn these stops!' Or sometimes to ask Ichac, 'How's my little mouse? Take care she doesn't escape.' This particular little mouse was going to be a godsend to Indian doctors. It belonged to a strain of which pure specimens, no longer to be found in India, are essential in the study of certain types of malaria.

India at last! There was a perfect moment when, looking at the view through a window, I could conjure up the ancient city of Mohenjo Daro, the invasion of the Aryans, and that earliest monument of mankind, the Vedas.

Our Ambassador, Monsieur Daniel Lévi, and the staff of the Embassy at New Delhi were on the landing-ground at Palem to welcome us and help us with all the official complications. At the Indian Customs they had never before seen an expedition arrive lock, stock and barrel by plane.

'I wish to see a complete list, in English, of everything you are taking with you, with details of the weight, value, size . . .'

'But there are more than 50,000 items!'

Without so much as listening the official added: 'You will be admitted in transit. Upon your return you must bring everything through the Customs again.'

But hadn't we got to eat while in Nepal? And suppose we were to lose or give away a gun or a tent . . .

It was clearly a difficult situation. With an accommodating smile the Customs officer made a new suggestion:

'Your equipment can all be impounded for the duration of your expedition. It will come to no harm!'

'And what about us?'

'You can proceed to Nepal. You can pick up your stuff on the way back.'

I was in despair at the way things were shaping. 'The Himalaya?' our Customs man seemed to be asking himself, as he rolled his eyes, 'All very well for pilgrims—'

We certainly were pilgrims, I thought to myself, pilgrims to the mountains. But I dared not interrupt the reflection in which he was plunged.

'Well . . .' (I felt sure everything was about to be settled), 'now in this case I shall impound the aeroplane as well.'

I turned round to see whether our pilot had fainted.

Like everything else in India the problem would be solved, provided there was no hurry. Ichac kept right away in a corner, for he is very quick-tempered and didn't trust himself. He took his revenge by making a sketch of the Customs officer's skull.

'A perfect geometrical figure, but difficult to express as an equation,' Couzy whispered.

Eventually we cleared the Customs after two days of negotiation, and proceeded to load up our gear at Old Delhi station. It was no light job. The work was done at night, with lamps throwing a faint light upon the dismal rows of stalls; acetylene lamps with their bright, blinding glare, flickering and smoky oil lamps, lit up the passing crowds, and threw fantastic shadows everywhere. I was nauseated by the foul smell. Everywhere was an infernal din, and I was constantly in danger of being knocked over by bicycle-drawn rickshaws.

Rébuffat and Terray were given the job of accompanying and looking after all the equipment that could not go by air, while the rest of us took the plane for Lucknow. We were hardly in our places when three magnificent Sikhs got in, colossal figures, with a noble bearing and flowing beards. They wore enormous turbans, and with their swarthy complexions and deep-set eyes they looked very fine indeed. Beside them we felt like little boys in shorts.

'Gosh! They're the pilots,' exclaimed Oudot. We were all amazed by their competence, and by their smooth piloting during our short journey from Delhi to Lucknow.

At Lucknow I met for the first time Angdawa, the youngest of our future team of Sherpas, and his chief, Angtharkay. The rest of them I met at Nautanwa, which is the last straggling Indian village before Nepal and the terminus of the narrow gauge railway. It thrilled me to see these little yellow men, with their plump muscles, so different from the lankier Indians. These Sherpas, whose loyalty and unselfishness is proverbial, would in fact be our climbing partners, and I should see to it that they were treated as such: their equipment and their well-being would be exactly the same as our own, and their safety, like that of my friends, would always be in the forefront of my thoughts.

8

Angtharkay, their sirdar or chief, was very energetic, and assumed undisputed authority over his companions and the porters. He was a convinced and ardent Buddhist, and his moral influence with them was considerable. The other Sherpas—Dawathondup, Angtsering, known as Pansy, Sarki, Phutharkay, Aila, Angdawa, Ajeeba—had all had a certain amount of experience. The expedition was to give them plenty of opportunity to show what they were capable of.

Beneath a torrid sun we got out at Nautanwa, where we met our new Sherpa friends. The four-and-a-half tons of our equipment were added to the one-and-a-half tons of food which, thanks to Noyelle's foresight, was already waiting for us at the railway station. On April 5th we were at last admitted within the gates of Nepal. Nepal lies higher than any other country except Tibet, and numbers within its forbidden frontiers eight of the fourteen highest peaks in the world. This country of 7 million inhabitants straddles the great Himalayan rampart for nearly 400 miles, and is 120 miles across. Its Indian border, the Terai—the zone lying below the foothills—is overgrown with tropical vegetation. It is an astonishing region, sometimes sweltering under a burning sun that parches everything, sometimes flooded by torrential monsoon rains.

The Nepalese—Buddhist in the north, Hindu in the south, but all suspicious of foreigners—have prospered within the shelter of this formidable natural fortress. They have great respect for tradition and have preserved intact the spiritual estate of their forefathers. From these hill-people we have learned to expect upstanding character and readiness to rise to a great occasion.

The jeep took us along a dusty stony road. About six miles away was Kapilavastu (now called Ruminn-Dei)—a simple and not particularly impressive place, at the foot of Kipling's beloved Siwaliks. There, thousands of years ago, a man was born whose youth was traditionally as full of poetry as his whole life was of wisdom. Gautama Buddha spent his early years in this country which now lay before my eyes, and he who had founded one of the wisest and most beautiful of all religions had perhaps trodden the paths we were now following.

At Butwal, the first village in Nepal, which marks the end of the great plain of the Ganges and the beginning of the mountains, we had to get our money changed, for in these mountainous regions, particularly in the remoter districts, the natives have no faith in notes and insist upon silver, the standard coinage in most Asiatic countries.

Lachenal and Terray, who formed the advance-party, inspected

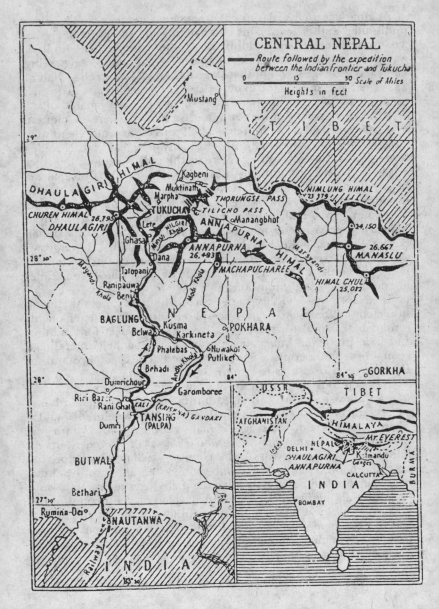

CENTRAL NEPAL

Route followed by the expedition
between the Indian frontier and Tukucha

0    15    30  Scale of Miles
Heights in feet

the wretched horses brought out for them. The preparations of the main party dragged on endlessly beneath a burning sun. The loads were being gradually made up to weigh one mound each, 80 lb., and then distributed to some 200 coolies.

'Bara Sahib, umbrella, please?'

A fine-looking Nepalese obligingly offered me his umbrella—a protection in these countries against sun as well as rain—and in this casual way I made the acquaintance of G.B.Rana, who soon became a real friend. G.B., as we all called him, was deputed by the Maharajah of Nepal to accompany the Expedition wherever it went. For many years he had served as an officer in Gurkha battalions, crack units of the British Army.

Suddenly we heard wild galloping hooves drumming on the cracked sun-baked ground. The two horses belonging to Lachenal and Terray, all in a froth and without their saddles, rushed towards us from the gorges of the Gandaki[1] and made for their stables.

'Real climbers, you see,' Lachenal explained later, with dignity, 'real climbers find such artificial means of transport entirely obnoxious.'

On the evening of this first march G.B. conducted us to a rustic rest-house.

'It belongs to His Highness,' he informed me deferentially.

'We are indeed honoured.'

But on this point the Maharajah is rather like the Marquis of Carabas; later we were to realize that in Nepal everything belongs personally to the Maharajah.

On the 10th the main body of the Expedition reached Tansing, the capital of the province, and stopped for three days. Here we had to reorganize, check the loads and recruit fresh coolies. Ichac was down with dysentery and we left him in camp in the care of the Sherpas. The rest of us—as soon as camp was pitched and roped off to keep away the crowd of sight seers climbed the hill overlooking the village from which the distant mountains were visible. It was a wonderful moment at last to set eyes on the object of our dreams!

We had all read a great many books on the Himalaya, and had talked endlessly with our friends who had been to the Karakoram in 1936; we had put the most ridiculous questions to Ichac, the only Himalayan veteran among us; everyone had formed his

[1] A large river, a tributary of the Ganges, which we were to follow to Tukucha (map, p. 10).

own personal idea of these mountains. Were we going to be disappointed?

In reality the sight which awaited us at the top of the hill far exceeded anything we had imagined. At the first glance we could see nothing but filmy mist; but looking more closely we could make out, far away in the distance, a terrific wall of ice rising above the mist to an unbelievable height, and blocking the horizon to the north for hundreds and hundreds of miles. This shining wall looked colossal, without fault or defect, with seven-thousand-metre peaks leading up to the eight-thousanders, and we were quite overwhelmed by the magnificence and grandeur of the sight. This was the Himalaya, our promised land, and from now onwards we would carry this vision with us wherever we went.

The problem now seemed quite simple: to reach the mountains as quickly as possible and come to grips with them. As we lay in our tents that evening, we all did a lot of thinking.

We left Tansing in two detachments, the advance-party, consisting of Lachenal and Terray, going on a day ahead of the main body. Soon after we had started, about noon, I suddenly saw a wild figure loping towards me with long strides. With a shock I recognized Terray *en tenue népalaise*—that is to say, in a minimum of clothes—his head shaven, his face gleaming with sweat. He looked very angry, and was vigorously brandishing his ice-axe so that everyone stood respectfully aside to let him pass.

What on earth could be the matter? Had there been an accident? Suddenly I felt anxious about Lachenal—Biscante, as we called him, using the Savoy word for cider. I called to Terray:

'Where's Biscante?'

'He's back up there. The coolies have gone on strike.'

'What about the loads?'

'Biscante is up there keeping an eye on them. Anyway I don't think the coolies mean any harm. They want more pay. They want . . . I don't know what they want, I don't understand a word of their gibberish. But there they are near Waiga at the side of the track. They just refuse to go on; they've put down their loads and they won't budge an inch. It's blackmail.'

'All that is G.B.'s pigeon,' I said.

'I don't see how he can get us out of it.'

'Well it'll show us whether he has any real authority over these types.'

We left at once and by the end of the afternoon we came in sight of the strikers. Lachenal, usually so cheerful, looked thoroughly depressed. Upon the arrival of our officer, the porters drew closer together, and addressed him noisily, probably telling him exactly what they were claiming. As for us, we settled down calmly to eat and drink at our leisure; we felt that a refusal to be rattled would add to our prestige, and with remarkable nonchalance took off our boots to rest our feet, performing every movement with studied slowness.

Now it was up to G.B. For half an hour he treated the coolies, to a flow of eloquence which we shall always remember, though it was quite impossible for us to understand what he was saying. The quiet, measured tone in which he began grew steadily louder, then suddenly it rose to a tornado which echoed in the cathedral-like gorge. Magically the loud complaints of the coolies were transformed into diffidently advanced reasons to which G. B. replied with vigour and assurance. There was no question about his authority. Suddenly a coolie said something, probably abusive. We were amazed to see our officer hurl himself upon the offender and beat him until he took flight. This rough handling produced quick results: one by one, as we watched, the coolies took up their loads and continued on their way.

On Sunday, April 16th, we arrived Baglung, the last considerable village before you climb to the high valleys. There remained only another three or four marches before Tukucha, but these would be the hardest, for we should have to rise from about 2000 to 8000 feet.

Next morning Noyelle woke us early:
'Come and look—Dhaulagiri! Dhaulagiri!'
Dhaulagiri at last! Noyelle was outside yelling for joy. Could he really see it? Everyone was out in a flash, covering up his nakedness with the first thing that came to hand. Some went out in their sleeping-bags, hopping as in a sack race, others had a handkerchief by way of pants. Lachenal distinguished himself by using his knitted cap.

An immense ice pyramid, glittering in the sun like a crystal, rose up more than 23,000 feet above us. The south face, shining blue through the morning mists, was unbelievably lofty, not of this world. We were speechless in face of this tremendous mountain; its name was familiar to us from all our talk about it, but the reality so moved us that we couldn't utter a word. Then slowly the reasons for our being here at all took precedence over our own emotions and our aesthetic response, and we began to examine the gigantic outline from a practical point of view.

'Just you look at the east arête, on the right!'

'Yes, it's not even worth thinking about.'

This was rather a blow.

The sight was utterly magnificent, but from a mountaineering point of view there was not a hope on this south face.

'If you're good, I'll show you Annapurna in two days' time,' said Ichac who, with Couzy, had just been taking careful bearings.

Seated in the shade of some great banyan trees, I held a pay parade which lasted all day long. The coolies, interested but wary, shoved their noses close to the beam of the scales. Each of them received six rupees and one packet of 'Red Star' cigarettes, acknowledged it with hands clasped, Hindu fashion, and then signed his name on G.B. Rana's list. (In front of what he is told is his name, written by the babu, each porter presses his thumb previously dipped in ink.) As the list lengthened, supplementary bits of parchment had to be stuck on—by the time the operation was finished it was getting on for four yards long!

Terray allotted the loads to the coolies before they passed the check point. He felt their calves and their biceps, and inspected their lung-expansion, just as he used to do on his farm at Les Houches. The 'strong man', as the Sherpas called him, handled the heaviest of the containers with disconcerting ease, and the porters treated him with great respect. They came forward one by one, gauged the loads at a glance, and tried their weight, with sidelong glances in the direction of the others. With considerable ingenuity they made frames for the loads out of bamboos and lianas, and in time everything was picked up. The coolies carry and balance the loads by bands round their foreheads, and in this way our six tons of gear was carried over 120 miles of mountainous tracks to the scene of action. Now, on to Tukucha!

The coolies filed ahead of us as far as the eye could see, along the banks of the Kali Gandaki. Towards midday we came to a large tributary; the Mayandi Khola. Marcel Ichac couldn't make it out.

'Why, it's as big as the Gandaki. If it drained only the south face of Dhaulagiri it would be just a stream.'[2]

And in fact, judging from the map, the proposed route up Dhaulagiri from our headquarters at Tukucha would, without any apparent difficulty, follow a valley running up into the north face. But if instead of going towards Tukucha this valley should descend in a westerly direction, as we were now beginning to suspect—judging

[2]See maps, pp. 22 and 23.

from the extent of the waters draining it and pouring into the Mayandi Khola—then there must be a ridge, not marked on the map, cutting Tukucha off from the north face of Dhaulagiri, which would certainly be an obstacle to our proposed plan of ascent.

'Well, yes,' I had to admit, 'the Mayandi Khola ought to be far smaller than this before the monsoon.'

'I think I have it,' suggested Ichac with remarkable intuition, 'it drains all the north side as well as the west.'

'But what about the map?'

'There's no doubt, it must be wrong.'

This logic struck me as plausible. However, before questioning the map I would wait for more positive proof. This we were going to be given; a month later the puzzle was cleared up.

Next day, April 20th, as we passed through Dana we tried to pick out the lesser peaks and ridges of Annapurna.

'Well, aren't you going to show us this Annapurna of yours?' I reminded Ichac.

We couldn't see Annapurna, but right opposite us there opened out the deep winding valley of the Miristi Khola. On the map was a clearly-marked path which followed these gorges to the Tilicho Pass from which a short arête led to the summit of Annapurna.

'This Tilicho Valley doesn't look very attractive,' said Schatz.

'There's a path marked on the map.'

Noyelle came back looking gloomy after having asked some shikaris or hunters for information.

'Nobody's heard of the Tilicho Pass.'

'That blasted map again!'

'It would be too much to expect,' said Rébuffat, 'a pass over 19,000 feet high with a good path and a 26,000 foot peak just at hand!' Later, when we came to explore the country, we found that the Miristi gorges were impassable and the famous Tilicho Pass was not where it was marked.

Meanwhile our path skirted the cliffs. Looking down through the conifers we could barely make out the wild, rumbling waters of the Krishna Gandaki; tremendous waterfalls gushed here and there from the limestone cliffs. We gained height imperceptibly, and realized it by the party's heavier step and slower pace.

At Ghasa it began to get chilly, for we were now about 6500 feet up, with another 1600 feet to climb up to Tukucha. There were no longer any bananas or rice, only a few poor-looking crops, mostly barley. A little further on we saw the upper slopes of Dhaulagiri, streaked with blue ice. The south-east ridge running down towards us, of which we had had some hope, extended endlessly, as sharp as the blade of a knife and bristling with ice pinnacles and snow cornices—absolutely impregnable, as seen from here.

We all craned our necks to get a view of the gigantic walls which disappeared nearly four miles up into the clouds and the blue sky. The rock was dark brown, the snow dazzling, and the light so intense it made us blink. To try to pick out a route seemed presumptuous. Nevertheless we couldn't hide our pleasure, so happy were we to be in the mountains and able, from now on, to devote ourselves to the real object of the whole expedition. As for myself, I should at last be able to give up a role which was more that of a carrier or impresario than leader of a mountaineering expedition.

At Lete we passed, with some surprise and feeling, through a pine-wood which reminded us astonishingly of our own mountains—the same trees, the same scattered blocks of granite and cool mosses. I could not know that two months later this beautiful idyllic place would witness my sufferings.

We came out on to a long stony plain formed during the centuries by the impetuous and irregular flow of the Gandaki which had cut a colossal corridor right through the great Himalayan chain. Tremendous gales blew down this funnel and held up our advance. These hurricanes rage all the year round, and prevent any kind of growth. Columns of dust were whirled up into the air, the wind howled round this gloomy, rocky inferno, and Ichac, who was protecting himself as best he could, yelled in my ear, 'We might be in the Karakoram!'

The barefoot coolies doubled themselves up and kept together in tight little groups for mutual protection. Everyone was in a hurry to reach Tukucha.

Angtharkay soon felt quite at home. He is an ardent Buddhist and he had just caught sight of Larjung with sacred streamers flying from its housetops, their prayers agitated by the wind.

In the distance, at the far end of the stony desert, we could see a village gay with hundreds of prayer masts and encircled by what looked like fortifications.

'Tukucha, Sahib!'

We all hurried on, forded the swirling torrent—the Dambush Khola, of which we shall hear more later—and so made our entry into Tukucha.

There were, after all, far fewer people than we had expected

Numbers of dirty children surrounded us, observing our every move with curiosity, and playing about in the water conduit in the middle of the village in which the women washed their pots and got the water for their tea. The old men remained on their doorsteps, suspicious and mistrustful on these white men who were here with such obscure intentions. We were through the village in a few minutes, and before us lay an open stretch. On a Buddhist temple with rose-coloured walls flags flapped in the wind. Although it was not a very prepossessing spot, and was made rather gloomy by a naked grey cliff rising above it, it was the only suitable place for our camp.

The preliminary marches were now over. The date was April 21st and we had taken just over a fortnight to travel practically right across Nepal.

# 3

## The Hidden Valley

The programme now before us was clear-cut. First we should have to establish camp, unpack, check, list and sort out the equipment and food; for the next forty-eight hours everybody would have a definite job. They were soon at it, dirty, noisy and cheerful. Ichac delved into his precious crates of films and equipment, Oudot was deep in his dressings and medical supplies, and the Sherpas were pitching the tents, fixing up their kitchen, and helping the Sahibs stow everything away.

The weather was superb, and this first day at headquarters the mountains were looking their very best. It was marvellous to get at last a proper view of the peaks all round us. The Gandaki Valley is a long rift between two immense mountain groups: the Dhaulagiri massif on the west rising to 26,795 feet, and the Annapurna massif on the east rising to 26,493 feet. Mist often lies in the depths of this rift, giving even greater majesty to the inaccessible walls that towered over us. The shapely Nilgiris,[1] the 'blue mountains', glittered nearly 15,000 feet above us. Towards the north the sky was much clearer, and as far as we could judge, vegetation was sparser up there towards Tibet.

Tukucha is a maze of alleys, and the houses, regular little fortresses, are mostly caravanserais where passing travellers can find lodging for the night. The majority of the 500 inhabitants are Buddhists, whose piety can be judged from the wall of prayer-wheels, 50 yards long. Our Sherpas never omitted, when passing, to give a joyful turn to the metallic cylinders upon which sacred texts are engraved—a far more practical idea than the reciting of lengthy prayers.

A caravan surrounded by a host of children had assembled not far from our camp, and everyone was talking hard—Tibetans, no doubt. The women wore very becoming coloured aprons, and their typically Mongolian faces were adorned with pats of cowdung applied to both

[1]This impassable chain (not to be confused with the Nilgiri Hills of South India) forms an immense screen between Tukucha and Annapurna. To reach Annapurna one would have to skirt the Nilgiris to the south along the Miristi Khola, or to the north.

cheeks. Confident in their power to charm, they laughed, exposing all their teeth. A crowd gathered, and suddenly a wild dance started. The dancers were silhouetted against a magnificent background of snowy mountains. The ballet, which appeared to express the eternal dualism of joy and sorrow, life and death, was perfectly controlled. Its beauty was rough and primitive, for a dance always reflects the spirit of a people.

Abruptly they stopped. A Tibetan woman placed a copper dish in the centre of the circle; the dancers began to mime most expressively, and their gaze travelled from the dish to us and back again. With great dignity the Bara Sahib generously tossed in a few rupees. This was a great success. Immediately the dance began again, even wilder than before, and again they all stopped suddenly. The Bara Sahib was obliged once more to display his generosity.

Since our arrival at Tukucha we had all nursed a secret hope of discovering a safe and easy ridge that would lead us straight to the summit of Dhaulagiri or Annapurna. The south-east ridge of Dhaulagiri, which was clearly marked on the map, and which we had seen from Baglung, gave some slight encouragement to this hope, but no one was very certain. Then there was the north ridge; it was undoubtedly ice, but, judging from the general structure of the mountain, its moderate angle and slight rise in height would make it very suitable for an attempt. Now, by pitching a few intermediate camps, we might . . . As for Annapurna, its proximity to the Tilicho track seemed to make it easily accessible, and for that very reason it lost a good deal of its interest from the climber's point of view.

Next day Couzy left with Pansy on a reconnaissance to make observations from the 13,000-foot point that dominates Tukucha and should command a wonderful view.

At 11 A.M. I was in radio communication with them.

'Coucou speaking. Just reached the top. The view is marvellous; Dhaulagiri dominates everything. The south-east ridge looked absolutely frightful. Very long, with lots of ice towers. Camp sites dubious.'

'What about the north ridge?'

'Ice all the way. Looks very steep. Certainly great technical difficulties. The ticklish part is towards the middle, but there's another snag, how to get on the ridge. From here the East glacier,[2] which you

[2]The East glacier lies between the north and south-east ridges. At first sight it appeared to give access to both ridges.

19

would expect to be the normal approach, looks extremely broken up.'

'Can you see the north face?'

'Those great walls of seracs make it a very dangerous proposition. At its foot there is a relatively easy slope, which ought to give access to the north-west ridge, but from where I'm standing I can't see very well.'

'What do you think of the Nilgiris?'

'Absolutely sheer. Not a hope from this side.'

'Thanks, Coucou. See you later.'

'O.K., Maurice. Off.'

This first report did not do much to encourage optimism. When he returned we should proceed to a first examination of the problem, with the help of his sketches.

That evening in the mess-tent Couzy, between cups of tea, confirmed what he had told us by radio.

'We must find a way to the foot of the final pyramid,' began Rébuffat. On this point everyone was agreed. But on the means of getting there opinions differed.

What ought we to do? Ought we to go up this East glacier of Dhaulagiri, which was in a chaotic condition and was without question extremely dangerous? Or skirt round the Tukucha Peak, which marks the end of the north arête, and follow this Elbow Valley shown on the map,[3] in order to reach the northern basin of Dhaulagiri?

'We must reconnoitre in all directions,' I said, 'and to do so we shall obviously have to split up. During this period of reconnaisance, when we shall be working our way round Dhaulagiri and Annapurna, we need parties of two only.'

'There's certainly something to be done on Annapurna,' declared Schatz. Then, dreamily, 'A pass at 20,000 feet, a track . . .'

'Dhaulagiri has a nasty look. I'd prefer the other fellow,' admitted Couzy.

'Very well. Tomorrow, we'll all get going. You, Lachenal, and you, Gaston, will go and reconnoitre the East glacier. The M.O. and Schatz will take horses, and go up above Lete to get a view of the Tilicho Pass and Annapurna. Matha and I will take a little trip up to the top of the Elbow Valley, marked as the Dambush Khola. Perhaps we shall be able to see the north side of Dhaulagiri.

'And what about me?' said Couzy, deeply disappointed.

'You'll rest in camp. Don't worry, there'll be something for

[3]See map, p. 22.

everyone to do. It's now April 23rd, we've time enough before the monsoon breaks, early in June. You, too, Lionel, try to keep warm.'

'And stick to light food for the present,' advised Oudot.

Terray, who had been suffering from a stomach upset, was feeling a bit better already, but I still thought he looked very pulled down. 'And I suppose I'm to twiddle my thumbs?' asked Noyelle.

'Your excellency will be good enough to make contact with the big-wigs. And you and Coucou can finish organizing the camp.'

We were awake at 5 A.M. Lachenal and Rébuffat went off with two Sherpas, carrying skis and one high-altitude unit. This consisted of a nylon tent for two, two special sleeping-bags, two half-length air mattresses, a spirit stove and cooking utensils; the whole weighing roughly 22 lb. A shikari would guide them over the lower slopes of the mountain where otherwise they might well lose time in the valleys and forests.

Oudot and Schatz were up and about, and their horses were ready at 7 o'clock. I hoped that during the day they would be able to go high enough to see the famous Tilicho Pass and clear up the mystery about it. Then Ichac and I left camp, delighted at the thought of being in the mountains once more. In a few minutes we came to the Dambush Khola, whose valley we were to follow as high as possible.

'Certainly this stream's on the small side,' I conceded.

'I don't want to influence your judgment, Maurice, but to me it's practically a certainty: the drainage from the northern slopes of Dhaulagiri doesn't flow this way. There must be a valley on the other side. It follows that we must be separated from the north face by a ridge.'

'We'll soon see.'

Our route took us through a wonderful stretch of thick jungle. We were greeted by the first rays of the sun, and at this early hour a delicate scent rose from some pink flowers, and some recently felled fir trees gave out the familiar smell of resin. It was already pleasantly warm. Jumping from boulder to boulder, climbing the rocks that barred our path, scrambling over precariously balanced obstacles at the risk of falling into the stream, we rapidly gained height.

'The first snow!' shouted Ichac happily.

'More at home on this sort of ground, eh Matha?'

'What contrasts there are here, and how different from the Alps! Here it's only a step from jungle to snow.'

By keeping to the cliffs on the true left of the valley we hoped to

21

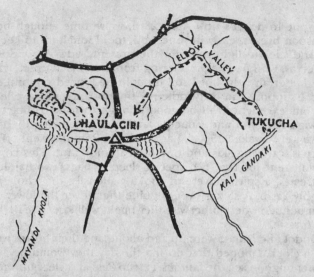

*THE RIDGES OF DHAULAGIRI — These sketch maps show the fundamental differences between the map of the Indian Survey, above, and the true lay-out, on the right. Tukucha had been chosen as our base on account of its proximity both to the Elbow Valley, which appeared to give access*

get some enlightening glimpses of the north face, and even perhaps a proper view. We had great hopes of this side, since we were aware that in the Himalaya north faces, for many reasons of geology and weather, often offer the least steep and least difficult means of access.

For some time we had been keeping along by the cliffs.

'It's like the Cirque de Gavarnie, only on a much larger scale,' remarked Ichac.

The Tukucha Peak, a 'seven-thousander', completely blocked the view with its grand and terrifying walls. All round us cascades spouted from the rocks, and banks of rotten snow clung desperately to the flanks of the mountain. It was the end of winter.

Who knows the secret of the renewal of life in such places? From beneath the snow as it melted and slid off, the vegetation appeared, stunted, twisted and flattened. Birds and insects were migrating to heights which once again could nourish them.

'Another few weeks and summer will be here.'

'The Expedition's arrived at just the right moment, don't you think?'

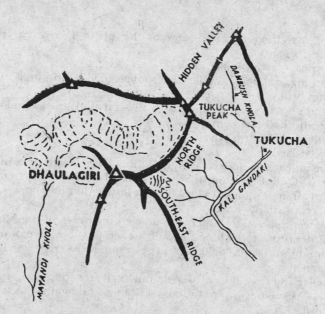

*to the north face of Dhaulagiri, and to the east face, where a small glacier lies wedged between the north-east and the south-east ridges. As Dhaulagiri has no true north ridge, we were accustomed to call the north-east ridge (which joins Dhaulagiri to the Tukucha Peak) by this name.*

Ichac took some bearings. The altimeter registered 11,000 feet. 'North Nilgiris 111° east. Tukucha Peak 270° west . . . This map is wrong! It's quite obvious. The great Dambush Khola *cirque* is contained on the north by a ridge coming from the Tukucha Peak. At the foot of Dhaulagiri on the north side there is another basin, that's all. But if we've got to cross the ridge to get to that basin before tackling the north face, then we'll still be here next year!'

I was beginning to be shaken, but we had to leave it at that if we were to reach camp that same evening. We made some long glissades down the snow, stopped to take a few pictures and pick up some stones for the geologists, and at 4.30, sunburnt and happy, were sipping wonderful tea with milk back in camp at Tukucha.

'What, didn't you even *see* Dhaulagiri?'

The others were astonished. No doubt they had been expecting a 1:20,000 map in relief, and coloured too, upon our return from the outing.

'You must never expect too much from a reconnaissance. Every thing's on such a huge scale. It's bound to take days and days of marching to get a view of the north face even from a distance ... .'

'No post?' asked Ichac.

'Nothing,' replied Noyelle; 'I've spoken to G.B. and he is making inquiries.'

'What about Annapurna? Have you seen it? I asked Oudot and Schatz who had just come back.'

'Only the very top part.'

'Ah, at last!'

'The little we saw looked all right. I think it impressed us favourably, didn't it, Oudot? Getting there, however, is quite another matter, and I'm afraid it's going to be a bit of a puzzle. But of course we only had a very distant view.'

'We were just able to pick out, above the gorges of the Miristi, a sort of depression which on this side looked possible. The other side is an unknown factor. We'd have to get a much closer view to be able to say anything.'

'You're right, we'll have to get a much clearer idea of it,' I said to Oudot. 'As soon as you're rested, you can go off again, this time for several days.'

For the moment we were completely in the dark. We discussed it all endlessly, but this didn't increase our knowledge by one iota.

'Hi, Maurice! Here's the boss!'

Noyelle came in with G.B. and a gentleman of forty or so, well-dressed, and wearing boots. He had fine drooping moustaches, and looked intelligent. It was the Suba, the head man of the district. There were Hindu greetings on both sides.

'*He* comes from Tinigaon,' our friend G.B. informed me with emphasis, pointing to a native who had held back until then. 'He's a friend of the Great Man.'

A searching interrogation began, for the man was a shikari who claimed to be perfectly well acquainted with the Tilicho Pass. We had to take him to look at our map.

'Tilicho Pass, at the foot of Annapurna? No? There. What?'

'But it's not possible—*north* of the Nilgiris? And not *south*? Isn't it along the Miristi?'

He must be muddling it up with another pass—the Thorungse, above Muktinath.

'No, look, he says no.'

'Let's see, it's most important. If the Tilicho Pass is to the *north* of the Nilgiris we should have to cross them to get to Annapurna, 'which could be impossible, or else make a big détour to the north.'

'Can he take us to the Tilicho Pass? Two days' march? Why, then, that alters everything. We'll soon see when we get there.'

'In point of fact, on the map there *is* a star marking a col to the north of the Nilgiris.'

'Look! The Tilicho Pass is clearly marked all the same between the Nilgiris and Annapurna. Perhaps the surveyors have made a mistake about the name? There must be a pass there all the same. Ask this chap from Tinigaon if there is a way between Dana and Manangbhot.'

'He's never heard of one.'

What *were* we to believe? There was only one thing to do—go and see the Tilicho of the man from Tinigaon. But this was all part of the exploration of Annapurna, and would be for later on. For the moment we were concerned with Dhaulagiri.


Next day Lachenal and Rébuffat returned, in high spirits. Their guide had taken them well to the right of the East Dhaulagiri glacier, practically underneath the Tukucha Peak.

'The shikari is a great chap,' said Lachenal, himself a good judge of a guide.

'That's useful to know for the future. Well, what about this glacier?'

Rébuffat explained the position.

'We went up to about the same height as Mont Blanc, after bivouacking at around 13,000 feet. The East glacier's just a great torrent of ice. All the same it should be possible to get up it, but it wouldn't be plain sailing.'

'Even supposing we did succeed in getting up the glacier,' continued Lachenal, 'I don't quite see how we should get on to the north ridge. My own view is that we shouldn't try. It's a regular Walker[4] with seracs stuck on!'

'It might be easier to get on the ridge from further south,' went on Rébuffat. 'The ridge itself doesn't look all that bad, seen from below. It's long of course but not very steep. We could see some ice towers through our field-glasses—but nothing unclimbable.'

'Anyway we were quite at sea over the scale of everything. It's all far bigger than we had supposed.'

---

[4] The north buttress of the Pointe Walker on the Grandes Jorasses is perhaps the most difficult climb in the Alps.

Clearly this demanded something beyond Alpine technique. A series of well-placed camps was called for, and individual initiative must give way to collective effort. Lachenal and Rébuffat were beginning to realize just what Himalayan climbing is and what it requires—a team. While they hungrily devoured bully beef *à la vinaigrette*, we talked over the situation.

It wasn't at all encouraging. But these preliminary reconnaissances had been the means of our making contact with the real Himalaya, and getting to the heart of the sort of problems they set. There was no question of solving them in forty-eight hours. Only now could we begin to make a serious attack on our objectives. While Couzy, Oudot and Schatz were examining possible approaches to Annapurna by the Miristi Khola, Ichac, Terray and I were going to explore the north face of Dhaulagiri and the approach to it from the Dambush Khola.

At dawn on April 26th the two parties left for several days' reconnaissance—our lot accompanied by Sherpas carrying high altitude units and skis. Lachenal's and Rébuffat's shikari guided us as far as the first névés which was as far as he had ever got. After a quick meal we sent him down again. The heat was overpowering; the snow became like soup; we put on our skis so as not to sink in too much. For the Sherpas, who went in up to their waists, it was a horrible ascent.

Five o'clock! The Sherpas, all except Angtharkay, were going down again; it was time to pitch camp. We couldn't take off our special glasses—the glare was too powerful for our tired eyes. The light which poured down the immense north face of the Tukucha Peak overwhelmed us. This was our first night at high altitude. The tents were minute: we called them 'coffins', and had to crawl in and out, but they only weighed $2^{1}/_{2}$ lb., for they were made of nylon and duralumin, and could be carried at the bottom of a rucksack. Lying on our stomachs on our air-mattresses, tucked in our sleeping-bags, Ichac, Terray and I did the so-called cooking. We had to be careful not to make any sudden movement, for every inch was limited. Your morale needs to be good to cope with so oppressively restricted a world.

The next day Terray set a rapid pace from the start. Perhaps he wanted to make up for having been ill. His upset had so weakened him that he had been able to walk only with considerable effort, but now it was as much as we could do to follow him. The slope was steep, at the maximum angle on which our sealskins would hold, and we were sometimes obliged to push with our sticks. The sun was already directly overhead. The ground became more difficult, and we stuck our skis upright in the snow, so as to be able to spot them on the way down. The height, which was about the same as that of Mont Blanc, was making us tired. In spite of a gnawing hunger we went on until we reached a little plateau. Terray was making heavy weather of it: had he over-estimated his returning strength? Anyway he had to summon up every ounce of energy to reach that plateau. He let himself fall heavily on to the snow.

'I'm as weak as a kitten!' he told us. 'I feel like death.'

To be on the safe side, he would go back to the first camp after having drunk some good hot tea.

'It's only mountain sickness,' said Ichac. 'You're not really fit again. If you go down lower you'll be all right at once.'

Angtharkay, after helping us to pitch our second camp, would go down to join him. We said goodbye to Terray and set off again, traversing some wide snow slopes overhung by great walls of seracs. The danger of avalanches was real but not excessive; we took the risk with our eyes open. We made over as quickly as possible to the side of the slope which might lead us to the pass, and embarked on a long pull up, which was very heavy going because of the altitude; we were not yet acclimatized. The pass was a long way off and we decided to send Angtharkay back. A little rocky island right in the middle of the slope offered a site for our tent. After putting down his load Angtharkay went off quickly so as not to be overtaken by the dark.

We soon began to suffer from splitting headaches, which are frequent above 16,000 feet, and were glad of the tablets of aspirin which Oudot, with foresight, had handed out. Although we were both very tired, we could not sleep a wink, and at sunrise we started in the direction of our wretched pass, leaving the tent up. We ascended much faster than the day before, and reached the pass in barely an hour. The morning sun made the ridge ahead of us stand out in extraordinary relief and bathed it in lovely clear colours.

'Bad luck—this isn't the true pass yet,' I said to Ichac, who was deeply disappointed.

Instead of looking out on to a valley, we had before us a basin of crusted snow.

'Maurice, look over there! The pass is the other side, at least two hours from here.'

In spite of our preliminary marches we were feeling our lack of training and acclimatization. It showed itself in our abnormal tiredness.

'Everyone, including the Sherpas, will have to go on reconnaisance and sleep out between 16,000 and 20,000 feet up,' I said to Ichac. 'Today has made me realize that without previous acclimatization, one can't go really high.'

An icy wind greeted us as we approached the pass. We put on our nylon anoraks and trousers, which were both snow- and wind-proof.

'Well I'm damned! This is most odd. A valley starting here—'

'It's not marked on the map,' said Ichac. 'It's an unknown valley.'

'It runs down in a northerly direction, and divides into two great branches.'

'No sign of Dhaulagiri! Surely it's not that pale imitation over there, that impostor opposite us?' said Ichac, pointing towards a 23,000-foot peak which had an odd likeness to Dhaulagiri.

Before us the 'Hidden Valley', as Ichac called it—he loved giving things names—ran gently downwards. It was broad, like a valley scooped out by a glacier, and the alternation of snow and yellow grass reminded one of a tiger's striped coat.

'To see the north face of Dhaulagiri, we'd have to go round to the left, right to the other end of the valley; it must be a terrific sight from there!'

But my words did not seem to arouse any enthusiasm in Ichac.

'It's too late now,' he replied, 'and we haven't got the necessary camping gear.'

'I suppose you're right.'

'Go on down a bit, if you like, I'll take a panorama and then we'll be off.'

On the other side of Tukucha, above the Nilgiris, there rose a mighty summit which Ichac identified as Annapurna. He made a rapid sketch of it while I was climbing up to him again. There was a keen wind from the north, and clouds were coming up, so after swallowing the contents of a tube of condensed milk, we started back.

Walking automatically, and looking straight ahead, we advanced in silence: we were both short of breath. Our minds wandered off into daydreams. I thought of the gentle valley of Chamonix with its trees, of so tender and restful a green, and its shady paths, so pleasant to stroll along. I felt my strength ebbing. The last rise before the pass was hard going, and Ichac made the trail. I tried to follow him; I just couldn't. Every ten steps I lay down in the snow. I couldn't go any further! Ichac cursed me roundly—the only thing that does any good at times like that. At last we got on to the ridge. God, what a relief! But we still had the whole descent before us.

To my great surprise, from the moment we started going down I felt as light as air. We went careering down to the camp, reaching it in a few minutes. This was a new experience for me: going up, one suffers from the height, the lack of oxygen and difficulty in breathing; coming down is quite a different story—everything seems dead easy.

While the water was heating for tea, Ichac told me a queer thing had happened while we were on the plateau:

'As I was ploughing along heavily, I thought I heard someone else behind me . . . a third man. He was following us. I wanted to call out to tell you. I couldn't. I glanced behind me rather furtively, to set my mind at rest. But like an obsession, the feeling of someone else there kept on coming back to me. Then everything was all right again. It happened at the same moment that you felt so groggy.'

'It just shows that when you're at a great height, your powers of clear thinking deteriorate very quickly.'

We were all in, our legs like jelly and our heads like lead. Then the sun began to reach us, through the ceiling of nasty-looking clouds.

'Angtharkay is coming!' cried Ichac, who had just seen a little black speck on our tracks.

'That's fine! He'll help us carry all this stuff.'

We were excited, and ready to put off for a while the joys of our super sleeping-bags. We got into our frozen boots as best we could, broke camp in record time and then burdened like donkeys we moved carefully down the slope of rotten snow.

'Salaam, Angtharkay!'

'Tired, sir?'

He wanted to carry everything himself, and it was hard to resist the temptation; my shoulders were being sawn through by the straps; but it was wiser to share the labour. On we went, striding down slopes which were just ready to avalanche and completely untrustworthy at this time of day. Here now was the ridge—Terray's nightmare—and our skis were still there. Angtharkay went on down to the lower camp on foot while we skied slowly down, describing elegant figures in the very uneven snow.

Next day we were given a triumphal reception at Tukucha. Terray, who had gone down the day before, was better, though still pretty exhausted. The others plied us with questions.

'Well, what do you make of Dhaulagiri?'

'Where do the waters from the north face drain?'

'They drain into the moon!'

# 4

## *The East Dhaulagiri Glacier*

Everyone was back in camp, except Couzy and Schatz, who were still off on the Annapurna reconnaissance, so it was a good opportunity to review the general situation. Oudot, who had only just left them, reported that on April 27th he had gone as far as the depression which we had first seen from Lete.

'It was hard work, but perfectly possible for porters. From there we saw Annapurna—but a long way off. From the higher ridges a spur runs down into the Miristi Khola Valley.'

'And the pass?'

'No sign of the Tilicho. I stopped there and let the other two go on.'

'What it amounts to is this,' I said after a moment, 'there are three problems. For Dhaulagiri we must explore the north side, and the way of getting there. The reconnaissance that Ichac and myself have just made gave us one glimpse into the unknown, but did not really clear up the problem.'

'It's not a problem', said Ichac, 'it's a mystery. I've my own ideas on the matter, but obviously we must go and see for ourselves.'

Well then, we must organize another reconnaissance over there. It's far away, and it's high. We'll have to make an all-out effort.'

'I'm ready to go,' said Terray, 'as soon as ever I can. I'm fed up with being sick. I made very heavy weather the other day with Ichac and Maurice. I want to get my own back. In two days' time I'll be perfectly fit again.'

'I don't want to push myself forward,' put in Oudot, 'but I admit I'd like to be off, too. I spend my time handing out Epsom salts to my panel patients in Tukucha.'

"All good for prestige. And anyway you've only just got back.'

'Our prestige is so high it can stand my absence for a few days.'

'Seriously,' I put in, 'I don't care for the Expedition's medical officer being too long away from Tukucha, but obviously it would be a good thing for you also to get acclimatized.'

'Then we'll go together,' decided Terray.

'Right you are.'

'I warn you,' said Terray to Oudot, 'I'm going on to the bitter end.'

'We'll get there together.'

'However long the route, however many passes there are to cross, whatever the difficulties, I shan't stop.'

"All that's necessary is for you to go to a point from which you can sketch the whole northern side of Dhaulagiri,' said I.

'Right,' said Terray, 'but I'm in earnest about what we'll need for this trip. I shall want two Sherpas, six porters whom we can engage locally, and at least eight days' supplies.'

'We'll go into all that in detail.'

'And what's the second problem?' asked Lachenal, who was obviously infected by Terray's fever to be up and doing.

'The second question is Annapurna. We'll have to go further into it, but before we can decide anything we must wait for Couzy and Schatz to come back. As for the third problem . . .'

'Ah, this is where we come in, Gaston,' said Lachenal to Rébuffat.

'You don't know what I'm talking about.'

'Oh, don't I?'

'The East glacier of Dhaulagiri,' said Gaston

'Exactly. Is it possible to make one's way up it, and then to get on to the south-east ridge on the left, or the north ridge on the right? Here again the reconnaissance that you made in this direction with Biscante wasn't pushed far enough for a definite opinion to be possible.'

'Far enough, all the same,' Gaston replied, 'to make us pretty dubious about it. I don't think going straight up the glacier would be at all easy. Judging from what we saw, it's a huge slope of ice cluttered up with seracs and seamed with crevasses. Avalanches sweep it continuously. I don't much like the look of it.'

'I shall go with you,' I said to Lachenal and Rébuffat. 'We'll ride up as far as possible on horseback, and pitch a small base camp at the foot of the glacier. It'll be surprising if we can't clear up the problem.'

The following day everyone rested. In the morning Ichac, Noyelle, Rébuffat and myself took the opportunity to climb up a hillock south of Tukucha from which we had a perfect view of Dhaulagiri. Through the glasses I picked out the frightful obstacles on the East glacier. By keeping to the left, that is to say, on the true right bank of the glacier, we should be able to avoid most of the seracs, except in the upper section. The problem was to reach one of the two ridges.

Dhaulagiri, as seen from here, was magnificent. The morning mists were still lingering in the valleys, but high up the snow and ice glistened and made us blink. The sky was pastel blue. On another rocky point barely 200 yards from us, a vulture was watching, motionless.

We had now been in Asia for a month.

Next morning we traversed the great rocky flats of the Gandaki on horseback. The Sherpas took us by way of Larjung, no doubt so that they could spin the prayer-wheels. This village, where the alleys are covered in by roofs—there must be a great deal of snow in winter—is extremely picturesque. Half a mile further on we left our mounts, and the party spread out over the grassy slopes. Numbers of yaks and cows were grazing hungrily on the lush grass. On the hill-side our way was lined by trees covered with sweet-smelling blossoms that ranged from pink to red. It wasn't easy to keep to a timetable in a paradise like this. Today—and the Sherpas couldn't understand it—we let the porters have all the halts they asked for. It was fantastic that only a few hours after seeing these giant flowers and this inviting turf we were to be walking upon glaciers of such a scale that our cheerful assurance would suddenly change to awestruck respect. All day we climbed up.

We left the tree-line behind, and some patches of scrubby grass were the only sign of vegetation at this height; the névés increased in number. The porters came up steadily with their loads, and when evening came we pitched our Base Camp on the last patch of earth. The radio was set up—it enabled us to receive and send messages at a distance of over six miles—and contact with Tukucha was established. I listened with almost childish delight to Ichac's voice as he gave me the latest news and the current village gossip.

'Hallo, Matha? We've arrived safely. It's gloomy up here this evening in this weather. We're all spending the night here . . .'

'Noyelle is leaving tomorrow to join you. Couzy and Schatz are back.'

'Oh! What about Annapurna?'

'They went on for three days. They succeeded in reaching the bed of the Miristi Khola.'

'Excellent!'

'They crossed it and then ran up against a subsidiary ridge coming down from Annapurna.'

'The same one they saw with Oudot on April 27th?'

'That's it. This ridge seems to be huge. After a plausible-looking start it probably links up with the main ridge, but this junction wasn't visible from below.'

'Did they go any further?'

'No. They thought it would be quite impossible to skirt round the ridge to have a look at the north face.'

'So they didn't see the Tilicho Pass?'

'Not the ghost of a pass. If there really is a Tilicho Pass leading to the foot of the north face of Annapurna, it's somewhere else.'

'The man from Tinigaon was right! I hope they're not too tired.'

'They're resting. What sort of weather have you got up there?'

'Very cold. We're in the clouds. Greetings to everybody.'

'Cheers, and good luck.'

Next morning at daybreak we proceeded rapidly in the direction of the great ice-fall. From close at hand, and in the half-light, it was extremely impressive. The party consisted of myself, Lachenal and Rébuffat, and the Sherpas—Angtharkay, Phutharkay and Sarki. It would be the first time on this expedition that they had come up against considerable technical difficulties.

The day was one long search for snow-bridges over the crevasses: we wound in and out between immense barriers of ice or alongside gaping crevasses. We were obliged to make our way beneath gigantic seracs that threatened to collapse at any moment, for there was no alternative. As we climbed, cutting steps, or walking up on our crampons, we often glanced uneasily, out of the corner of an eye, at these huge, precariously balanced blocks of ice.

The slope steepened considerably, and we cut a lot of steps. The Sherpas laboured beneath their rucksacks, which weighed over forty pounds. The weather had been threatening since 11 o'clock, and it now grew suddenly worse. We had to find a level spot, sheltered from falling seracs, on which to pitch camp. It was 2 o'clock, we were only half way up the glacier, and it started to snow. The afternoon was lost. We spent a pretty restless night; my companions couldn't sleep a wink.

We were up very early in the morning, for every day the weather was liable to break any time after 2 P.M. Then the noise of the thunder would echo ceaselessly among the surrounding walls and rumble away until the evening.

Day was breaking and the first rope climbed in the ice slope above the camp. Various bits of ironmongery—ice-pitons, hammers and snap-links—clanked in our sacks: we were prepared for anything.

At such an early hour the ice was very hard. The Sherpas used their crampons correctly, but were slow. As we had observed the day before from our lookout point, the best, if not the only, route ran along the true right bank of the glacier.

Round about 16,000 feet our breathing became laboured. When the Sherpas halted they would double themselves up over their ice-axes and empty their lungs with a deep whistle to which we soon became accustomed even during the preliminary marches some of the porters used to breathe like this.

Although there is no hard and fast criterion in the matter, it seemed to me that I suffered less from the lack of oxygen than Lachenal and Rébuffat: probably the happy result of those recent nights spent at 16,000 feet. This consideration convinced me of the need to make everyone go up to between 16,000 and 20,000 feet before a major assault.

It was already midday, and we were still 300 yards from the plateau which marked the end of our difficulties. A glacier is like a river; the level places where it spreads out tranquilly are succeeded by turbulent falls. The possibility of crossing these 300 yards was doubtful.

'Looks bad,' said Lachenal.

'Not reassuring. Look at the blocks of ice that have come down already!' said Rébuffat.

'Bare ice everywhere,' I said dejectedly. 'And what a slope! We'll have to go right across the glacier and try the left bank.'

'Before committing ourselves to that side, we ought to have a look just above, and to the left near the rocks,' advised Rébuffat.

'Go and see whether there's a way, both of you. I'll wait here with the Sherpas.'

In a twinkling they were up the first slope, which was green ice and extremely steep.

'Well done! Nice work!' I couldn't help calling out to them.

Their skill cheered me greatly, and the Sherpas were amazed. After a few minutes Lachenal shouted:

'Maurice! Don't go over to the left. You can come up, we're going to have a look over to the right.

'O.K. Be careful!'

The sky was livid—it was the daily storm coming up. Lachenal and Rébuffat were on extremely dangerous ground. At any moment they might be caught under a serac.

'Let's go on,' I said to the Sherpas, who were not feeling too happy. I was obliged to cut plenty of big steps as well as holds for the hands, for their cumbersome sacks tended to tip them outwards. The angle was so steep that a man standing upright could lick the ice without the least difficulty.

'Nothing doing,' a voice called to me from above.

'There's an enormous crevasse right across the glacier,' yelled the other. I could hear them cursing.

'Won't it go?' I said, using the mountaineers' term. 'Well then, we'll have to cross over. Perhaps there's a way on the other side.'

It was snowing a little, the cloud ceiling was low, and thunder growled ceaselessly, setting our nerves on edge. All six of us were in the middle of gigantic seracs; we were overwhelmed by the unexpected difficulties with which the mountain was confronting us. Sinister cracking noises shook the great blocks of ice on which we moved. The glacier was pallid, the light grew dim.

Although they were obviously uneasy, Lachenal and Rébuffat made a gallant attempt in the direction indicated while the rest of us waited in complete silence, trying to keep cool and impassive when the glacier was shaken by significant shocks and tremors. The others returned looking glum.

'No way there,' they told me.

'It's not very cheerful,' I said doubtfully, 'but . . . if there's nothing doing . . .'

'Maurice, we'd much better get down,' insisted Rébuffat, 'it's not healthy here.'

Suddenly we heard a loud, prolonged cracking. We tucked our heads in: but it wasn't our turn yet!

'Come on! We'll be caught,' yelled Lachenal, 'down we go.'

'Let's get out of this,' shouted Rébuffat.

The endless rumbling of the thunder added to the general alarm. It wasn't a retreat, it was a flight from the mountain, which was preparing to strike.

'If we're not caught, we shall be lucky,' Lachenal just had time to gasp as he flung himself down the slope with a Sherpa on the end of his rope.

'Get a move on!'

I swore at my chap, who was too slow for my liking. Down the ice wall we went one after the other. Then a violent hailstorm broke, and we had to check ourselves from going too fast for safety in this place where every move demanded care.

'Mind out for the Sherpas. Don't let them come off,' I called into

35

the wind to Lachenal, who was setting rather too hot a pace for his man.

'We'd go the hell of a long way!' he flung back at me without slowing down.

The hail slackened: now, safely down the wall, we were out of danger.

'Hell! We so nearly got there—!'

'You can't push on when it's like that.'

I reflected that even if we had reached the plateau, it would have been madness to try to bring the main body up this way. The risk was far too great; no victory would justify loss of life resulting from such deliberately taken risks.

The hail turned to snow; and we were surrounded by mist which reduced visibility to five yards. Grey shadows loomed up from time to time as ghostly figures went their headlong, way down towards camp. Avalanches of fresh snow fell continually, with a frightful din. The inferno receded, but for us it would always remain a nightmare memory.

About five o'clock, down at Base Camp, we were drinking tea which Noyelle had brewed as soon as he had spotted us.

'So you came up yesterday?'

'I found the way quite easily. When I got here I sent young Angdawa down to Tukucha—an unnecessary mouth to feed here, and Terray needed him.'

'What day is it then? We've lost all notion of time.'

'It's the third.'

'What, May 3rd already! Just a month more before the monsoon.'

'And nothing decisive has been discovered about Dhaulagiri. To settle the whole question once for all we'd have to explore those buttresses of the south-east ridge lying just in front of us.'

'Perhaps we could go,' exclaimed Lachenal.

'Right. As soon as your skis arrive, go and have a look at the big snowy point at the end of the ridge.'

'A ski trip—that sounds all right.'

'I'll be able to take some pictures of the south face.'

Noyelle suggested that we should get into radio communication with Tukucha.

'I spoke to Ichac a couple of hours back, but there was such a buzzing from the aerial that I thought it best to switch off.'

'Afraid for your precious set?' Biscante teased him.

A few minutes later communication with Tukucha was established.

'Herzog speaking. What's the news from Tukucha.'

'Ichac here. All's well in camp. Nothing to report. Lionel and Oudot went off this morning. But what about you?'

'We haven't reached the top of the glacier, but we know where we are.'

'Then you've found a possible route?'

'Not on your life! These mountains are unclimbable! No expedition could ever get through this way.'

'What are you going to do?'

'I'm going down tomorrow. Rébuffat and Lachenal will go on skis to a small point of about 18,000 feet on the south-east ridge of Dhaulagiri. From there they will be able to see the whole of the south face.'

'Do they need anything?'

'Send up extra food supplies and three pairs of skis.'

'O.K. If you come down tomorrow you'll have *thar* for lunch.'

'*Thar?*'

'Himalayan chamois. G.B. and the Suba have been hunting—with our rifles—and shot three. There's one for us.'

'Well, then I'll come down tomorrow for sure. And Lionel . . . did he go off just the same?'

'Don't worry—he took a good big hunk with him!'

'See you tomorrow.'

'Greetings to everybody. Off.'

Early next morning I left the others upon the grass beside the camp, giving the Sherpas a lesson in ice-technique, and made my solitary way back to Tukucha. The descent was pure delight. I tried not to lose too much time, but I couldn't resist stopping every hundred yards or so. My heart was full of joy as I passed beneath the trees with their wonderful red blossoms and then, humming to myself, went striding down grassy slopes covered with budding spring flowers.

Between two fir trees, and modestly concealed by wooded hillocks, lay a green lake in whose limpid waters was reflected the graceful picture of the Nilgiris. The larches round it looked less severe than the firs, and its banks were covered with soft moss. Rough tracks led down to the stony plain of the Gandaki. The waters had risen, and I should be obliged to get my feet wet. I didn't want to get blisters, and so I hesitated. By good luck a Tibetan came along just then, and took in the situation at a glance. In the admirable manner of the country, he took me gently on his back and then, despite his load and the current, he crossed the flooded streams of the Gandaki barefoot on the stones and deposited me on dry ground. How could I show my gratitude? I held out a rupee. Very respectfully he bowed to me several times in succession. Poor devil! Generosity can't often be exercised in this wild part of the world.

'Look, here's another.' He couldn't believe his eyes. Bowing deeply, he came up and kissed my feet! I was rather embarrassed and didn't quite know what to do. I struck a dignified and lordly attitude, and then went off feeling a bit ashamed of myself. At 1 o'clock I reached Tukucha where Couzy and Ichac gave me a cheerful welcome.

'Fresh meat, for once,' I said between mouthfuls. 'Congratulations to G.B. for the *thar*.'

I was in splendid form and my appetite rivalled Terray's.

'Was the East glacier all that bad?'

'Technically, it must be much about the same as the north face of the Plan, but incomparably more dangerous. That's what Biscante thinks too. We had some really nasty moments up there. We came whizzing down; the Sherpas all came off several times.'

'Not very funny, that sort of thing,' said Couzy.

'But at any rate no harm's been done.'

'Yes it has! Time—the days are flying by. Dhaulagiri is putting up a very good defence.'

'There's no knowing we shan't find a route tomorrow.'

Ichac gave Couzy a long glance, then answered me:

'Tomorrow—that would surprise me. We've got to find a way, but what's worrying me is that none of us has yet seen even the glimmer of a hope. The reconnaissance stage is far from finished.'

'There are still possibilities of access by the south-east ridge. On the other hand the East glacier, which stopped us yesterday, might be turned by the left-hand wall.'

'Now, Maurice, forgive me, but really . . .'

'Yes, I'm a bit sceptical, too,' I had to admit.

'Schatz and I could go,' said Couzy.

'That's true. Are you rested now?'

'I should say we are!'

'Well, you shall kill two birds with one stone: get acclimatized to the altitude, like the rest of us, and make a final reconnaissance of the upper part of the East glacier.'

'Don't you think that would just be duplicating the object of the trip which Lachenal, Noyelle and Rébuffat are making to the snowy peak?' asked Ichac.

'No, they'll not be able to see much more than the possibilities of the south ridge and the south face.'

'From one face to another, and one ridge to the next, we shall finish up by going all round Dhaulagiri,' concluded Couzy. 'So we'll be off tomorrow.'

'Congratulations on the *thar*,' I said to G.B., who had come into the tent. He was very proud of being a good shot.

I noticed he felt like talking that evening. He seemed to be at a loose end. With some difficulty we started a conversation about Nepal, the Gurkhas, and the Rana family who are all-powerful in this country. From his wallet he pulled out his instructions, which were now a month old: he might have shown them to me earlier! He held out some parchment (made of bamboo paper) covered with Sanscrit writing and adorned with several complicated seals: it looked like the ancient charters of our early kings.

The next day, May 5th, at about 8 o'clock Couzy and Schatz left camp. It was their turn to go and rub their noses on the East glacier! Suddenly everything became very quite. Ichac and I alone remained in Tukucha.

'There's a soldier going down to Tansing! Any letters?'

Of course we had a whole pile. But where was our mail from France? For more than five weeks we had been without any news. With G.B.'s help we wrote a letter in Gurkhali for the postmaster to try and clear up the matter.

A telescope with a magnification of twenty-five diameters was mounted on the camera tripod, and we were not long in discovering our friends at about 16,000 feet, high up on the snowy peak we christened the White Peak, getting ready for the descent. Ichac and I wrangled for turns at the telescope. They were now giving a fine exhibition of the French style of ski-ing, in spite of the snow apparently being in poor condition. I recognized Lachenal by his style as he executed some dazzling turns before the startled eyes of the Sherpas who, themselves, preferred to descend on their backsides.

On his return Rébuffat gave us an awestruck account of what he had seen from the White Peak.

'What's the south face like?' asked Ichac; and without waiting for the answer I added:

'When we saw it from Baglung it looked terrific.'

'If you'd seen it from close up you'd have seen something! A monstrous slope, several miles high, and without a break—something like the north face of the Matterhorn, which as you know isn't exactly an attractive place, only three times as big.'

We all looked at one another in consternation.

'The best thing is just to write off the south face.'

'At least now we know where we are. What about the south-east ridge? The other day when we saw it from the East glacier, you were the most hopeful, you said . . .'

'I was absolutely wrong. To begin with, it's incredibly long, it's all very high up, and above all it's technically very difficult: great walls and towers of ice, some rock, broken ground, gendarmes - there's no end to it.'

'Any possible camp sites?'

'None.'

'Well,' I said, 'all that's not very encouraging.'

'Oh,' he replied, 'there's absolutely no question of going *that* way.'

'I don't think any of us had many illusions about the south-east ridge,' said Ichac, 'any more than about the south face.'

'What's the verdict?'

'We must put a big cross against both these routes.'

Dejectedly we went off to get ready for dinner in the mess tent.

The next day we received a visit from Buddhist Lama whom we had already seen at Baglung. His claret-coloured robe was of doubtful cleanliness, but his expression radiated jovial good nature. Ichac, who much enjoys the simplicity and naturalness of Buddhist Lamas, gave him plenty to eat. Our Lama spoke enthusiastically of Muktinath. Our conversation with him was carried on with Angtharkay as intermediary and was very quaint indeed. This is about how it went:

'Are you going there now?' we asked him.

'I'll be there tomorrow.'

'But it's a long way from here.' Even though he was a Lama, and a man of oracles and prodigies, I didn't think he would have seven-league boots!

'You must come there,' he began again, 'every day there are miracles: flames come out of the ground, the priests make prophecies.'

'We'll certainly come. In a few days perhaps . . .'

Ichac suddenly had a wonderful idea: 'Shall we climb Dhaulagiri?'

Here was a chance to show off his talents! The Lama reflected deeply. He began to tell the beads of an enormous rosary. He gazed up into the sky, then down at his hands. This went on for more than five minutes while we remained silent and motionless. Were we about to witness some extraordinary feat of magic? Had we not been told that these Lamas were supernatural beings?

Very slowly, the Lama seemed to be coming back to earth: he brought himself to utter:

'Dhaulagiri is not propitious to you . . .' Then he added after a minute: 'It would be best to give it up and turn your thoughts towards the other side.'

'Which side?' asked Ichac.

For us the question was of some importance!

'Towards Muktinath,' he said, as though it was obvious.

Did he mean Annapurna? The future would soon show us.

Lachenal now turned up, bronzed by the sun. He had left Couzy and Schatz at the glacier camp, and as the radio was out of order, we should be without news of them for some days. About 5.30 Oudot and Terray 'landed' (the word is no exaggeration) from the cliff overhanging the camp. Terray was wildly excited; he'd grown a beard which made him look quite frightful.

'As for Dhaulagiri, my lads, you can think again!'

His lips were protruding even more than usual in his efforts to find the right words. In a loud, exasperated voice he burst out:

"Look here, Maurice, it's absolutely unclimbable, that Dhaulagiri of yours! It's fiendishly difficult!'

'Come and sit down and have a drink. You're all dust and sweat!' I said this in the hope that they would calm down a bit.

'Isn't there anything to eat?' Terray demanded.

'They're getting you something. Well, what did you see?'

'I'll tell you what happened from the beginning,' said Oudot quietly. 'On the third we pitched our tents at about 14,700 feet, between your two camps. The next day we spent the night in the Hidden Valley. When we got to the pass the porters gave us a bit of trouble. They were frightened: they had never been beyond this point. Yesterday morning, very early, Lionel and I reached the pass which you had seen from a distance and which overlooks the northern basin of Dhaulagiri. And there . . .'

'Well?'

'It still gives me the creeps.' Terray could not stop himself from shuddering, 'And there were the most terrifying gorges!'

'But where?'

'In front of us was Dhaulagiri,' went on Oudot, 'the real one—not what I had mistaken for it on the way up—and straight down below us was a huge glacier, heavily crevassed . . .'

41

'The foulest-looking piece,' put in Terray.

'. . . flowing down a canyon with walls thousands of feet high!'

'You see, I was right,' said Ichac, with modest triumph, 'so it *does* all drain into the Mayandi Khola!'

'It's all on such a terrific scale, it's a world in itself,' added Terray. 'As for the north ridge, which you see separates this glacier from the East glacier up which you went, it's half rock and half ice, and very steep. The north-west ridge, which we had never seen before, runs down into the canyon.'

This was most disappointing. 'So you really think it won't go?' I asked.

'The Lama,' said Ichac briskly, 'has informed us "Dhaulagiri is not propitious for you. Go towards Muktinath." Well?'

'Well, we must go towards Muktinath,' I said firmly, 'and tomorrow morning at that!'

'Towards the Tilicho?' asked Gaston.

'We'll cross the Tilicho, the pass *north* of the Nilgiris, the one spoken of by the man from Tinigaon and we'll take Annapurna in the rear.'

'Why not make use of the Couzy-Oudot-Schatz reconnaissance of the Miristi Khola? They saw Annapurna.'

'Yes, but only from a long way off. And they didn't see the north face. To reach it isn't going to be easy. And the ridge they saw there doesn't seem to me to be worth it. They don't think so either . . .'

'Look at the map,' interrupted Ichac: 'if we go by the Tilicho we shall save several days' march.'

'You'll see,' said I, 'we'll arrive plumb on the north face—and north faces in the Himalaya are often the easiest. We'll go just as far as is necessary to find Annapurna! As far as Manangbhot if need be.'

'Well, so that's what we've come to!' concluded Ichac, quite disillusioned, 'Just *looking* for Annapurna!'

*Left:* Houses in
Tukucha

*Below:* Dhaulagiri
and Tukucha Peak
from the east

*Above:* Camp high up in the valley of the Dambush
Khola: The Nilgiris in the background

*Left:* Fist reconnaissance in the Dambush Khola, north-
east of Dhaulagiri

15,000 feet up, Herzog catches sight of Annapurna,
on the right of the photograph

*Left:* The snow-blinded Terray returning to Camp II supported by Angtharkay

*Right:* Ajeeba carrying Herzog across the flooded Miristi Khola

*Facing page:* North Face of Annapurna, seen from the buttresses of the Great Barrier.
*Inset:* Facsimile of Herzog's message announcing the decision to attack Annapurna

*Left:* Camp III among the seracs

*Bottom right:* A sherpa crossing the ice slope below Camp IVA at about 23,000 feet

*Bottom left:* Climbers knee - deep in new snow on the way to **Camp III**

# 5

## *Looking For Annapurna*

'Hurry up, Oudot, I'm starving.'

Lachenal and Terray were not enjoying themselves much that morning: Oudot was using them for various important tests-tests of metabolism, and Flack tests[1] - and the proceedings had gone on for an hour or more. The tests had to be done on empty stomachs, which was hard luck, for people have pretty good appetites after getting back from a reconnaissance. While Terray was being put through it, Lachenal, who had finished, cut himself enormous slices of saucisson . From time to time Terray cast a sidelong glance in his direction.

'Go away, Biscante, You hog, with Your *saucisson.*'

'Shut up, You'll spoil the results,' said Oudot unsympathetically. At first I'd been a bit apprehensive that Oudot might be keener on climbing than on doctoring, but I need not have worried: he turned out to be a brilliant combination of the two. He kept me regularly posted about the physical form of my party and about the progress of their acclimatization. May all future expeditions have an Oudot !

While Terray was feeling sorry for himself, Ichac, Rebuffat and I were getting ready to leave for Manangbhot. An attempt on Annapurna by the Miristi seemed very problematical. From Manangbhot it should, by rights, be rather easier.

'You can give Tilman our love,' said Lachenal, who had    finished his snack. Tilman is one of the great names in the Himalaya; it was he who had conquered the highest summit so far climbed by man Nanda Devi, 25,645 feet high - and we thought the world of him. On our departure we had been told that he was preparing to explore just this district round Manangbhot. I felt that, given the party he had with him, his objectives would be a reconnaissance of the approaches to Mauaslu[2] and Annapurna. Climbers always like

[1]This unpleasant test left us disagreeable memories; it consisted of blowing into a tube and maintaining in it a pressure of four centimetres of mercury. The session comprised about twenty different tests.

to keep their plans dark beforehand; but it would be absurd if two expeditions were to attack the same summit.

Phutharkay left in advance to get quarters ready at Tinigaon. We were taking supplies for eight days; and before our return Oudot and Terray would have had time to go up to the Dhaulagiri glacier, if Couzy and Schatz should not meet with any success. These two rest days did me good; they gave me time to send news to France, to bring the Expedition's accounts up to date, and to see that the organization of the Camp was running smoothly. But the sedentary life really didn't suit me and I was very glad to be off again.

Along the route to Tibet there straggled a number of caravans carrying salt and rice. We made a triumphal march through the little village of Marpha, where the prayer-flags were fluttering and the people crowded cheerfully round us. There were more Tibetans here than in Tukucha. All the Expedition's sweets were distributed to a rabble of children; Marpha should retain happy memories of us ! Later on we reaped the benefit of our open-handedness, for a great many coolies from the valley offered their services when we had need of them. We came upon a number of prayer walls adorned with slabs of rock upon which we read the classic inscription : *Om mane padme hum*[3]. We were careful to respect the religious observances of these peoples, and to pass on the left of the walls. Little by little the look of the country changed; it became far more desolate even than the regions we had just left. Northward the contours were softer; hills covered with reddish coloured stones, a new luminosity in the atmosphere, and a growing feeling of desert country, showed beyond all doubt that we were approaching Tibet, though the frontier was a good day's march from this point.

At dusk we entered the wretched village of Tinigaon. The natives, extremely primitive and revoltingly dirty, stared suspiciously at us. A howling ragged mob, worthy of the *Cour des Miracles* of medieval Paris, escorted us to the only decent house in Tinigaon. A smiling Phutharkay was there to receive us; he had already made himself at home and was giving this orders, with his usual gentle kindliness, to numbers of women who crowded round him. We were in the house of the head man, the chief personage of the village, whose home served as a halting-place for the caravans. He was an astute trader, adept at procuring at an advantageous rate all that the village needed.

It was still dark when Angtharkay brought us breakfast next morning. A few stars were shining in a very clear sky: a promising sign. There

2 Another 'eight-thousander', 26,640 feet, to the east of Annapurna.
3 'Hari, the jewel in the lotus flower.'

**44**

in the distance, a beautiful and moving sight, was Dhaulagiri, rising solitary above the shadows and already lit up by the sun. Its wonderful architecture stood out astonishingly, seen from here.

The shikari who was to guide us professed to be quite familiar with the Tilicho Pass, but he did not know how long it would take to reach it. We walked up in single file, bent under our loads. Angtharkay, Phutharkay, Pansy and several Tibetan porters came with us. To enable them to go faster, we had lent them boots, but these for economy's sake they carried slung over their shoulders until we reached the snow.

After several hours' march the shikari no longer seemed very confident of his previous assertions: though we plied him with questions he didn't appear to know where the Tilicho Pass really was. In fact, this shikari was just an ordinary shepherd; and all he really knew was the way up to the grazing grounds. His role and his self-importance tended to diminish with the altitude, and, in the end he walked quite happily along behind us. In this manner we came to the much talked of Tilicho Pass.

Here we had a surprise. According to the map we ought to have been at the opening of a deep valley coming up from Manangbhot. Where was the wonderful view of Annapurna we ought to have had on our right? In some bewilderment we gazed at a dazzling scene of snow and ice where a galaxy of summits scintillated against the clear sky. It was a winter landscape, with something of fairyland in its brilliance and clarity.

On our right, instead of Annapurna, rose a gigantic barrier of mountains with many summits of about 23,000 feet. Before us opened out no deep valley but a vast plateau in the centre of which was a great frozen lake covered with snow, its size difficult to assess. On the left, cliffs fell sheer to the immense white expanse of the lake.

'But where the devil *is* Annapurna?'

'There can't be much doubt, Matha. It's almost certainly behind that handsome triangular peak, over there—look to the right, in the distance.'

'I'm not so sure,' said Ichac.

'Nor am I,' said Rébuffat.

'And the Tilicho Pass—where's that?' went on Ichac.

'At the far end of the plateau, on the other side of the lake. It must overlook the Manangbhot Valley, which lies just beyond.'

'Well, I shall have to verify that, but I'm not at all sure that you're right.'

In any case we should have to go down towards the Great Ice Lake, as, for want of any better name, we already called it amongst ourselves. An hour later we were on its edge, and while Pansy cooked a meal, the discussion continued.

'No sign of a lake on the map! And it's at least four miles long.'

'Oh, the map . . . Are all those summits marked on it?'

'Where do you think the waters flow down to?'

'This place is a regular funnel.'

'Like the Mont Cenis Pass.'

'I tell you the waters flow down towards Manangbhot!'

Everyone had his own idea, and insisted on putting it forward.

The main thing was to get to the other end of the lake. We took up our sacks, and the party proceeded along the left-hand bank until the superb red cliffs forced us out on to the ice. The coolies weren't very keen on this diversion. Ichac belayed me with a nylon rope and I ventured out some fifty yards from the bank. There I jumped up and down and danced, and banged with my ice-axe to break the ice and measure its thickness. Then I called out to the others:

'It's like a billiard table. Come on, the lot of you!'

All the same it was better to be safe than sorry: so we roped up into two long parties, with the porters and Sherpas spaced out at intervals of at least twenty-five feet. They could not understand that we did this to secure the safety of one and all; being roped up like this prevented them from grouping together. The first rope started off in my wake. I began a wide circular sweep so as to come off the ice again on the other side of the cliffs. Behind me, one by one, the porters, bent under their loads, hesitantly approached the edge, then braced themselves to it as if they were plunging in water. Fervently gabbling prayers, they followed exactly in my tracks, the eyes of every one of them riveted to the ground. The operation went off all right, and henceforth the porters would now have the slightest wish to part company with us, for if they did they would be obliged to come back over the Great Ice Lake!

Safely across on the other side, we climbed up the slopes and reached a pass that corresponded to the one we had reached earlier that morning. We christened it the East Tilicho: its height was about 16,400 feet.

As I had suspected, there was no outlet here; this end of the lake was blocked. At our feet a deep valley opened out going down to Manangbhot. Here again I had made an error in estimating distances. I had imagined Manangbhot as lying at the bottom of a huge basin,

46

but in fact the lie of the land was far more complicated: miles of moraines ran down steeply from where we stood, and the valley was blocked by a high mound of detritus. The only outlet here was a narrow defile which gave passage to the Marsyandi Khola, a torrent which rises at the Tilicho Pass and flows down beside the Great Barrier on which we hoped to find Annapurna. Beyond this obstacle, the ravine widened out gradually and here and there among the grey of the stones, shale and moraines were a few patches of green, islets of native cultivation.

To the right, along the continuation of the Great Barrier, were other peaks even more graceful and elegant than those we had seen above the Tilicho Lake; to the left, above the red cliffs, the Muktinath range rose to a number of 20,000-foot peaks. Behind us was the lake plateau over which we had just come, and at the far end the West Tilicho Pass which we had crossed that morning.

We settled down to a council of war. Ichac was of the opinion that, contrary to the map, Annapurna was possibly not situated on the Great Barrier.

'These clouds have come just at the wrong moment. They're blocking out all the higher summits. We can't discuss things we can't see.'

'We had a glimpse just now,' I said. 'Of course I know the map's a bit erratic, but I should hardly have thought it could make quite such an error; one doesn't mistake the position of a peak over 26,000 feet high.'

'So you think Annapurna's on the Great Barrier?'

'Yes, behind the big triangular peak in front of us.'

'Well, I'm prepared to bet the Great Barrier isn't marked on the map.'

'Even though it's over twelve miles long and has about fifteen points of 23,000 feet or over.'

'Fifteen? Come, come,' protested Ichac.

'Well, there are quite a number.'

'So, in short, you think the long ridge we see, and the ridge marked on the map, aren't the same. Then there'd be two long ridges, wouldn't there?'

'I suppose so.'

Thereupon Ichac made some calculations about distances which, according to him proved that it was quite impossible for Annapurna to be on this main ridge. I was shaken by his arguments, but not convinced.

Where on earth *was* Annapurna?

'Well,' I said at last, 'let's pitch camp here.'

'Fine,' said Ichac.

'You can stay here tomorrow, and the day after as well.'

'As long as you please . . .'

'You can check your opinion by making all the observations you want to.'

'And what are you and Gaston going to do?'

'Go down to Manangbhot. No doubt Annapurna will turn up just there!'

'I don't really know whether that would help matters or not, but as far as I'm concerned I'd rather stay here.'

'Right. We'll take advantage of our trip to buy tsampa for the porters. Phutharkay and Pansy will come with us.'

'Perhaps we'll see Tilman, too!'

Next morning at dawn Rébuffat and I set off early with light sacks. We counted on finding provisions down at Manangbhot. Without bothering about the stonefalls that we started, we set off at a rush down the great ravine.

Jumping down from rock to rock, we soon lost height. We followed the turbulent waters of the Marsyandi Khola, which was fed by a big hanging glacier under the Triangular Peak. The lower down we went the more we realized the size of the cliffs barring the foot of the valley. Soon we were forced to admit that the bank we were following wasn't really a practicable route and that we should have to cross. Gaston was over in a second. I hesitated. Let's see, if I stuck my ice-axe into the bed of the stream and used it as a pole . . . One foot on that rock . . . hum! that's not too safe . . . One . . . two! My muscles relaxed, the ice-axe twisted and the stone rolled over, and into the icy, frothing water I went.

The two Sherpas, Pansy and Phutharkay, had had a bright idea. They had made for the top of the cliffs and we could see them going along a vaguely marked track without any difficulty.

The great scree slopes which we had seen from the Tilicho Pass now barred our way, and from where we stood we could see no visible track or path. It was hard work climbing up. The slope seemed to be too steep for the stones to stay put, and the least movement was liable to start a regular avalanche. Far behind us we could see the Tilicho Pass, where we had been a few hours earlier.

The stones were all the same size as though they had been put through a sort of sieve with an enormous mesh. When at last we reached the head of the gorge, we were suddenly brought up short by a steep ravine of hard earth.

'There's no doubt, we'll have to cut steps,' I said to Rébuffat, somewhat puzzled.

'I'd rather it was ice!'

It was a chance to see how the Sherpas would manage. Phutharkay went ahead on to the slope, ice-axe in hand. He stood in perfect balance and cut steps with quick blows. Pansy followed, quite at ease. We had only to follow in their tracks.

After this ravine we had expected to find grass slopes, but when we reached the crest, a second ravine confronted us, then a third, and a fourth. In the end we were obliged to cut steps for a good hour before we reached the easier slopes of green. We went down some immense screes, glissading in clouds of dust.

It was past midday, and we stopped by the edge of the clear waters at the lower end of the gorges, and made a quick lunch. It was rough going along the banks of the torrent, and at times we had to climb up several hundred feet in order to find a way through the thick jungle growth.

This was a completely different world from the Tukucha Valley; here it was much hotter, there was more vegetation, and the contrasts were greater. From time to time flowering trees gave to the scenery a softer and more friendly aspect.

Man had already penetrated here, and the various ill-defined tracks now converged to form a path. Manangbhot was still a good way off, and as we had no camping equipment and very little food we must reach it that evening. At a bend in the path we suddenly came upon some habitation, sheltered behind a dip in the ground. A Buddhist *chorten* adorned with prayer flags marked the entry to the village of Khangsar. Ragged children, black with filth, caught sight of us and rushed up. It was the first time they had seen white men and they stared curiously at these apparitions from the mountains. They could not conceive that we had come from the other side of the range. In fact they didn't know there was another side. The only path known to the natives here is the pilgrims' track to Muktinath which goes over the Thorungse.

Pansy asked for the Suba. A noisy procession preceded us along the foul-smelling lanes. The Suba came out to meet us. He showed no surprise whatever: for centuries Buddha has taught the art of remaining impassive in face of the most extraordinary happenings. I asked him to procure tsampa for our coolies who had remained up in the mountains. With loud lamentations he replied that Khangsar was very poor: not a pound of tsampa to spare, nor a handful of rice, much less a chicken. We must go on to Manangbhot: it was only an hour's march, he told us, and then the sahibs would find everything they needed. Manangbhot at once became a paradise, and without waiting any longer we continued on our way, in spite of the heat and our hunger and thirst.

As we left the village we came upon the completely bare skeleton of a yak, lying across the path. No one would dream of moving these sacred bones: there they had been for months and there they would stay until they turned to dust. Everyone reverently skirted round them.

A series of steps hewn out of the rock and a very steep slope brought us down to the torrent again, and we made our way rapidly along its banks.

'Manangbhot!' said Pansy.

The town was perched on the cliffs after the manner of the ancient towns of Tibet. From the river we could see nothing but walls, and it looked as if we were going up towards a fortress. A plank across the water showed that we were now in a civilized country.

We followed a series of alleys which brought us to the centre of the town where we found an immense prayer wall about fifty yards long. The villagers came running up on all sides and surrounded us: the usual wretched-looking children, an old woman with a very curious portable prayer-wheel which she turned continuously, and young men—most of them very good-looking, and with a different type of face from those in the Tukucha district.

Here all were Buddhists. They were all crying out something, I couldn't make out what, but I didn't worry. I had learnt that to say 'good morning' in this country everyone finds it necessary to make a long speech at the top of his voice. After discussions lasting a quarter of an hour, a man went off in search of the Suba. Meanwhile Pansy had found us lodgings on the second floor of a barn. We climbed up to it by a ladder made of a thick plank in which notches had been cut. We all left our sacks there and Gaston and I returned to the square.

The villagers gathered round gesticulating:

'Americans?'

'No, French.'

'—?'

'Yes, French.'

As if this were conclusive proof, they nodded approval:

'American!'

'No, there are Americans, and there are Englishmen, but we are French.'

'Oh yes! But you're Americans all the same!'

I gave it up.

Most of them were Gurkhas who had served with the British army. We were the first white men to come here.

But as for Annapurna, not a thing was known about it. A summit of 26,000 feet doesn't pass unnoticed. Even if it were further along the range the locals should at least have known of its existence. Perhaps its name here was different—perhaps it was called after some other god.

The sun was sinking; it had already gone behind the splendid summit—our Triangular Peak—which towered above Manangbhot. Through Pansy, who questioned the inhabitants closely, we learned that the mountain in question was Ganga Purna. The two other summits on the left were Tchongor and Sepchia. Coming back from a stroll through the narrow alley-ways of the village, which had at last quietened down, Rébuffat and I met our Sherpas who reported sadly that the country was very poor. It would be extremely difficult for us to find supplies.

At that moment along came the Suba, an old man with a long beard, dressed very simply, and looking intelligent. After being introduced we sat down. Immediately the conversation opened on very practical lines. He would provide ten kilos of tsampa, and that was all. He gave us so many reasons that he got quite muddled himself. No hens, only four ridiculously small eggs; no milk and no rice. It was a very small amount of the tsampa so essential for our porters at the Tilicho Pass.

This serious news compelled me to send Phutharkay back to the pass first thing next morning. I scrawled a note to Ichac.

Dear Matha,

Phutharkay is just off on his way back to you. It's a very very long way down here. Results up to date:

Beyond the great Triangular Peak, which is called Ganga Purna, is another summit, Tchongor, a snow and ice peak of 23,000 feet. Then the range appears to drop down to the valley at a distance of about two miles from here, near a junction with another river, the Choundikiou, at the little village of Chindi. From where we are we can see another big summit on the right bank of the Choundikiou—this is Sepchia.

But where is Annapurna? It's still a mystery. Nobody here knows of it. *Programme:* Gaston, Pansy and I are going to Chindi in the hope of collecting information to

51

place Annapurna. If we get it we shall examine the possible approaches and estimate the difficulties, then return immediately by way of Muktinath.[4] If what we discover makes it clear that we ought to proceed with our intended reconnaissance to the top of the Great Barrier, which should be easily accessible and which we should do together, then we will return to the camp on the 12th, that is to say, tomorrow.

If we don't turn up, you break camp on the morning of the 13th and return to Tukucha.

Yours ever,
MAURICE

Meanwhile Ichac, after having seen us off to Manangbhot, set out with Angtharkay at about 9 o'clock the same day from the camp on the East Tilicho Pass. His objective was a point to the north-east of the camp, on the Muktinath Himal, looking towards the Great Barrier. When he reached a suitable spot at about 18,000 feet he took a series of compass-bearings and photographs. While he was engrossed in this, Angtharkay set to work to build a cairn, with such skill that he managed to construct an impressive monument over eight feet high. The clouds which had covered the sky at dawn now returned and the party had to make its way back to camp.

Lying flat on his stomach in his tent Ichac, with as much accuracy as the conditions and his equipment allowed, transferred the triangulations he had made to the map.

'There we are—I've got it clear at last.'

He had collected evidence that the chain stretching to the south of the camp, which we called the Great Barrier, was in fact the Annapurna Himal. Our famous Triangular Peak—the Black Rock whose topographical importance we had suspected—was the starting point of the further system of ridges from which rose Annapurna. So the only possible conclusion was that Annapurna must lie on the other side of the Great Barrier from the camp.

Rébuffat and I, therefore, had gone off after a ghost mountain. If only we had realized . . . But that is exploration: a great deal of hesitation, doubt, error and then, quite suddenly, a discovery.

Up in the past it was a very cold night. Dawn shone through the tent and heralded fine weather. Ichac took advantage of the clearness of the atmosphere to take bearings of the enormous peaks to be seen beyond Manangbhot, among them Manaslu, one of the eight-thousand-metre peaks of Nepal, a formidable pyramid that stands out strikingly from the other summits.

The clouds came down and the wind began to blow. The party

[4]The way round by Muktinath would save a day's march.

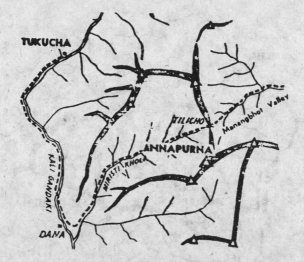

THE ANNAPURNA RANGE—*according to the map of the Indian Survey, with the Tilicho Pass incorrectly situated.*

either remained in the tents or kept a look out through glasses for the return of the Manangbhot party. Towards 3 o'clock Phutharkay arrived and gave Ichac my message. Ichac read it quickly—he knew already that he would learn nothing from it. There would be no point, he reckoned, in going up the easily accessible summit of the Great Barrier. It was preferable to go in the other direction as high as possible up a magnificent glacier he had discovered the previous day, and try to see Annapurna over the top of the Great Barrier.

On the morning of the 12th the weather was magnificent. Ichac explained to Angtharkay that they would go up together in the direction of the Muktinath Himal. At 7 o'clock they reached the cairn built the day before; at 7.30, with clouds beginning to cover the sky, they set foot upon a gently sloping glacier and started to climb it. A layer of new snow covered the ice and made the going slow. The altimeter rose gradually. They came to a zone of crevasses.

It was not the moment to embark upon anything difficult but simply to get as high as possible in the shortest possible time. Here and there a few steps had to be cut in the ice, but the difficult bits were short, and finally they emerged on to the upper slopes. They reached the ridge in thick mist.

Where was Annapurna? Visibility was nil. Ichac did not even know

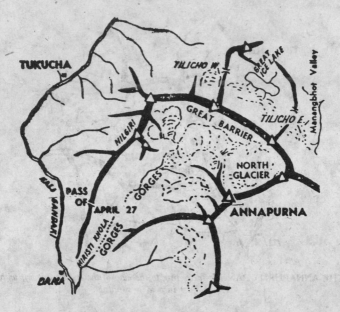

THE ANNAPURNA RANGE—*shown correctly.*

exactly where he was himself. He waited in vain for an improvement in the weather. It was 12.30 and the altimeter registered 20,300 feet. They did not suffer badly from breathlessness, which showed that they were beginning to get into training. This point reached by Ichac was the highest so far attained by the expedition, and was our first summit of over 20,000 feet.

The weather did not improve, and at 3.15 they began the descent, following in the tracks made on the way up which remained visible in spite of the sleet. It was 4.30 when they reached the camp. Here they found the leader of the Expedition snoring heavily in his sleeping-bag! Now just what had happened?

At Manangbhot, at dawn on the 11th, the little party had wakened with difficult. After a frugal breakfast Phutharkay went off with his sack and my note to Ichac. Rébuffat and myself, with Pansy, left shortly afterwards to go down the valley of the Marsyandi Khola in search of our elusive Annapurna.

Ahead of us, and a good distance off, a peak stood out which we

54

identified as Manaslu. Our intention was to skirt round the Great Barrier as far as possible. But we had to be back at Manangbhot that evening. At midday the little village of Chindi came into view and beyond it the valley narrowed and I could guess at the deep gorges that enclosed the river. To go further would have been useless. I was quite sure we were not on the right track—Annapurna was not down in these parts.

The inhabitants, and the shikaris from whom we asked for information, had never heard tell of it. They explained at some length that the word meant 'Goddess of the Harvests'. There was nothing for it but to return to Manangbhot, which we had to do on empty stomachs as our provisions were all finished.

Clouds collected over Tchongor and Sepchia and prevented us from taking the photographs which we should have liked to bring back as evidence. A halt was indicated to give them a chance to clear. Everybody found a comfortable nook, and Rébuffat was not long in falling asleep. Pansy smoked his last cigarettes. I kept watch like a sentry ready to give the alarm the moment our summits should appear.

At last Tchongor and Sepchia came out of the mist. Rébuffat took photographs and then we went on our way back to Manangbhot.

It was hot and we found it pretty hard going. Every time we met anyone Pansy would ask about the possibility of getting some provisions, but it was hopeless. The afternoon was well advanced when we reached our barn.

'So we're going back empty-handed,' said Rébuffat dejectedly.

'At least we know it's not over here.'

'We'll have to get back at once.'

'There's scarcely any food. Take what there is and push off with Pansy to Muktinath over the Thorungse. That will save you the ascent to the Tilicho Pass and you'll be back a day earlier at Tukucha. You'll be tired after travelling on an empty stomach, so with the remaining rupees you can hire ponies.'

'What about you?'

'Don't worry, with a slab of chocolate I'll manage to get up to the Tilicho camp.'

'It's a hell of a long way!'

'I'll be there tomorrow morning. I'd like to go up with Ichac to this "Accessible" summit.'

We had a little to eat and then went on our separate ways.

I was all alone. With a slab of chocolate as my only food I should have to be pretty nippy to get up from 9000 feet to over 16,000! My plan was to go as fast as I possibly could, to run when possible, until I couldn't go a step further.

An hour later I was at Khangsar. Without losing a minute I followed the path which gradually faded out along the left bank of the torrent. I made my way between the cliffs, going up and down to avoid obstacles. The hours went quickly by.

I found the steps which Phutharkay had cut in the limestone. Then I started up the great scree-slope and at last came to the stream which had to be crossed. Jumping was out of the question, so I took off my boots and hung them over my shoulder. It was getting dark and a slip into the icy water would be extremely disagreeable. I entered the water gingerly, testing every stone with my feet.

The current was very strong. Suddenly I slipped, tried to save myself only to fall in deeper, and ended by going right over altogether. This time I was soaked to the skin. With considerable difficulty I got up on to the opposite bank and began wringing out my clothes and emptying my boots. Still shivering and with my teeth chattering, I got dressed again. It would take me four hours to reach the camp and I had scarcely more than an hour of daylight left. Staggering on, I crossed a long steep slope of hard earth, where more than once I narrowly avoided slipping.

A piercing wind blew up from the valley and I shivered with cold. I could no longer see to go on, so I looked for a grassy place where I could spend the night, and ended by sitting down on a tuft, spreading my cape so that it covered me completely. My legs were icy cold and my knees knocked together. With my hood over my head, I hesitated between eating my last bit of chocolate and keeping it for the morning. I chose the first course, and then I allowed myself the last cigarette.

I was lost in the heart of the mountains, over 14,000 feet up, soaked through, weary and starving. Should I have the strength to climb up the last fifteen hundred feet? A treacherous wind found its way through every gap in my clothing, and snow began to fall. I closed my eyes, relaxed my muscles, and composed myself as I always do in mountain bivouacs.

Long and monotonous, the hours went by. Below me the full rumble of the torrent shook the ground and the noise echoed back and forth interminably in the valley. The damp rose up and went right through me—a horrible feeling when one is already chilled to the marrow, and I had to fight against it. From time to time I had a look round. The weather was not improving. If the clouds came down I should not be able to recognize the way.

Though numbed and half asleep, I welcomed the first streaks of dawn with real delight. I should have to wait for it to get a bit lighter, and how hard those last minutes were! Folding my anorak, I started off again with a painfully empty stomach. It was very cold and I hoped to warm up as I walked. The weather had improved slightly and I frequently stopped on the pretext of picking out the way ahead. My legs were trembling and refused to make any effort, but all the same I managed to gain ground. I could see patches of sunlight shining on Manangbhot, but up here I was still in shadow.

At every halt, before starting off again, I picked out ahead a comfortable stone for the next stop. The stops became more and more frequent, and longer. I began to wonder if I should ever get up. Whenever I came to a flat rock I sank down on it, and immediately felt a bit better. After a few seconds rest I would see the absurdity of the situation: how could I possibly give up with only a few more yards to climb? I would pick out another rock, drag myself up off the first, and take a few steps—to myself it was as though I were racing along, but actually I was going extremely slowly, and I threw myself down the moment I reached my successive objectives. Yard by yard I gained height, and presently there remained only two hundred yards to the camp, which was just not visible from this point.

I tried to call out, but no sound came from my throat. It was difficult to stand up without wobbling; it was safer and easier down on all fours. My head swam, and I wanted to sleep. Then, mustering my last ounce of strength, I threw myself heavily down on a rock on the ridge. Time slipped by. When finally I opened my eyes it seemed as though a century had passed; I raised my head above the ridge. There was the camp, barely twenty yards away! In vain I tried to attract somebody's attention, but the coolies were chatting quietly round a good fire. If only they could see me! If only one of them would turn his head! I dropped some stones in the hope of making them look up, but they didn't hear, and I couldn't call them. My head was like lead and my ears were buzzing.

Now that I was certain of getting there, I gritted my teeth fiercely and managed to crawl along on all fours like an animal. Suddenly Phutharkay turned round.

'Bara Sahib!'

Quite thunderstruck, he watched me crawling along. Then everyone got up and came running towards me. I was saved!

They laid me down, trembling all over, on an air mattress. I drank, and ate a little, and learned that Ichac had not yet returned, but that he wouldn't be long. I asked them to get a meal ready for me. With the assistance of the porters, Phutharkay opened an impressive number of tins. The fire burned merrily and the capacious cooking-pots began to simmer, giving out such an appetizing smell that to control myself I had to remain motionless and half asleep.

When the meal was ready, I began to eat straight out of the pots, which was not at all what Phutharkay was expecting—he had been cooking for the whole camp! For over an hour-and-a-half, without stopping, delightedly, and at high speed, I consumed the biggest meal of my life. I was like the snake who swallowed a fat sheep in the dream of the Little Prince, in St Exupéry's story. I settled back in my sleeping-bag with relief.

'Hullo, Maurice, good morning!'

I pulled myself together.

'Matha!'

'We've just come down from a peak of over 20,000 feet!'

We exchanged news. Everything fitted in with Ichac's deductions and confirmed them, and the whole northern side of the Annapurna massif had been explored.

'There's no question of it,' I told him. 'The key to Annapurna lies in the south, along the route that Couzy, Oudot and Schatz took on April 27th, up the Miristi Khola.'

'So there's nothing more for us to do here,' concluded Ichac. 'We must get back quickly to Tukucha.'

Next day we packed up. The porters were delighted to be leaving this spot where they had spent three days completely cut off and with nothing to do, and there was no need to hurry them on or show them the route. In a few minutes the loads were made up and allotted, and while Ichac and I set out, still talking, the porters went off quickly under the supervision of Angtharkay who led them straight towards the Great Ice Lake. This time, without any fuss, they traversed its entire length.

In three days the snow which had formerly covered the ridge leading to the West Tilicho had melted. At the pass, we paused a little to look at the Great Ice Lake, the immense amphitheatre surrounding it, and above all at the remarkable Great Barrier. Never should we see it all again. We ran down the hillside and came out on to the lower slopes in the middle of a magnificent forest of deodars.

A strong wind got up, but it was blowing the right way, and soon afterwards we reached Tinigaon.

Next morning we passed through Marpha; and after six exhausting days we were very glad indeed to get back to headquarters at Tukucha. As we neared the camp Oudot came towards us.

'Hallo, Doctor! Any news?'

'Everybody's here and very fit. What about you?'

'Have you seen Gaston?'

'He got back yesterday.'

'Good. It is May 14th, we'll have to make up our minds. We'll have a meeting this afternoon.'


Meanwhile what had been happening on Dhaulagiri during our absence? On the evening of Monday, May 8th, Noyelle had come racing down from the camp on the East glacier. Excitedly he explained that while going up the glacier with a Sherpa, he had seen the Couzy-Schatz rope in a very steep snow couloir. The point of this route was that it ought to have enabled us to by-pass the enormous and dangerous seracs of the upper part of the East glacier. Actually it was just as difficult and as dangerous as the other route, since the couloir was threatened by avalanches. One look upward revealed tremendous walls of blue ice, 1500 feet above. At the very moment when Noyelle was watching the movements of the other two an enormous unstable block of ice heeled over. Tons of ice shot down the slope with a fearful noise, just missing our liaison officer, and were pulverized on the plateau of the East glacier lower down.

'And to think my camera wasn't set,' he said regretfully.

Couzy and Schatz had insisted upon going on. They were not to be deterred by a little thing like that; however, their efforts to get out of the couloir and set foot on the rocks proved fruitless. They pressed on with their attempt but were unable to advance more than a dozen yards: the rocks were slippery and unsafe. Schatz had one small satisfaction: he was able to hammer in his first piton in the Himalaya at over 16,000 feet. After having exhausted all the possibilities, they gave it up, and on the 9th they came down.

The following day Oudot and Terray went up in their turn, and though they met the Sherpas coming back, this did not stop them. They pitched a camp on the East glacier, at a height of 16,500 feet, up against a big rock wall on the right bank. During the night a stone tore right through their tent.

On the 11th Oudot and Terray broke camp early, at 3 a.m., and so they had all day before them to devote to the problem. Putting on their crampons, they started up and with great difficulty succeeded in advancing a few yards. After considerable effort they reached the foot of the big ice wall which the first reconnaissance parties had climbed, and which Couzy and Schatz had passed on their right. Instead of going up the wall, on which steps had already been cut for a good part of the way, they went towards the left bank of the glacier. Cutting steps and climbing up with exhausting trouble, they reached the same height as the previous parties' furthest limit. Soon they saw a possible way that had been invisible from the point these parties had reached. As they went up they were able to skirt round a number of seracs and gain height, and, taking dangerous risks, they reached the place where the glacier levelled out.

In front of them stretched a tangled maze of crevasses and snowfields with no way through. Further away on the right the slope steepened again and ran up into the north ridge of Dhaulagiri, which rose before them, clear cut and inaccessible.

Oudot and Terray rightly judged the difficulties and dangers to be far too great. What was the use of going on, only to be forced to give up later? The way up Dhaulagiri did not lie over this glacier, and if there were no other way, then the mountain would never be conquered. Having thus reduced our visionary hopes to their proper proportions, and realizing very well the bitter disappointment it would be to us all, the two decided to give up the attempt. That evening they made their way wearily back to Base Camp at the foot of the East glacier, and the following day to Tukucha.

If we were to launch the full strength of the expedition against Dhaulagiri, it would be a tremendous hazard full of uncertainty and peril; and we could only decide on this course after very carefully weighing all the reasons for and against it. We should have to examine the whole question soberly and judiciously.

On May 14th the entire expedition assembled in the mess tent at Tukucha for a solemn council of war.

# 6

## Council of War

The heat was oppressive, and the glare outside blinding; the greenish light that filtered through the canvas of the mess tent where we assembled offered a pleasant change. Throughout our deliberations Angtharkay kept us supplied with coffee.

Everyone looked serious. I realized very well that behind all Lachenal's light-hearted joking and nonsense there lay a very understandable impatience and uneasiness. Well, in an hour's time we should have come to some decision.

The Sherpas made themselves busy. They guessed that something was up—all the Sahibs were there.

'It is now May 14th,' I began. 'In spite of all our efforts since April 22nd, no real possibility has turned up: we have no route in prospect, we aren't even clear in what direction we ought to set out. We aren't sure of anything. Time's short. The moment has come to take major decisions.'

Nobody said a word.

'These mountains are extremely tough propositions. The climbing possibilities are limited in every direction. As for Dhaulagiri by the Dambush Khola and the Hidden Valley, it would be pretty risky to plan a route which would involve crossing two passes of 16,000 feet, and then traversing a huge and extremely difficult glacier and all this just to get to the foot of the mountain. A route up the East glacier would be even more problematical. I don't wish to take the risk of sending the Expedition over such dangerous ground. There will be quite enough danger, wherever we go, without deliberately running into it at the very start. There remains another possibility: the Tukucha Peak, which we haven't yet reconnoitred. But must we really first get up a seven-thousand-metre peak in order to climb an eight-thousander? It would be a counsel of despair—and the longest route, if not the most dangerous.'

'I'm never going on that mountain again,' said Terray, his recent experience among the rickety seracs and treacherous snow bridges of the East glacier fresh in his mind. 'Dhaulagiri will never be climbed,' he declared, and added firmly: 'I wouldn't go up there at any price.'

Schatz made a face. 'The chances seem pretty thin. I, for one, don't really see any possibility: the south-east ridge is out of the question. What about the north ridge?'

'The north ridge!' exclaimed Terray. 'No one will ever get up it—it's bare ice and the angle is so steep that hand-holds would have to be cut.'

'When Couzy, Oudot and Schatz were up above the Miristi gorges on April 27th, they brought back sketches showing the average angle of the north ridge of Dhaulagiri. It looked perfectly reasonable. Moreover, the steep part didn't look to me to be more than 15,000 feet high. On the left flank, looking towards the mountain, there are crevasses which would give shelter for camps. And why not place some fixed ropes.' Although my argument was based on reasons of a technical nature it didn't convince anyone. After a long silence Rébuffat replied:

'In any case we'd have to reach this ridge somehow. So what?'

None of this was encouraging, but I wanted to appear to be defending possibilities which I really knew were hopeless, because I felt a tacit and unanimous opposition to them. Once we had abandoned Dhaulagiri, I did not want the party to have any regrets on the score of not having fully explored the question. Before turning the page I wanted the problem of Dhaulagiri to be well and truly settled.

Another long silence; everyone was thinking but didn't want to be the first to speak. Then Couzy leant forward, and looked hard at me, searching for the right words:

'Maurice, on Annapurna there are at least *some* possibilities.'

The tension relaxed, and tongues were loosened. Everyone thought it rather courageous of Couzy to broach the question. Indeed, it was to Annapurna that we must now turn our attention.

'What we *do* know about Annapurna is that the only possible line of attack is from the north. But we must first get there. The way to the upper basin of the Miristi Khola is a problem we have already solved. From the farthest point reached, three routes were seen: first, the north-west ridge, and it is on this that, in theory, we ought to launch our first attack. Secondly there is the West glacier of Annapurna—it looks as if we ought to be able to follow a couloir from it up to the junction of the spur with the main ridge. And finally there is the glacier that no one has yet seen, but which, we can infer, flows down the whole of the north face of Annapurna.'

'You see,' said Oudot, 'that spur is the shortest route. In two days we ought to be able to reach the summit ridge at a height of 20,000 to 21,000 feet. Of course between the top of this spur and Annapurna itself there is a bit that we haven't yet seen. If there should be a gap, it would always be possible to get round it by taking to the West glacier, that is, to the right of the spur when you look at the mountain.'

'Yes,' added Couzy, 'I'm all in favour of this route, because we ought to be able to gain considerable height without any special difficulty.'

'And after all,' continued Schatz, 'it is only the middle part of the route that is still an unknown quantity. The upper slopes of Annapurna appear to be quite easy. There seem to be places level enough for tents. I'm sure. Let's have a go, in three days we'll have it in the bag!'

I was in complete agreement with Schatz; it struck me as an entirely reasonable plan.

'What's your view, Matha?'

'I'm not here as a climber, Maurice. I'm your photographer.'

'When you go out on reconnaissance you're a climber all right. What do you think, Oudot?'

'It strikes me that Dhaulagiri is altogether too dangerous. I'm for Annapurna.'

Noyelle was of the same opinion.

I turned to Rébuffat.

'Do you think there'd be any chance of getting up the Tukucha Peak?'

'I've already told you, Maurice: I think we ought to have begun by going up it, the summit must be a perfect viewpoint. But now it's out of the question.'

Once a decision had been taken, the Expedition would, single heartedly, throw all its strength into the attack. Every voice had been heard: now it was for me, alone, to decide. It was a very heavy responsibility.

'Instead of immediately making an all out attempt on Annapurna, we'll send out a large reconnaissance party to find the best route up. This party will carry ten days' food, and will be re-provisioned, on a limited scale, until further notice. As soon as the advance party see a possible route the whole reconnaissance will, upon definite orders from me, be transformed into an assault party. And right away we'll make arrangements to ensure that this transformation can be effected without wasting a single day.'

'Well, now that it's all settled,' exclaimed Schatz, 'let's be off at once.'

'Wait a minute!'

Everyone was quiet.

'It's a long way from being settled. You must all know exactly what you've got to do. Three of us know the route taken on April 27th. Each of these three will accompany a party during the four days' preliminary march.

'Matha, Gaston and myself are only just back from Manangbhot, and we are very tired. And I've got a lot to do here, with letters and accounts—I must bring them up to date so as to know whether we shall need more money for our return journey. Lachenal and Terray will leave today, with the Sherpas Ajeeba, Angdawa and Dawathondup, and Schatz to show them the way.

'A second group—Gaston and myself, guided by Couzy—will follow a day later. Noyelle will see to the regular provisioning of these groups, Ichac and Oudot will wait for instructions from me before coming on, and as this won't be before six days at least, they will have time to go over together to Muktinath.'

'What about Angtharkay?' asked Ichac.

'You can take him with you. And Noyelle and G.B. Rana will constitute the rearguard, and must not move up until I send word. Noyelle, you must prepare all the loads that are wanted for the reconnaissance, for the assault and the return, and organize the recruitment of porters against the time they're needed.'

'What about our equipment?' inquired Lachenal.

'Divide everything into four lots. The first, which you will take with you, must be very light—you must reserve your strength. The second lot—climbing gear, warm clothes, toilet things, etc.—will be carried by porters. The third lot will consist of everything necessary in the event of the reconnaissance being transformed into a full scale assault. That is to say—spare clothes, heavy equipments such as camp boots and sweaters. Finally the fourth lot, which will consist solely of what we need on our valley marches, will be put into containers labelled with your names and will remain at Tukucha.'

So everyone knew just what was in store for him, and what he must do. I called Angtharkay over and explained the plan. The camp immediately became a hive of tremendous activity. The first party was due to leave as soon as it was ready. Though they were not carrying much weight, the diversity of the objects they were taking gave rise to consultations, preparations and visits from tent to tent.

The doctor collected everything needed by the first group for a fairly long trip, through the jungle or high up on the mountains, in good or bad weather: the anti-toxic serum and the aspirin, sunburn cream and maxiton, vitamin B2 and bicarbonate of soda. He passed everyone as fit: it had taken three weeks for us all to get acclimatized and back to our normal form.

Terray sorted out his belongings most conscientiously: he painted his name on the container which would remain at the camp, and then got busy with the provisions. Lachenal, our equipment man, measured ropes and sorted out pitons.

Noyelle looked a bit worried: the negotiations with the Suba and G. B. Rana were difficult. He explained to them again and again that the horses asked for must really be produced at once. Eventually he got his way, but the wretched animals did not inspire much confidence: one was bandy-legged, another too old and his head nodded dismally. They did not look as if they could hold up even the length of the village!

Rucksacks were closed and the horses saddled—with what saddles! Our steeds were certainly not 'pawing the ground impatiently'—still, they were there. Everyone ran through his list of things in his head, praying that nothing had been forgotten. The Sherpas took up their loads, with a lot of kindly help from their friends, and shouts of 'Good luck' from those who were staying to those who were going. Then they were off.

While waiting for dinner in camp, I brought my accounts up to date and wrote a letter to Paris.

Tukucha, May 15th, 1950

My dear Devies,

We are just back from a long and tiring reconnaissance to the north of Annapurna, and I am writing at once to give you our news.

To begin with you can tell all our families that we are all very well indeed. Everybody's in grand form, and Oudot's tests confirm it. We're all working splendidly together as a team. I can now report that the period of exploration is practically at an end.

*Climbing:* Upon my return we went thoroughly into the technical situation: the various routes on Dhaulagiri are not only extremely difficult but also, on certain sections, highly dangerous. On the other hand Annapurna offers several possibilities.

So yesterday I took the decision to direct the Expedition's efforts towards this objective, and to send off a large-scale reconnaissance at once, which can be transformed without loss of time into a definite assault.

Actually, while Dhaulagiri rises alone like a monstrous pyramid, Annapurna dominates a mighty range comprising about fifty summits over 23,000 feet high, some very hig¹ ridges, and an almost inaccessible upper basin, with probably only one line of weakness—a depression by which we shall make our attack.

Yours ever,
MAURICE HERZOG

Why did we all feel so melancholy? Was it because some of our friends were already off on the adventure? Or was it because there was still some element of indecision? Or was it simply that we were tired? I couldn't say. So while Gaston snored away conscientiously in his sleeping-bag, I worked late on figures, making estimates and drawing up my budget till my eyes closed.

The camp slowly came to life next morning; people got up and began to get busy.

The second party was due to leave early in the afternoon. The kitchen smoked and the Sherpas bustled around the tents, while the village children stared wide-eyed. One of the locals placidly twirled his distaff as he looked on, another had his eye on an old tin which spelt treasure to him, and a third blew into an old tube of condensed milk and burst it with frightful pop.

The porters began to arrive one by one. They had been told to come in the afternoon, so of course they turned up in the morning; they would just have to wait and watch us. Pansy, Sarki and Aila had their heads deep in their wide-open sacks. I kept an eye on them because, with an excess either of prudence or mistrust, they tended to take all their belongings along with them. I thought it quite unnecessary for them to be burdened with three pairs of trousers, but on the other hand I did not hesitate to load them up with extra ropes.

Sounds of Indian music reached me from the mess tent where Noyelle was trying to get the news on the wireless. This renewed contact with the world beyond turned our thoughts away for a moment from our tasks. What news had they of us in France? Here we had heard nothing from home—not a word; in spite of all our inquiries, complaints to the Nepalese, and special messengers, the mystery of our mail remained unsolved.

When our meal appeared we threw ourselves upon the food making free, while we had the chance, of all condiments, vinegar and anything spicy.

Now it was time for the second party's departure; yesterday's scenes were repeated in an atmosphere of mounting excitement Rébuffat supervised the provisions and Couzy the equipment. The horses arrived; by good luck the porters were there.

The afternoon was already well advanced, hot and thundery. Saying goodbye to Ichac, Noyelle and Oudot, we dug our heels into our horses' flanks.

It was our turn to set out on the great adventure.

# 7

## *The Miristi Khola*

We passed along Tukucha's main street at a gentle trot, through a crowd of lousy children, women scouring their pans and old men who observed us from their doorways; the Sahibs were up to something new.

The crossing of the Dambush Khola was a tricky operation. Perched up on our mounts we tried to avoid getting our boots wet and might have managed it if we had not been obliged to keep close to our horses' heads to guide them firmly through the rushing river, and if the local saddles had not had the disagreeable habit of slipping round the animals' bellies, or the over-taut girths had not chosen the most inconvenient moments to give way. Rébuffat, who has long legs, crossed over boldly, with his feet in the water.

'It's better to get your feet wet,' he explained, 'than be soaked all over.'

On the broad plain of Tuckucha we urged our steeds to a decent pace. One of the straps of Rébuffat's saddle broke and he completely lost his balance; he did not seem to be aware of the comic figure he cut as he clung to his horse. I offered to change mounts with him but eventually we got things straight and galloped on.

Passing through the familiar villages of Khanti and Larjung we came to the little village of Dhumpu—extremely primitive, but with most friendly inhabitants—and then started up the slope to Lete. The *garawalas*, or grooms, who were waiting for us there were getting anxious: it was late—how were they going to get the horses back to Tukucha? Since the path was good, why should we not proceed with the horses and so save time? The grooms could trot along behind us. The moment came when we really had to dismount. The *garawalas* came up dripping with sweat and did not conceal their satisfaction at seeing the end of the gallop—nor did we, for that matter.

We started off along a poorish track which struck off to the left and which, according to Couzy, should lead us to the hamlet of Choya. Soon we came in sight of the village; there was a lot of coming and going at the first house, and coolies were climbing up and down a ladder. The sounds of laughter, singing and general hilarity led me to suspect that *chang*—rice-alcohol—was being generously distributed. Its sale is forbidden in Nepal; but that was no good reason for giving one's guests a poor welcome!

Not long after we had left the village we came upon the main body of porters—whom I had sent on ahead, in view of the long march—comfortably settled in the cool grass with their loads lying round them. We shouted at them, and in the twinkling of an eye the loads were picked up and the porters disappeared with a rapidity of which I should not have thought them capable. As darkness fell we skirted some large boulders and came out on to an alp perched on the edge of a precipice. Sarki and Aila quickly got the tents up, unpacked the evening's provisions and lit a great fire. It was late, and we ate our meal in silence and then all got into our sleeping-bags.

Next morning we soon found ourselves all together on a narrow track leading down to the river-bed. It was at this spot that, later on, Marcel Ichac and Jacques Oudot met a band of monkeys going up the valley. We now followed a path along the side of the cliff and after a steep descent we emerged suddenly beside the Chadzion Khola, not, at this season, a very large stream. There was no difficulty about crossing it, but even for those who had been there before, it was quite impossible to make out the slightest vestige of a track on the other side where a stretch of thick and apparently impenetrable jungle seemed to run far up the mountain side. Couzy informed us that this was the last water until the evening of the next day, and we filled up every available container. The Sherpas and the porters went on drinking indefinitely, like camels.

The ascent began with a climb up a vertical slab of rock. The track went up in steep zigzags, obstructed by bamboos, dead tree trunks and trees which straggled over the path in an attempt to reach the light, and the air was damp and heavy. Couzy and I embarked on a long discussion: we had got as far as Bergson and Junger when we came upon a delightful meadow bright with snowdrops and a variety of other flowers.

'It was here that Oudot, Schatz and I bivouacked on April 27th,' said Couzy. Mountaineers are great lovers of routine, so we had lunch there. Tubes of condensed milk were passed round. Those who were not sick of this form of nourishment sucked concentrated fruit tablets, and while the last of the sweating porters were still arriving, the smoke curled up from our cigarettes. Couzy had grown meditative as a result of our discussion and Rébuffat thought of his little Dominique, of whom he had received no news.

69

Resuming our march, we suddenly found ourselves, at a turning of the path, in a grove of trees resplendent with brilliant coloured flowers whose names I did not know. No vaulted roof could have been more magnificent. The track went on across a beautiful clearing. Round us was a cemetery of charred deodars whose trunks rose well over a hundred feet high, and giant rhododendrons bordering our path hung out great clusters of pink and red flowers. The Sherpas rushed up to some trees like red birches, made holes in the trunks with their ice-axes, fixed an empty tin underneath and so got a few mouthfuls of fresh water.

We now climbed painfully up a desperately long and steep couloir full of loose stones.

'There are lots of marmots here,' said Rébuffat.

But though I kept my eyes skinned I did not see a single one. At the top, which must have been about 13,000 feet high, we stopped again to smoke a cigarette while we waited for the porters. They had gone splendidly so far, but I could see they were tired. The ground was becoming more difficult and their loads, which were held by straps round their foreheads, tended to make them overbalance downhill. It was rough and painful for their bare feet and they did not feel at all safe. Further on, we had to cross a large patch of snow where we enlarged the track and stamped it down, but our porters, doubled under the weight of the containers, looked most unhappy. I felt vaguely guilty as I walked along in my comfortable boots.

The weather turned really bad and it rained solidly. We kept together so as not to lose each other, and advanced by guess-work over the gentle slopes of an alp up to the cairn which marked the pass that was the goal of this day's journey. We pitched the tents in an indescribable muddle; our only thought was to get under cover the minute they were up. We had climbed over 6000 feet in the day to reach the pass which we decided once for all to call 'Pass of April 27th'. Couzy, Oudot and Schatz, who discovered it, deserved great credit for picking out the various vague tracks and following them up to the end.

The day's route was planned to cross the buttresses of the Nilgiris, always keeping well above the Miristi Khola. When impassable ravines barred our way we went higher up and then descended again right to the river's edge where the gorges became practicable once more. Endlessly we carried out these flanking movements, going up and down the ravines, crossing streams, large and small. Here and there, by good luck, we found boulders which had been up-ended. These guiding marks were dotted along the route taken by the first party the day before, and on a patch of snow I read the time at which they had passed, written by Schatz. Roughly speaking, we were keeping to the same time-table.

We were covered in cloud and I could get no general view of the ground over which we were passing. Early in the afternoon we got to a point from which any further progress appeared very difficult, so we hailed Couzy, our guide: he hesitated a bit, retraced his steps, then called to us triumphantly: on a small boulder, held in place by some stones, was a pennant of the Club Alpin Français which marked the beginning of the descent to the Miristi Khola. We started down some steep grassy slopes where the porters, whose morale was not very good, kept on slipping. It rained and snowed and the way seemed interminable. Suddenly I heard a shout, and as I went forward I saw a wood fire, and round it, the porters of the first party who, having deposited their loads, were returning to the valley. Conversations began in Gurkhali. Once more I noticed how well this language of short words and guttural sounds can be understood at a great distance.

The slope continued over steep rock slabs, and then skirted along cliffs in which we could make out some enormous caves. Couzy assured me that the previous time he had been that way a herd of thar, taking things easy by the entrance to these grottos, did not even trouble to move as he went by. But today I had the rifle, and of course there was not an animal to be seen.

A few minutes later we were all assembled on the banks of the Miristi Khola, a turbulent river that drains all the waters from the upper basins of Annapurna, the Great Barrier and the Nilgiris. From now on the route lay along the opposite bank, so we had to cross over. I spotted some tree-trunks which the others had placed the day before, but our coolies refused to venture on them with their loads. Rébuffat and I did not hesitate: we would take the stuff over ourselves.

Now Rébuffat was transformed into a porter; he had the straps supporting the containers placed round his forehead, and his head, his neck and his long body swayed dangerously. He approached the torrent, started across with Couzy's support, then balancing by himself took a few steps over the foaming water, and stretching out his arms reached me where I was standing on a boulder sticking out of the water: from that point I could take the loads on safely.

This manoeuvre was repeated a number of times, but one of the loads made me anxious; it was very heavy and very awkward, consisting of two base camp units and one high-altitude unit. Rébuffat advanced, hesitated, lost his balance, just managed to regain it, and advanced again, slowly. Then the strap round his forehead slipped, the load was hurled into the water, and in a flash I foresaw the irreparable loss of our tents.

Couzy and I reacted in the same way: from our opposite banks we each tried to grab the tents, and madly hopped about from boulder to boulder. I missed once, jumped along further, and just before a big eddy which held up the load, managed to stick the point of my ice-axe into a bit of stuff and pulled the load out. The rest of the operation went off perfectly.

Next day, in appreciably better weather, we left early. I went on about an hour ahead of the rest of the party and, towards midday, met Marcel Schatz, who had come out to look for us. He gave me the latest news: Louis Lachenal and Lionel Terray had left that morning on a reconnaissance of the north-west spur of Annapurna. Near the Base Camp the moraines flattened out, the valley of the Miristi widened, and there was a better view of our surroundings. The spur which ran down and petered out a few hundred yards from where we were did not look too bad, but without quite knowing why, I did not feel keen on this route. Since our experiences on Dhaulagiri I was suspicious of ridges. I was afraid that even if it did not present any insurmountable difficulties, this ridge would be troublesome, and I could not bring myself to turn the reconnaissance into a full-scale assault until we had completed our exploration. This meant, practically speaking, not before we had set foot upon the upper plateau of Annapurna. Schatz and I arrived at Base Camp, which was pitched among the moraines in the midst of a vast stony desert with little blue-green lakes dotted about in the hollows. From here it would be a day's march to the Great Barrier which blocked the horizon to the east, or to the Nilgiris on the north. Snow was falling and we sheltered in one of the tents where hours passed in prolonged discussions . . .

There were sounds of stones displaced, ice-axes clanging against the rocks, bad language—evidently the Lachenal-Terray party had arrived. A flap of the tent was jerked back and a boisterous greeting flung in: the pair were clearly in full cry I could see they were very tired, but resolute and optimistic. They pulled off their snow-covered clothes and while they sipped their tea told me what they had done during the day. This celebrated partnership, which had conquered all the finest and most formidable of our Alpine faces, was today living up to its reputation.

'It's not exactly a picnic,' said Terray.

'I should say not!' put in Lachenal vehemently. 'There are pitches which are easily grade 5.'[1]

'Grade 5!' I was horrified. 'How on earth do you think Sherpas can climb pitches of that difficulty?'

'There are only sections here and there.'

'We can fix ropes and by pulling and pushing the Sherpas we'll manage all right.'

'We'll see. And apart from these pitches what's the ridge like?'

'It's certainly very long,' said Terray, 'and the further you go the more difficult it becomes.'

'And no doubt becomes impossible beyond the point you got to!'

'I don't really think so. We stopped at about 11 o'clock this morning, climbing since dawn up to somewhere near 18,000 feet. A bit higher up the ridge steepens again and becomes snowy. After that we could see no more, but I think, and Biscante agrees with me, that it must run up into the upper plateau of Annapurna a few hundred yards higher up.'

'Perhaps!' I remarked sceptically.

'Listen, Maurice, it's quite simple. All we have to do,' proposed Terray, 'is to go there in strength. Tomorrow we'll all set to work and move Base Camp to the summit of the grassy saddle and then begin the assault.'

'And we shall have saved several days of indecision,' added Lachenal.

'And perhaps we shall have spoiled all our chances,' I replied. 'If the attack upon the spur should be unsuccessful we'd have to move Base Camp again and come down into the valley and then start up once more. It's out of the question. I've no intention of hazarding the whole strength of the Expedition on a route we know so little about. Let's push on further with the reconnaissance you have already made; tomorrow let's go beyond the point where you stopped—on until we are certain that it's practicable right up to the summit. We won't make the final decision until then.'

'You *are* an obstinate old devil!'

Lachenal and Terray stormed away at me. They thought we ought to decide to attack at once, and kept on insisting how sure they were

[1] Rocks are graded according to their difficulty from grade 1, the easiest, to grade 6, the hardest, reaching the limits of the possible. Only very few climbers get to grade 6. Most of the classic expeditions in the Alps are grade 4. In the Himalaya where the altitude makes every movement more of an effort, parties do their best to avoid all climbing difficulties. Where these are met, they do not generally exceed grade 4.

this route would go. I knew my friends well and had my doubts of their wild enthusiasm; they were in a very excitable state after their day's exertions. I was the responsible person and it was up to me to supply the element of prudence: I stuck to my decision. Tomorrow morning we would all go up the spur, taking light camping gear, and we would return only after we had made sure. Base Camp would remain where it was for the moment, and our explorations would be on the scale of a strong reconnaissance party. While my friends dried themselves, tidied up, and got things ready for the next day, I wrote a note for the rearguard:

May 18th, 1950

Dear Noyelle,
    I am now at the Base Camp. Lionel and Biscante have just come back from the spur, and are fairly hopeful about it. We are keeping to the same tactics: we remain a strong reconnaissance party. At the moment the weather is bad, and this threatens to delay operations considerably.

*Provisions:* I'm afraid I may be a bit short. Please send up at once three Base Camp containers, three high-altitude containers, and one container of heavy[2] tins.

*Equipment:* 10 rock-pitons, 10 ice-pitons. 300 feet of nylon line and 3 50-foot full-weight ropes. 2 high-altitude units.

*Porters:* Pay off the porters of the first party and give them all the same baksheesh. Pay off the second party too: full baksheesh to those who have a note for you. The two old boys half baksheesh, and nothing to the others as they didn't go well.

*Future provisions:* After the dispatch of what I have asked for, could you, unless you hear to the contrary, send up three more Base Camp containers, and three high-altitude containers?

*Matha and Oudot:* For the moment, there's nothing to tell them; bad weather has so far prevented me from seeing Annapurna. As soon as there is any news I will send it.

Greetings from us all,
MAURICE

On May 14th, the day on which we had held our council of war, after we had made the decision to turn our attention towards Annapurna, Ichac had told me of his wish to pay a visit to Muktinath with Oudot. I said goodbye to them on the 15th, before leaving for Annapurna. They set off next morning, accompanied by the Sirdar Angtharkay, for whom Muktinath was the holy of holies. A fervent believer, zealous in all his religious practices, he took this as a unique opportunity to go on a pilgrimage so many of his brethren had had

[2]Expedition slang: tins containing main meals.

to renounce. All day long the little party ascended by the right bank of the Gandaki and by the end of the afternoon they came in sight of a large group of buildings: white houses, red temples, the whole dominated by a ruined Tibetan fortress. Angtharkay, in transports of excitement, announced: 'Muktinath!'

As they approached this marvellous city the fine buildings turned out to be dirty and dilapidated. At the end of the village were a few bedaubed chortens. Where, then, were the temples, the monasteries and the multitudes of Lamas? Over to the east Marcel Ichac saw some rather newer buildings protected by zinc roofs. Making some inquiries, he discovered that Muktinath consisted of only five or six buildings, and that this was Chahar. It couldn't be helped, the pilgrimage would have to be put off to the following morning. They found shelter for the night in a ruined castle, made a quick meal and went to bed before the interested gaze of fifty natives.

Next day at crack of dawn they started up towards the holy place. After leaving their horses at the door of the first building, they passed by a rock on which there was a vague imprint, something like the shape of a foot.

'Buddha, Sahib!' Angtharkay cried out, throwing himself on the ground.

They passed by a first temple, rather like the one at Tukucha, and came to the sacred fountains: water from the stream ran along a horizontal conduit and fed some sixty spouts in the form of cows or dragons. In the centre of the square was a Nepalese *gompa*. Some pilgrims came to fill up their vessels and drink. Angtharkay, carrying one of the expedition's water-bottles, made a tour of every fountain, and our two friends were not able to use the bottle for the rest of the trip.

A little way to the south they visited another temple guarded by a dozen maidens, dressed in coloured robes. A stone was lifted up and Ichac and Oudot were shown two narrow apertures. Along them came the sound of the flowing water, and in them flickered the blue flame of a natural gas which burned perpetually. The vestals sang and danced, and the Sahibs offered their mites; Angtharkay showed himself particularly generous with the Expedition's cash.

Early next afternoon the pilgrims were back at Tukucha where Noyelle was awaiting them impatiently, for he, too, was very keen to go to Muktinath. His turn came next day, with G.B. Rana. Then on May 20th at 9.30 Angdawa and Dawathondup arrived, bringing the message written at the Base Camp near the spur, after Lachenal and Terray had come back from their reconnaissance.

# 8

## The Spur

We were up and doing before dawn on May 19th, in our provisional Base Camp at the foot of the spur.

It was still pitch dark. The Sherpas could not make out what this untimely commotion was all about. On other expeditions they had never left before sun-up! Still half asleep they prepared *Nesthé* and *Tonimalt* while Rébuffat, Terray and Schatz packed their sacks. Then the climbers went off one by one across the moraine and disappeared into the night. I was not long in following and, my eyes still heavy with sleep, I stumbled over the loose stones which I could hardly see in the dark. I made for the foot of the spur, and the clink of ice-axe on rock soon told me the others were not far away; we had one more moraine to cross. We were all heavily laden with equipment for three camps and several days' food. The Sherpas would carry the loads up as high as they could and then go back to the Base Camp as quickly as possible so as not to use up the high-altitude provisions. It was daylight when we reached the snow—it was hard, and my vibram soles held nicely. Our progress was slow, and somewhat laboured, but we gained height steadily.

Was it really going to be fine? Since leaving Tukucha I had barely seen a glimpse of blue sky, and at the risk of slipping on the hard snow of this steep slope, I kept on turning round to admire the view. We were completely overwhelmed by the Great Barrier whose average height I put at nearly 23,000 feet. Its defences culminated in a gigantic and inaccessible keep, right in the centre, and its precipitous walls rose 10,000 feet above the camp. The rock was smooth and offered no irregularity, no line of weakness on which the trained eye of a mountaineer might hope to trace out a possible route. Annapurna was a giant fortress and we were still only on the outer defences.

We were in a savage and desolate cirque of mountains never before seen by man. No animal or plant could exist here. In the pure morning light this absence of all life, this utter destitution of nature, seemed only to intensify our own strength. How could we expect anyone else to understand the peculiar exhilaration that we drew from this barrenness, when man's natural tendency is to turn towards everything in nature that is rich and generous?

We were nearly as high as Mont Blanc, and it was extremely cold. Everybody was out of breath, and went at his own pace. When we reached the saddle the sun had risen, and whereas a moment ago those stupendous walls had been dark and ominous now they glowed with light. We had to make for the foot of the ridge proper, and Terray, who had come with us in spite of his previous day's exhaustion, pointed out the line of attack. We took the ropes out of our sacks, and tied on. The previous day's party had left a rope fixed here all ready for us, and we started up rock which, though limestone, was relatively firm. Sarki was on my rope; Rébuffat followed with Ajeeba, Terray with Aila and Schatz.

If the solution of the problem lay up the spur we must reach it quickly, and we determined to go all out. The plan was that as soon as the ground became too difficult for the Sherpas they would put down their loads and go down again, while the four Sahibs would go on and pitch a tent as high as possible, where Rébuffat and I would sleep. Terray and Schatz would go back to the shoulder, where Lachenal would join Terray in the evening, after resting from his exertions the day before. As for Schatz, he would return to Base Camp and come up again the following day with Couzy, and so make a third assault party; they would organize a camp on the shoulder.

The first part was soon accomplished: we sent back the Sherpas, who lost a great deal of time on the difficult rock. I noticed, however, how quickly they adapted themselves to the terrain, though up till now they had had little experience of this kind of thing. Sarki in particular, I thought, would be capable of leading a party on quite difficult rock. After they had gone we gained height rapidly: we surveyed, as from an aeroplane, the continuation of our spur, which from here looked quite attractive. We could also see the glaciers flowing down on both sides of our ridge. The clouds, as usual, were low down, obscuring any view of the mountains around us.

The ridge narrowed and put us in mind of our own splendid Chamonix aiguilles. The rock was good, and if it had not been for our loads and for the height it would have been a really enjoyable climb. Then it became very cold and started to snow. We were certainly above 18,000 feet. I looked up the ridge and tried to spot a site for the tent. For the moment we could see nothing but some unsatisfactory-looking ledges, and these were few and far between. The weather was threatening and we had to come to some decision, particularly as it was getting late and Schatz and Terray wanted to go back. We were holding on with our hands to a blade-thin little rock ridge, while our feet dangled against the rock. The exposure was considerable—I couldn't remember anything quite so steep in the Alps. The few rocks sticking out from the slope were covered with ice. I could not understand how snow could ever lie on these slopes and I realized why avalanches were so frequent.

After this delicate traverse we came to a small triangular snow-covered shelf. The weather had now turned really bad, and we straightaway decided to pitch our tent here, setting to work at once, hurling the snow off either side of the ridge and so starting avalanches; some ice-covered rocks went the same way. But even after this clearing of the decks there was hardly room for two of us to sit down. We tried to prise up some rocks embedded in the ice, hacking away in turn, or plying our axes as levers. Terray angrily grabbed my axe and struck such furious blows that the rock seemed likely to split—alas, it was the axe that gave way; the blade was literally bent double! Fortunately he succeeded in straightening it again. The site now looked more promising, and Terray and Schatz could leave us. In five minutes they had disappeared from sight. But I was worried about them—climbing at this height in fresh snow is highly dangerous.

Rébuffat and I were now alone. We went on working away at our emplacement for all we were worth—that is to say, as quickly as our want of breath would allow us. We prised up an enormous stone and placed it carefully on the edge of the slope to extend the surface at our disposal. We consolidated the whole with snow, levelled it and then at last began to get the tent up. We fastened it in front with pitons hammered into the rock, and at the back to our ice-axes driven in up to the hilt, and we fixed the guy-ropes to stones instead of to pegs. The careful Rébuffat made a little wall on the edge of the precipice to protect himself from the wind, and prudently put in a good strong piton for us to belay ourselves to. To this piton we remained roped all night.

Snow fell relentlessly, with never a break; the cold became unbearable. Had there ever been such an airy camp as this, we wondered, or one which had been wrested from the mountains with such difficulty? Tea cheered us up a little. We had very little appetite, but dutifully swallowed the vitascorbol and B2 vitamins advised by the doctor. The wind howled, the tent shook; our thoughts went round and round in circles; we could not get to sleep for a long time.

At dawn it was still snowing slightly; the rocks had quite a thick covering of powder snow which discouraged any hope of our being able to go on. We decided to wait for better weather, and if it did not improve we would go down at midday, leaving everything in place for our return to the attack. The most difficult pitch was directly above our tent. It consisted of a block split at the top by a little crack which had to be reached—but heaven knew how, for everything was covered with snow. Rébuffat thought it was hopeless and was all for going down at once. But I wanted to exhaust every possibility and so avoid any future regrets. If the weather improved the snow might melt quickly and allow reasonable progress.

'They're coming! Listen, that's their ice-axes.'

Lachenal and Terray appeared on the ridge.

'What the hell are you doing here?' they asked. 'Are you resting?'

'Can't you see the snow?'

'We've seen just as much as you have. More than you, for we've been climbing since dawn to get here.'

'You're a pair of sissies,' growled Lachenal crossly.

'It would be mad to go on,' retorted Rébuffat. 'I've no wish to come off here.'

'We'll show you who's coming off,' said Lachenal, quite beside himself. And without waiting another minute he flung himself at this pitch which he had already climbed two days before. He began a traverse to the left on particularly insecure snow; it was just lying loose on the slope, but when he stepped on it, it packed and adhered to the rock. At the very end of this ledge was a crack up which he climbed for about ten feet; all the holds were covered with ice. I glanced at Terray, to whom he was roped, and saw that he had him well belayed. Lachenal now set to work on an outsize open corner and cleared a crack which he tried to use. His feet slipped, and only by a miracle did his hands hold. He came down hammered in a piton which wobbled and inspired no confidence, but he stepped on to it without any hesitation. How on earth was he to get any higher? He took his ice-axe, which was all wet, jammed it an inch or so in the crack and pulled on it hard to see if it held: the axe moved up and down in the crack, but by jerking it he succeeded in jamming it firmly in. Then he hung on by both arms to the shaft of the axe, took his foot off the piton and made a desperate effort to gain a few inches. I was not at all happy: it seemed to me that it was wrong to take such risks in the present conditions. I kept close to Terray in case it should be necessary to hold Lachenal on the rope, but had

79

hardly time to say a word before Lachenal was up, having surmounted the difficult stretch in a really masterly fashion. Without losing a second Terray followed and fixed a second piton and some nylon line.

Closing the tent and shouldering our packs, Rébuffat and I started off too, and a few moments later joined the other rope on a comfortable stance protected by a great shelter stone. Here, of course, was where we ought to have pitched our camp, but the filthy weather of the previous day had made it impossible. Today we were still surrounded by clouds, but through some rifts I was able to see, over on my left, the final ice-fall of the north Annapurna glacier of which I had so far had only indistinct views.

We held a brief consultation. The only one to take an optimistic view of the route up the spur was Lionel Terray. Lachenal, having made such a to-do when he joined us, was now of the opinion that we should never finish with this endless ridge. Rébuffat was pessimistic. As for myself, I had come to the conclusion that in all probability the spur would not prove to be the way up Annapurna because, even if we found later that the route itself would go, it would be out of the question to bring the whole Expedition up it. Obviously, the route was so long and difficult that, in the event of prolonged bad weather, the premature arrival of the monsoon, or any injury to a climber which involved carrying him down, our situation might well become highly dangerous.

Much the same reasoning had already made me give up Dhaulagiri. Lionel Terray was so confident, so enthusiastic, that no arguments in favour of caution had the slightest effect on him. I found it hard to discourage so much perseverance, and in particular that burning desire, which I could so well understand, to go all out on the mountain. On the other hand I did not wish to delay future operations by even one single day.

As I looked once more at the glacier, and the enormous ice-fall down below, I felt in my bones that if there was a way up Annapurna, that was where it lay. So another plan began to take shape in my mind. Rébuffat and Lachenal, who had not the least wish to continue up the spur, would go back as quickly as possible to the temporary Base Camp. They would then take a Sherpa with them, and attempt to force a way—which to all appearances would be found along the right bank—up the glacier to the plateau which, we guessed, lay beyond the ice-fall on the north face. If they were successful they would have to send us word at once. Meanwhile, Terray and I would continue up the spur to set our minds finally at rest over the possibilities of this route. So Lachenal and Rébuffat left us, taking with them instructions for Couzy and Schatz to come up the following day either to back us up, or to help us get everything off the spur.

Terray and I put the tent up. I looked forward to spending a night high up with him for the first time. The weather was very poor. Our aim was to take as little with us as possible and to press on with all speed in order to settle once for all the question of the spur.

We slept like logs, but Terray, who always wakes on the dot, was up and moving soon after dawn. Snugly installed in my sleeping-bag I played at being the Bara Sahib: Terray made the tea, opened tins and served me my breakfast in bed. We stepped out into the fresh snow, which had been falling thickly for two days. We felt the height badly while we were still cold. Although we were carrying very little, it was a tremendous strain at first; but we gritted our teeth and went on, for we did not want to lose a minute. We felt it was a sort of commando raid we were engaged on.

After an easy chimney we came out again upon the ridge which gradually became so narrow that we could not walk along it in balance. So we followed the crest, hanging on by our hands, as though we were traversing an immense horizontal bar, with our feet dangling against the steep sides. We progressed like this over a precipice of some six or seven thousand feet. Gradually we approached the famous snow ridge which Lachenal and Terray had told us about. Their remarks had been so contradictory that I had every reason to be anxious about this obstacle. In fact, as we came nearer, it showed itself to be very high and very steep. Without hesitating a minute Terray went ahead and I followed a short distance behind him. The slope began with an elegant crescent moon, then it did indeed become excessively steep, and soon I felt not only snow under my crampons but hard ice lying just beneath. While Terray was cutting steps with tremendous whacks, I stuck some ice-pitons into the slope to belay him. Luckily the thin layer of snow was extremely hard, and it was not necessary to make very large steps. By skirting round to the left we were able to avoid a steep ice wall. I hammered in an ice-piton regularly every rope's length, and Terray did the same, and as I came up I collected the pitons—we had to be very economical since we were carrying only a limited supply of them. Our noses were right up against the slope, and often hand-holds as well as foot-holds had to be cut in the ice. We now came to the first rock gendarmes of the ridge—they were overhanging. What a series of disappointments!

Terray traversed boldly to the right to reach a crack in the rock, where he put in a couple of pitons. He belayed himself securely, then, leaning over backwards above those plunging ice-slopes, he brought me up. We were in shadow now, and shivering with cold. In turn I belayed Terray, who continued his traverse to the right to avoid a rocky projection. The going was pretty tricky, and the general feel of the climb not too good. Soon we were again together, this time in the sun, but the situation was most uncomfortable and indeed precarious, for the few rays of warmth had been enough to turn the hard snow into a treacherous mush. The last slopes of bare ice gave us some trouble; and then we found ourselves at the top of the ridge, at about 20,000 feet. The weather was now brilliantly fine, and I took some photographs. Annapurna looked only a stone's throw away.

Our spur continued towards the summit of Annapurna, but the jagged ice ridge, that looked like a cluster of cauliflowers, was scarcely any nearer to us now than when we had started up the spur—the clearness of the atmosphere quite falsified distances. Terray and I contemplated the difficulties that lay ahead, which we were now in a position to appreciate, and realized that it would take several days' climbing to complete the route, even at the same pace we had kept up so far. Nature was too powerful, and the obstacles with which she confronted us were out of all proportion to our resources. No long exchange of opinions was necessary. Even if no other obstacles cropped up to hinder our progress—we were thinking of the possibility of a gap in the ridge—it would have been madness to launch an expedition on this route. No Alpine climb had ever presented us with the number of difficulties we had encountered here, and never in the Himalaya had men engaged in such acrobatics. With all my heart I hoped that the Annapurna glacier would give up its secret to Lachenal and Rébuffat. From our present situation it looked quite feasible and we had a good view of the plateau which they aimed to reach. Should they be forced to retreat, our last hope would have gone. Would all this activity, all this effort, all this trouble, result only in some quite secondary achievement? If so, we should be bitterly disappointed.

Without further delay—for we knew the hardest part still lay before us—we began the descent. Cautiously we moved down in turn, placing pitons whenever possible, for the rock was far from good. It was scorchingly hot in the sun, but in the shadow the cold was intense. We traversed across the slope, then started on the great ice ridge. This time the snow no longer held—it was quite loose and we would rather have been on bare ice. Terray started off; I belayed him with pitons, but the limited number we had with us forced me to take most of them out. So I had to go down by myself, with no belay, under the watchful eye of Terray, who knew very well that if I slipped I should inevitably drag him off too. When it was his turn I watched him go down face outwards with slow, carefully studied movements so that he should always be in perfect balance. He told me later that twice he had begun to slip and twice been able to pull himself up. My technique was different: I went down face to the slope, using my hands as much as my feet. With my right foot I felt the ice, searching for a good hold and putting my foot in position without being able to see what I was doing; my left foot held, in spite of the soft snow, by the two front points of my crampons. With my left hand I pressed the wet snow against the ice, using this as a sort of little hold; with my right hand I used my ice-axe as an anchor, with the pick stuck a few millimetres into the rock-hard ice. When my right foot was in position and my balance re-established on three points of contact, such as they were it was the turn of the left foot to repeat the operation. It was an extraordinary reptilian progress, a kind of balancing trick, in which I held the mountain very gently without jolting it either by speed or movement.

'Hullo, you up there!' It was Schatz's voice. He was coming up to help us. Terray, who was nearer to him, called out that we were giving up.

'Hi, Schatz, take the tent down, we're going back to Base Camp.'

Schatz heard, and watched our progress from a little way off. The clouds were now all round us, and the mist was down and everything melted into a dull uniformity. We put in pitons, judged the distance still left to go, and fixed our spare rope for a rappel. I watched the piton as Terray went down first on the doubled rope; it curved and bent over at each jerk, but came back to its original position, and the ice was so hard that I did not really worry much. Then in my turn I put the rope round myself in the usual way and quickly joined Terray who had prepared a landing-place for me with his ice-axe. I brought down the doubled rope by pulling on one of the ends, and soon we reached the rocks. We could not conceal our relief as we took off our crampons. A second later we started on the traverse of the rock ridge with such enthusiasm and such a strong wish to get down at least as far as the saddle by evening, that what had taken us half an hour up in the morning now took only a few minutes.

A race against time began. Terray and I tore along the easy bits of the ridge, sliding down chimneys and shooting down couloirs. In spite of the cold we were soon sweating hard. In record time we reached the camp we had left that morning, and found Schatz and Sarki who had just finished taking the tent down. While we swallowed beef in tomato sauce, and mougat, and sipped the excellent tea which Terray had just made, we summed up in jerky sentences the significance of the enterprise. Those thrilling and inspiring moments, which were yet so exhausting, had led only to a useless victory on a minor spur of the mountain. Nevertheless, as Terray declared later, nothing would ever equal those desperate days when he gave so freely of his courage, strength and resolution.

The cloud ceiling was low, but we hoped the weather would become more settled. We soon reached the pitch where we had left the nylon line, and one after the other we went down into space and then re-assembled again on the narrow platform where Rébuffat and I had spent the night before last. The four of us carried two entire high-altitude camps over difficult and dangerous ground, but this did not slow up our pace. Sarki was terrified at our speed, but was not long in adopting a rhythm as rapid as that of the Sahibs. There was thick snow on the spur and we had to take all kinds of precautions. As soon as we were over the difficult pitches we raced on again, for all of us were keyed up by the rhythm of action. The saddle was getting visibly nearer, we negotiated the last pitches and then ran down the grassy slopes now covered with fresh snow. Soon we all reached the advanced camp which had been established during the assault on the shoulder of the spur. We came down in a few hours what it had taken us two days to get up. The Base Camp on the moraine in the bed of the valley was plainly visible—the yellow of the tents stood out distinctly against the uniform grey of the surrounding stones. The rain, or rather the wet snow, which had been falling a few minutes earlier, had now turned to a light drizzle. Terray and I glanced at each other in agreement; in a second we had collected from the two Base Camp tents as much equipment as we could, made up our sacks and sprung off down the slopes. Schatz and Sarki tried to keep up with us, but we had apparently been transformed into human projectiles, hurtling down in spite of our sacks, which threatened to throw us off balance. We controlled our speed by jumping against tufts of grass and any irregularity of the ground. Traversing left we reached a tongue of snow lying in the bed of a little valley: without hesitation we glissaded down, describing some magnificent slaloms. By this elegant and rapid method we gained the moraine a few minutes later.

Schatz must have been wondering why we went at such a rate—to tell the truth there was no reason at all. Instead of taking a quarter of an hour we might just as well have come down quietly in an hour. It was all due to the exhilaration produced by this splendid day of hard climbing.

At Base Camp we were greeted with sensational news. Lachenal and Rébuffat had sent back their Sherpa with a note: the right bank of the glacier was practicable, and they guaranteed to reach the plateau which they had so far not been able to see. On the other hand they had been able to see nothing of the upper part of Annapurna. From the point Terray and I had reached on the spur, at a height of about 20,000 feet, I had been able to see the whole of the section which had remained invisible to them. I knew that the plateau was level and would present no difficulties.

For the first time during the expedition we had real grounds for hope. Were our perseverance and our faith at last to be rewarded? In a few hours the fate of the expedition would be decided.

For the moment we dried ourselves—all our clothes were soaked with rain, melting snow and sweat. Schatz arrived with Sarki and plans for the next day were immediately drawn up.

'I've spotted my own little route,' said Schatz. 'Give me two Sherpas and . . .'

'Two Sherpas,' cut in Terray. 'And what next?'

'Two high-altitude units and three days' provisions.'

'The Chief wants his own expedition,' said Couzy, using the nickname given to Schatz in Alpine circles on account of his passion for organization.

'Give him a chance to speak: what's your idea?'

'To go up the glacier by an easy ridge which I've spotted, and which would avoid the seracs on the right.'

'He's right,' I said. 'Supposing Lachenal and Rébuffat don't succeed, what would you do next? You'd be extremely glad to have another string to your bow.'

At dawn next day Schatz went off, full of hope. He had been one of the discoverers of the route along the Miristi with Couzy and Oudot, and he now looked forward to being in the lead again and opening up the decisive route to the top of Annapurna. Terray and I, as well as Sarki, were worn out with our recent exertions, and we gave ourselves the next morning off. Early in the afternoon we would set off to rejoin the advance party, under the guidance of Ajeeba. This time I had great hopes and it took all my good sense to allow myself to 'waste' those few very precious hours.

'Couzy, you are going to have a thankless job . . . '

'What's that?'

'You will have to pack up the advanced camp on the spur, move the present Base Camp and establish a permanent Base Camp where I tell you—that is to say, at the furthest point we can get the porters up to.'

'It certainly doesn't sound much fun, but if the job's really got to be done . . . '

'Yes, it must be done, you know. And what's more you'll have only one Sherpa.'

'It doesn't sound like a picnic.'

'You'll have to carry loads yourself.'

For several days, Couzy, the youngest of the party, would, in spite of all his ardour and enthusiasm, be condemned to stay low to carry out an essential but unspectacular job. He did it to perfection and without a single word of complaint, although he knew that, when the final attack was launched, he would not be sufficiently acclimatized and so would lose the chance of being on it. It is this admirable spirit of self-denial which determines the strength of a team.

A very pleasant evening began in spite of the wretched weather. We were warmed by our hopes. Conversation flowed easily, and we vied with each other in good humour and courtesy. The hour of decision was drawing near.

The rain beat with deafening noise on the taut canvas of the tents, but we fell blissfully asleep, beautifully warm in our sleeping-bags. In my sleep I heard cries, the clanking of pitons, hushed voices, the sound of a stove, the noise of a tin being opened, stones rolling over: it was Schatz getting ready with Pansy and Aila. While it was still dark, he came to my tent.

'I'm off, Maurice.'

'What's the weather like?'

'The sky is full of stars.'

'Good luck, Marcel.'

'Thanks, goodbye.'

For a while I heard the noise of stones as the others moved off. How wonderful it is to stay in the warm when other people are at work! How pleasant just to be able to dream, with no sense of time, when you know that in a few hours the pleasant idleness will give place to action. Since the start of the expedition I had never had a moment's quiet; this morning I had the chance to take things easy, and I thoroughly appreciated it. I got up and went round to the other tents: Terray, who had become possessed with the demon of orderliness, was sorting, tidying, selecting and organizing: on the eve of the critical time ahead he did not want to be caught unprepared. Before becoming immersed myself in this work I took a look at the mountains: the sun was already high, the temperature warm. It was a good day.

But everything comes to an end—even the best moments. I had one big worry. We were getting short of food, and I was anxious to make a list of what remained. We collected our stock together; then, squatting in the tent, I sorted things into different categories, spread them out, counted up and calculated. With the figures in my head, I could now have an easy mind. Early in the afternoon we set off carrying enormous sacks. I felt in grand form; the morning off had completely rested me after the last eight days of uninterrupted action, and the fine weather held.

The exhausting and monotonous moraines went on for miles, and several times one or other of us slipped on the stones which treacherously concealed hard black ice. Presently we saw a man coming to meet us: it was Ajeeba, bringing wonderful news. Lachenal and Rébuffat had reached the glacier plateau. Rébuffat added in his note that the way lay over rocks on the right bank which were easy to climb. So the great ice fall of the north Annapurna glacier had been overcome. With hope in our hearts, we hurried on. The temperature was quite tolerable and the nearby rocks reflected the warmth. The walls of the Great Barrier, in whose direction we were going, gradually came nearer: they were smooth and unclimbable, a slaty sombre grey. The moraine on the true right bank of the glacier, as so often happens, offered a quick easy route. Ajeeba was guiding us now, and by mid-afternoon we came to a sort of flattening of the moraine which spread out and abutted against the Great Barrier.

We now had to climb up the walls of the right bank. I decided this would be where the porters must stop, and made a quick sketch to indicate as near as possible the future site of the Base Camp. It was getting late and we wanted to make the plateau that evening. After leading us along at a good pace, Ajeeba brought us to the foot of the Great Barrier. A system of ledges cut by chimneys extending into couloirs enabled us to reach the top of the ice-fall of the Annapurna glacier. We were pretty exhausted by this march at high altitude and our sacks grew heavier and heavier. Dusk had fallen when at last we came to the foot of a big wall of ice where the first party had pitched their tent—the future Camp I—at a height of about 16,700 feet.

They welcomed us in the highest spirits. We could see nothing at this time of night, but they told us:

'There's not a shadow of doubt; we ought to be able to get up Annapurna.'

# 9

## *Annapurna*

An astonishing sight greeted me next morning. Lachenal and Rébuffat were sitting outside on a dry rock, with their eyes riveted on Annapurna. A sudden exclamation brought me out of my tent: 'I've found the route!' shouted Lachenal. I went up to them, blinking in the glare. For the first time Annapurna was revealing its secrets. The huge north face with all its rivers of ice shone and sparkled in the light. Never had I seen a mountain so impressive in all its proportions. It was a world both dazzling and menacing, and the eye was lost in its immensities. But for once we were not being confronted with vertical walls, jagged ridges and hanging glaciers which put an end to all thoughts of climbing.

'You see,' explained Lachenal, 'the problem . . . is to get to that sickle-shaped glacier high up on the mountain. To reach the foot of it without danger of avalanches, we'll have to go up well over on the left.'[1]

'But how the hell would you get to the foot of your route?' interrupted Rébuffat. 'On the other side of the plateau that we're on there's glacier which is a mass of crevasses and quite impossible to cross.'

'Look . . . '

We looked hard. But I am bound to admit I felt almost incapable of following Lachenal's explanations. I was carried away on a wave of enthusiasm, for at last our mountain was there before our eyes.

This May the twenty-third was surely the Expedition's greatest day so far!

'But look,' insisted Lachenal, his knitted cap all askew, 'we can avoid the crevassed section by skirting round to the left. After that we'll only have to climb the icefalls opposite, and then make gradually over to the right towards the Sickle.'

The sound of an ice-axe distracted our attention for a moment; it was Ajeeba breaking up ice to melt into water.

'Your route isn't direct enough, Biscante,' I told him. 'We'd be

[1] See sketch, p. 93.

certain to sink up to our waists in the snow: the route must be the shortest possible, direct to the summit.'

'And what about avalanches?' asked Rébuffat.

'You run a risk from them on the right as well as on the left. So you may as well choose the shortest way.'

'And there's the couloir too,' retorted Lachenal.

'If we cross it high enough up, the danger won't be very great. Anyway, look at the avalanche tracks over on the left on your route.'

'There's something in that,' admitted Lachenal.

'So why not go straight up in line with the summit, skirt round the seracs and crevasses, slant over to the left to reach the Sickle, and from there go straight up to the top?'

Rébuffat struck me as being not very optimistic. Standing there, in the old close-fitting jersey that he always wore on his Alpine climbs, he seemed more than ever to deserve the name the Sherpas had given him of Lamba Sahib, or 'long man'.

'But,' went on Lachenal, 'we could go straight up under the ice cliff and then traverse left and reach the same spot . . .'

'By cutting across to the left it's certainly more direct.'

'That should be quite feasible,' agreed Lachenal, letting himself be won over.

Rébuffat's resistance yielded bit by bit.

'Lionel! Come and have a look . . .'

Terray was bending over a container and sorting out provisions in his usual serious manner. He raised his head: it was adorned with a red ski-ing bonnet, and he sported a flowing beard. I asked him point-blank what *his* route was. He had already examined the mountain and come to his own conclusion:

'My dear Maurice,' he said, pursing up his lips in the special way that marked a great occasion, 'it's perfectly clear to me. Above the avalanche cone of the great couloir, just in line with the summit . . .' and he went on to describe the route we had worked out.

So we were all in complete agreement.

'We must get cracking,' Terray kept saying in great excitement. Lachenal, no less excited, came and yelled in my ear:

'A hundred to nothing! That's the odds on our success!'

And even the more cautious Rébuffat admitted that 'It's the least difficult proposition and the most reasonable.'

The weather was magnificent; never had the mountains looked more beautiful. Our optimism was tremendous, perhaps excessive, for the gigantic scale of the face set us problems such as we had never had to cope with in the Alps. And above all, time was short. If we were to succeed not a moment must be lost. The arrival of the monsoon was forecast for about June 5th: so that we had just twelve days left. We would have to go fast, very fast indeed. I was haunted by this idea. To do so we should have to lengthen out the intervals between the successive camps, organize a shuttle service to bring up the maximum number of loads in the minimum time, acclimatize ourselves,[2] and, finally, maintain communications with the rear. This last point worried me. Our party was organized on the scale of a reconnaissance and the total supply at our disposal was only five days' food and a limited amount of equipment.

How was I possibly to keep track of the thousand and one questions that buzzed round in my head? The rest of the party were all highly excited and talked away noisily while the Sherpas moved about the tents as usual. Only a couple of them were here, and there could be no question of beginning operations with just these two. So the Sahibs would set off alone and carry their own loads: in this way we should be able to get Camp II pitched the next day. When I asked the others what they thought they enthusiastically agreed to make this great effort, which would save us at least two days. Ajeeba would go back to the Base Camp and show the people there the way up to Camp I, which would have to be entirely re-equipped since we were going to take everything up with us for Camp II. For Sarki there was an all-important job: he would have to carry the order of attack to all the members of the Expedition.

[2]At the time I was thinking of the following points:
1.  that adaptability, and speed of adaptability, vary with the individual;
2.  that adaptability is determined to a large extetnt by previous appropriate training;
3.  that above a certain critical height, peculiar to each individual and capable of being progressively raised, people deteriorate—below it they recuperate.
4.  that for the majority of the party this critical height—owing to the policy followed since the beginning of the Expedition—should be at present between 16,000 and 20,000 feet.

With reference to this subject see the reports by Dr Oudot in the *Presse Médicale*:
(a) 'Observations physiologiques et cliniques en haute montange'. (59me année, n°. 15, 7 mars 1951, pp. 297-300.)
(b) 'Action des inhalations d'oxygène en haute montagne'. (59me année, n°. 17, 17 mars 1951, pp. 326-327.)

I took a large sheet of paper and wrote out:

Special message by Sarki, from Camp I to Tukucha. Urgent.

23.5.50

Camp I: Annapurna glacier

Have decided to attack Annapurna.

Victory is ours if we all make up our minds not to lose a single day, not even a single hour!

*Individual Instructions:*

*Couzy:* Move Base Camp as rapidly as possible and reorganize it, about two hours further on from present site, on a very big and very comfortable site just below an avalanche cone. Bring everything up. Send all high-altitude units to Camp I, as well as all possible food, wireless sets, Gaston's and my rucksacks, and Lionel's camp boots. (Give Sarki 15 rupees: you'll find them at the bottom of my *pied d'éléphant*[3] which you must bring up to me.)

*Schatz:* If Schatz comes down again from his ridge: organize Camp I, because Biscante, Lionel, Gaston and myself will take everything on to Camp II. The site is marked by a large cairn. It is just on the edge of the glacier. Bring up all possible food and equipment here.

*Matha:* Come up quickly. Have got small camera with me. Bring films and send them up to me. Porters can get up to Base Camp; you can leave reserves there.

*Oudot:* Come as quickly as possible to Camp I with essential medical supplies; leave further stuff (especially surgical equipment) at Base Camp.

*Noyelle:* Most important, without losing a *single hour*, send up to Base Camp: 10 high-altitude containers, 6 valley containers, all high-altitude camping units, the last walkie-talkie, one jerrican of spirit, 2 gallons of petrol, 1 100-foot 8 mm. rope, 2 50-foot 9 mm. ropes, 650 feet of 5 mm. line, 15 ice-pitons, 5 rock-pitons, 10 snap-links, all the head lamps, 2 hanging lamps plus reserve batteries. The Austrian *cacolet*,[4] 1 pair skis, 2 pairs ski-sticks, Dufour sledge, everybody's no. 2 rucksacks, Emerson set with wires, 3 pairs spare Tricouni gaiters, 1 pair *Ours* trousers, 2 valley tents (there will be 3 at Base Camp and 2 at Camp I), 4 pairs boots: 1 size 10, 2 size 9, 1 size 8.

As the valley camping units have got disorganized (sleeping-bags and air mattresses left at Tukucha), bring up what's necessary to fit them up again.

All reserves of gloves and socks—tsampa or rice for the Sherpas. Pack up safely what's left.

Prepare 10 high-altitude containers and 6 valley containers for future use. A Sherpa could see to bringing these up later.

Come along. Your headquarters will be at Base Camp. G.B. is free to do what he likes.

*Matha:* Send a wire to Devies: 'Camp I at 16,700 feet. Following reconnaissance have decided attack by north Annapurna glacier. Route entirely snow and ice. Weather favourable. All in fine form. Have good hopes. Greetings.'

HERZOG.

[3]Nylon bag for the legs to protect them from the cold.

[4]A carrying frame made of canvas and straps worn like a rucksack in which an injured climber can sit.

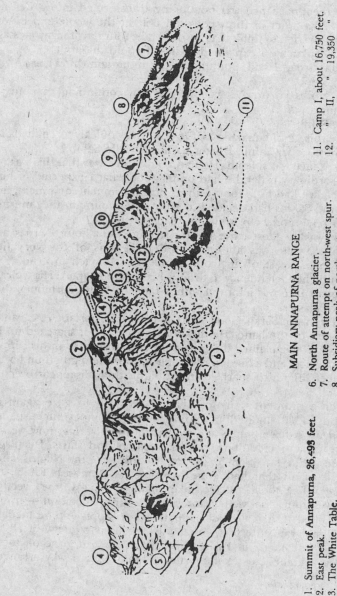

## MAIN ANNAPURNA RANGE

1. Summit of Annapurna, 26,493 feet.
2. East peak.
3. The White Table.
4. The Black Rock.
5. Buttresses of the Great Barrier.

6. North Annapurna glacier.
7. Route of attempt on north-west spur.
8. Subsidiary peak of north-west spur.
9. Summit of north-west spur.
10. Cauliflower Ridge.

11. Camp I, about 16,750 feet.
12. " II, " 19,350 "
13. " III, " 21,650 "
14. " IV, " 23,550 "
15. " V, " 24,600 "

The reconnaissance was now being transformed into a definite assault. This order of the day would delight the whole expedition, but I was worried to think that it would take four days for my message to reach Tukucha. I explained as best I could to Sarki:

'Annapurna,' I said, pointing to the mountain. '*Atcha now!*' [5]

'Yes, Sahib.'

'All Sahibs go now,' I said in English, continuing to point to Annapurna.

'Yes, Sahib.'

'Like this,' I said, making as if to run, 'very quickly to Tukucha for all Sahibs: Couzy Sahib, Doctor Sahib, Noyelle Sahib.'

Sarki's face was solemn. He had read in my eyes that this was not just an ordinary order, he had understood what I expected of him. He knew we had little food with us and not much equipment, and that if the Sahibs had decided to go up the mountain they must be able to rely upon help from the rear.

Sarki was the most active and the strongest of all our Sherpas, and this mission he was about to undertake was of the very first importance. He stood in front of me, his stomach protruding as though he had a tendency to dropsy, his legs wide apart. His typically Mongolian face was adorned with a blue balaclava surmounted by his dark glasses.

'Off you go, Sarki! Good luck! It is very important . . . ' and I shook him by the hand. He did not lose a second; snatched up his things, briefly explained the essential points to Ajeeba in his clipped guttural voice, and a few minutes later we saw them go off under the great ice cliff which sparkled in the light, then disappear over the moraine.

After a moment's silence I turned round to gaze again on Annapurna, all bathed in light. There was not much shadow around us. A few minutes ago we had been shivering, now we had to take off our eiderdown jackets, sweaters and shirts. Dhaulagiri towered in the far distance, nearer at hand were the Nilgiris, and I thought of all that had gone before—the Dambush Khola, the Hidden Valley, the Great Ice Lake, Manangbhot. We were very far from everything that we had foreseen: 'a light expedition'—'nylon', as we called it, a really fast expedition. To apply Alpine methods to a Himalayan enterprise—that was the basic strategy of all the plans we had made in Paris. The danger, we had gone on to say, lay in avalanches, so we must stick to ridges. And why arrange a

[5] We're going now.

94

route up the mountain fit for Sherpas? The Sahibs would undertake everything: no Sherpas; hence no need for complications. Heavens, how wrong we had been! Ridges were out of the question. Sherpas? We were not exactly sorry to have them with us. Lightness? Rapidity? The heights are so great that numbers of intermediate camps will always be needed. And then we had not paid sufficient attention to the question of exploration: you arrive in a district, burning with impatience to attack something—yes, but in which direction?

All four of us, Lachenal, Rébuffat, Terray and myself, got our things ready and filled our sacks with as much as we could possibly carry in the way of equipment, food, tents and sleeping-bags, leaving behind only one container with a few accessories which we did not need at once. We shared out the equipment: as usual, some preferred the heavier but less bulky loads, with others it was the opposite. It worked out at an average of about forty-five pounds apiece. At this height, where the least exertion is an effort, we felt crushed beneath our burdens. The straps cut into our shoulder and it seemed a physical impossibility to walk for more than five minutes. All the same we somehow struggled on, for although the packs were far too heavy, we reflected on all the time we were saving.

So the four Sahibs, in single file, and well spaced out on the rope, climbed heavily up through the snow of the great plateau at the foot of Annapurna. With the sun vertically above us, the glacier basin was like a furnace, with every ray reflected back from the surface of the snow. Walking soon became a dull agony. We sweated and suffocated. Then we stopped, split open some tubes of anti-sunburn cream and applied the paste thickly to our sweating faces. Lachenal and Rébuffat, who seemed to suffer even more than Terray and myself, made themselves white Ku Klux Klan cowls out of the cotton lining of my sleeping-bag. They assured me that this was admirable protection against sunstroke, but I was not convinced and they seemed to be stifled in them. Terray and I preferred to rely on the cream.

There was not a single breath of air in this furnace and we longed for the first slopes. Crushed beneath our loads, we had to summon up all our resolution to overcome our breathlessness and lassitude. We climbed up the *rognon*, a rocky outcrop in the middle of the glacier, under huge overhanging seracs which threatened us with a forest of icicles that turned the sun's rays into a rainbow of colour. Terray and I took turns at making the trail: the other two seemed utterly worn out. Our breathing was short and uneven as we approached the 20,000-foot level.

'We're not Sherpas!' said Lachenal bitterly.

'We didn't come to the Himalaya to be beasts of burden,' growled Rébuffat.

Terray was stung to answer:

'A climber ought to be able to carry his gear,' he said, 'we're as good as the Sherpas, aren't we?'

Lachenal was bent over his ice-axe, Rébuffat had flopped down on his rucksack. Their faces were scarlet and running with sweat; they didn't usually show their feelings, but now they looked really angry.

'If we wear ourselves out now with this ridiculous porterage, how on earth shall we manage in a few days' time? It isn't the Sherpas who'll be making a safe route through the seracs.'

At this, Terray saw red:

'And you call yourselves Chamonix guides! Just bad amateurs, that's what you are.'

'The more you're put upon, the more you like it,' retorted Lachenal. 'You'll tell me next that you're positively enjoying this job.'

'When I have to carry a load, I get on with it.'

I tried to restore peace:

'I know it's hell, but it's saving us two days. If the Expedition succeeds it'll perhaps be on account of what we're doing today.'

Rébuffat spoke again:

'You and Terray can manage your loads, we just can't.'

'You're supermen,' went on Lachenal, 'real supermen, and we're just poor types.'

After this outburst, which seemed to relieve him, we went on. The 'supermen' took turns at making the trail. We were extremely tired, and our legs barely held us up as with slow, uneven steps we tried to wrest a few yards from the mountain. Each step was automatic, eyes glued to the heels of the man in front, and we had to resist the temptation to stop or relax our effort. Everyone knew in his heart that Terray's hard words were justified even if not strictly necessary.

For some minutes we had heard yodelling behind us: it could only be Schatz. The route he had planned joined ours here. Had he discovered the perfect way up? Anyhow it was an excellent pretext for a good halt: we stuck our ice-axes in up to the hilt and wedged our sacks behind them to make comfortable seats. We opened some tins and seized upon our water bottles, but the sips were rationed for we had only a limited supply.

Schatz came up with his two Sherpas.

'There you are! God, I'm tired!'

There were certainly signs of considerable fatigue on his face. No doubt we looked much the same, but he had been alone with his Sherpas.

'Well, how did you get on?'

'The route's no good. If yours is at all reasonable we must rule mine out.'

'Too difficult?'

'Yes, and dangerous. Instead of being able to traverse easily from the top of the little spur to the plateau, we came to a secondary glacier, very steep and with magnificent seracs. We pitched our tent last night as best we could on a microscopic site. Then, this morning, we had to pass beneath a wall of seracs on the point of crashing down, and finally go up a very steep snow slope which I wouldn't like to descend at any price . . .'

'And then?'

'Look here, isn't that enough for one man? Then I caught sight of you, so I wound in and out between the seracs to join your tracks. But you're making me talk when I'm dying of hunger.'

While he hastily swallowed a laboriously prepared lunch the mist came down on us—forerunner of the usual daily storm.

'On we go,' said Terray.

As we went up visibility decreased. Everything was blurred in the mist, and snow began to fall. The trail that Terray and I made by guess-work was certainly not very rational, but what did it matter? All we had to do that evening was to pitch Camp II somewhere towards the centre of the plateau, out of danger from avalanches. It was snowing heavily now and we took our thick capes out of our sacks. With Terray behind me, I could manage to steer some sort of a course. I must not turn round in a circle as I had once done in similar circumstances. As far as we could judge we had now reached the centre of the plateau, so we decided to pitch the camp where we stood—for the night, at any rate.

In ones and twos Sahibs and Sherpas arrived at the site and put down their loads. We took hasty stock of the situation: it would not be wise to let the Sherpas go back by themselves to Camp I. So Terray, who was in good form, proposed to accompany them. It was late and still snowing very hard. Terray was in a hurry to leave, for the tracks of our ascent were already almost obliterated. He intended to bivouac at Camp I in Sarki's sleeping-bag, after sending the Sherpas on down to Base Camp, which was easy to reach, and these men would then be available for carrying up more loads.

'Lionel's crazy.' Lachenal made no bones about expressing his view of the matter. 'He likes to make a martyr of himself. Gaston, would it ever enter your head to spend the night lying on stones that stick into you everywhere rather than go down to Base Camp and sleep in comfort—and on top of it all to boast about it?'

Rébuffat's silent gesture was eloquent: the performance struck him as absolutely pointless. But climbers are all tremendous individualists; there is no more obstinate breed of men.

Our poor little Camp II was completely lost among the snow and ice. We were deafened by the continuous roar of avalanches and could not determine their whereabouts. For that night we would have to put up with only relative security. Amid flurries of snow and gusts of wind we got the tents up, fixed in the pegs and constructed some sort of level platform; an hour later we were all warm and snug inside.

I was with Schatz in the experimental tent that had served as a model for the construction of the other fourteen. It was slightly larger and Schatz assured me that with our heads at the back we should be ideally comfortable. All the same I had never spent such a bad night, and I would not for anything have repeated this miserable experience during which I was half suffocated; I prefer to have my head near the opening of the tent and so be able to adjust the ventilation. In other respects Schatz was a perfect companion. Snug in my sleeping-bag I watched him do the cooking; he served me with a substantial dinner where I lay. Sleeping-pills soon brought our conversation to an end.

Whilst we were thus making the best of the situation, Terray, bivouacking down at Camp I, was kept awake for part of the night by a violent wind. The thickly falling snow covered him up completely, so he shut himself right into the cowl of his cape, at the risk of being suffocated. After several hours he relaxed and slept the sleep of exhaustion with his head resting on the stones.

When we woke at 9 o'clock in Camp II, at 19,350 feet, it was already very hot, and the tents were suffused with golden light. But it was hard work to get our frozen boots on—they were just like blocks of wood. In future I put them at the bottom of my sleeping-bag. I poked my head out—the sky was blue and the view magnificent: a wonderful chain of peaks and ridges stood out round us at a height of 23,000 feet. Quite close above us was that jagged ridge which we called Cauliflower Ridge. It was a continuation of the north-west spur on which we had spent ourselves to no purpose. We could now see its whole length; we had, in fact, climbed only about a tenth of it! And to our surprise there was an enormous gap in the centre, cutting off all possibility of progress. So we had no more regrets.

Shining in the distance was a mountain of crystal—Dhaulagiri; and nearer us were the proud and inaccessible Nilgiris. To the right, towering above our Lilliputian camp, was the Great Barrier with its flanks falling directly to the basin of the upper Miristi Khola. To the extreme right, a great swollen glacier and a jolly looking peak—the Triangular Peak or Black Rock that we had seen from the East Tilicho Pass. I turned round: an enormous ice face bristling with seracs and seamed with crevasses sparkled in the sun. Far above, so high that one had to tilt one's head backwards to see it, was Annapurna, resplendent, dominating everything as a goddess should.

I inspected the face we had to attack with some anxiety. It was all so disproportionate, on such a different scale from our puny resources. What was to be our plan of campaign? I had to estimate the party's fitness, take into account the rather sketchy equipment we had at our disposal up here, and allow for dangers and difficulties and, above all, the time factor. There were such hundreds of things to bear in mind. But I had made up my mind to push on actively, establishing camps, whatever the weather, short of an actual blizzard. It could all be reduced to a mathematical formula: to pile up the maximum weight per distance during the day, at the same time taking care to conserve the physical form of the climbers for the final assault. On this last stage to the top deterioration would be bound to set in: at that moment we must be able to call up all our reserves of energy and resolution, without losing sight of the needs of the descent.

By morning we had forgotten the previous day's weariness and were all ready to take advantage of the fine weather to go up and establish Camp III. Over the gaiters which we wore above our boots we adjusted the extra-light-weight crampons, which from now on we used almost continuously. We took one tent with us, leaving the other where it was, with some food. We each carried about 22 lb. Before leaving camp we took a last look at the whole of the ice face, all unknown ground. On starting out we tried to pick out in advance a route between the many ice walls blocking the way, for once among them we should be hemmed in and unable to see more than fifty yards ahead.

We roped up in the same order in which we had camped—Lachenal and Rébuffat together, and Schatz and I on the second rope. It was nearly 10 o'clock—high time to start. After carefully closing the one remaining tent at Camp II we steered towards the snow-shoot at the foot of the great central couloir which descends from the summit slopes. On the section of the plateau between us and the couloir there were few crevasses, so our route was straightforward. When we put our feet in the snow they were numbed by the cold, yet the air was so warm that we soon took off our eiderdown jackets. The gigantic wall of snow and ice seemed to tower higher and higher above us. On the left a ridge of bare ice, typically Himalayan in its formation, surprised me by its transparent blueness, which was intensified by the lateral position of the sun. On the right the Cauliflower Ridge, immaculately white, proudly displayed its tracery and seemed to taunt us: 'If ever you get as high as me . . . ' In this strange world where everything tends towards the vertical, one's notion of balance is quite peculiar: all these vistas of chaos render one's first impressions unreliable.

After we had been going for an hour we had only got as far as the first slopes of the snow-shoot. But what worried me was what came next: thousands of tons of a titanic flood seemed to lie frozen in indescribable confusion. The nearer we got to the wall, the steeper appeared the average angle. Seracs crashed down with hideous din, and the rumbling of avalanches put us all on edge. For the moment there was nothing coming down the couloir. For some minutes we should be exposed to danger, for though we would cross it at a point where it narrowed—it was never very wide—every block that fell from the upper slopes would inevitably hurtle down this funnel. Lachenal crossed first. In turn, each of us followed in his tracks under the watchful eyes of the others waiting on the edge. Above us an enormous roof of ice, that turned a livid green as soon as the sun disappeared, constituted some slight protection. But would it be enough if an avalanche came down?

All went well, the danger zone was passed and we arrived out of breath on the opposite side. The place was scarcely suitable for a halt, for the slope was so steep that the snow no longer held firm, and we did not stop. The first party rapidly cut some tiny steps, barely sufficient for two spikes of our crampons. The ice was smooth and compact, like glass, and split off with a sharp noise beneath the axe. The chips broke off cleanly, went flying down into space and disappeared at high speed, starting up little avalanches. We continued to make over to the right under the protection of the seracs, and a rickety snow-bridge brought us to a snowy platform where we were at last able to stop. The fine weather held, for the time being, and we were cheered by the sight of a few healthy-looking clouds.

At our feet lay the plateau with Camp II which we now saw in its true dimension: we managed to pick out the microscopic tent only by following the tracks of our ascent. Higher up, the next part of the route was not very inviting, and 150 feet or so above our heads the way was barred by a huge vertical wall of ice. Not a hope either to the left or to the right. If we were to be held up like this so early in the climb . . .

Schatz and I went boldly to the attack. We sank in up to our waists, and the ice beneath the snow made us slide irresistibly down the slope. I seized hold of one foot with both hands and using the other knee as a fulcrum I brought my foot out several inches above the snow. Then I planted my ice-axe as high up as I could and pulled on it to free the other foot left behind. I slipped and came back to my original position. My heart thumped and I was weak for want of breath. Finally we had to clear a trough, and these 150 feet took us an hour to negotiate. We were now so close to the wall of ice that we shivered in spite of the heat. I examined the obstacle: a snow-covered ledge led up to a great overhang of ice. This proud colossus, smooth and chased by little avalanches, could be surmounted by cutting steps up it—a practical route after all. I told the second party that it would take at least two hours to reach the top of the overhang and that, during this time, they might as well skirt along the wall in search of an easier way.

For a second I took off my dark glasses, but I could not stand the dazzling glare all round us. Far away below, the green of the lower slopes gave a momentary relief to my eyes. My glasses were steamed up with sweat and melted snow, and I rubbed them with my handkerchief, then glanced at my waist to make sure the knot was all right, counted the number of ice-pitons, and saw that I had my piton-hammer. A glance at Schatz to satisfy myself that he was firmly placed, then:

'I'm starting. A bit of slack, please.'

'Go ahead,' replied Schatz, letting the rope out round his firmly planted ice-axe.

Unaccustomed effort at this height is terribly hard work, and each blow of the axe made me pant. First I cleared the ledge; the snow was hard and compact, but at last I had a stance at my disposal about a foot wide and three feet long on which I was obliged to crouch as my head bumped against the overhanging ice. I still had to advance horizontally for a couple of yards. I moved along inch by inch; the ledge became narrower and narrower, the wall above pushed me out further and further until I nearly overbalanced. I finished by crawling. I stopped to rest, lying on my stomach and clutching the shaft of the axe with which I held myself in. I now had to attack the ice on the roof. With one hand, and with nothing to lean against, I could not strike very hard. The splinters of ice showered down on to Schatz who stood stoically watching my every movement, ready to stop a possible fall. First I broke down the end of the little gutter in which I was penned. A few nicks chipped in the ice upside down served as a hand-hold for my left hand. Holding on thus with my left hand, I pulled myself up very, very slowly, scraping up against the overhanging ice, with a drop underneath. I could feel Schatz's eyes on me. With my right hand now free, I gripped my axe and made a better hold for my left hand on the bare ice of the roof itself. Then having driven in my axe, I made a lightning grab for the hold; now gripping firmly with my left hand, I withdrew my axe and with the utmost difficulty made two steps very high up for my feet. These were for use after I had got over the overhang, to enable me to remain a few seconds in position against the wall and to help me up. I let myself down again to my original position on the ledge, breathing hard, like a steam-engine this time. I dug my ice-axe in up to the hilt and while I clung to it Schatz came up, wriggling serpent-like along the ledge. Soon he was touching me, behind. As soon as I had gone up three feet he would take my place, belay me, and pass his axe up to me.

My turn to move now. I raised myself up and put my foot on the axe, which sank in, but all the same I managed to reach the upper hold with my left hand. I was completely out of balance. I used my piton-hammer, which I had taken out of its holster, as an anchor, though its security was purely illusory. Schatz made the next move as planned, took my place underneath, belayed me and passed me his axe. Without turning round I grabbed it and with a great swing dug the pick in hard a couple of feet higher up. There was not a second to be lost—my feet scrabbled in the air and I pulled up on my left hand-hold and upon Schatz's axe dug in the ice. It seemed an eternity;

I had to fight every inch of the way. My right knee reached the level of the lower of the two footholds, groped for it, found a lodgment—a terrific relief. With another spurt of energy I got my boot up to where my knee had been, but was I going to be able to heave my leg high enough to get the points of my crampon in? I was almost there—the crampon came up with hideous slowness, one point, two, just another heave to get them right in . . . I was up!

Careful not to make a wrong move or to lose my balance, I pulled on the axe, holding the shaft against the ice the whole time so that the pick should not suddenly jerk out. I found something for my left foot. I stretched out, pulled up once more, and there I was in the two steps prudently prepared in advance.

'Gosh! I'm up! . . . What a brute!'

Schatz, who had been desperately anxious, was waiting for this.

'Well done, Maurice!'

'Don't move! A yard of slack!'

Again, without a moment's rest, for it was a thoroughly unhealthy place, I hacked away harder than ever to make big steps in the good hard ice. A couple of yards further on the slope eased and I came to snow. I cut a large step where I could stand on both feet, and called out to the invisible Schatz:

'Wait a bit, yet. Give me ten feet of slack and I'll put in a piton.'

'O.K.!' The reply reached me through the wind which had just begun to rise.

My heart was thumping as though it would burst, my breath came in irregular gasps, and great drops of sweat poured off me. Before going on I leant on my axe and shut my eyes a second. Then I began cutting again; the ice became granulated and the work was not so hard. I was now above the overhang, with another yard to go to reach a good stance. With my axe I cleared a flat space in the ice in which to place the piton. Chips flew up: I wondered what Schatz was thinking still lying on his stomach on the ledge.

'Ready in a minute!'

Hanging from my waist was a spike, a kind of giant fish-hook, as long as a man's forearm and provided with inverted teeth. Using my hammer I drove this ice-piton in, with all my strength. The ice was so soft here that after a few blows it was in position. Would it hold? It would become firmer as it froze in. I now turned my attention to the spare rope—it was nylon, white and dry and clean. I opened my knife and cut off a six-foot length—enough to make a decent loop which I fixed to the piton. All this would remain fixed in place. The sixty-foot length threaded through the loop would run down the slope and hang freely out above the overhang. I tugged to test the piton. All was well.

It was my privilege to be the first to try it out. I hung on to the rope and regained my comfortable step, below and a bit to the right.

'Hallo, Schatz. You can come up.'

'O.K. I'll tell you when I'm starting.'

Schatz made his preparations. He put on his rucksack, which he had shoved under the overhang, and secured his axe to his wrist by a special bit of line which the others had made particular fun of. His voice rang out in the climber's familiar call: 'I'm coming!' I held him on a tight rope.

Schatz took hold of the fixed rope. I heard a jabbering, and a dirty cap appeared, then a dark face twisted into a grimace. He was not exactly handsome at that moment! He found a hold for a crampon, then drove his axe in, took fresh hold on the rope, pulled himself up, and there he was beside me. The obstacle had been overcome!

Suddenly it grew cold and clouds darkened the air. We got into our anoraks and long capes. But what were the others up to? We hallowed at them.

'We're over here,' came back the answer, in the tones of people who have been disturbed. They were sitting at their ease on the lower slopes. Their reconnaissance had come to nothing. Neither to the left nor to the right was there any possibility of turning the wall. The only solution was the way we had found. And so they were philosophically waiting to see what happened next. In a quarter of an hour they rejoined us.

The slow painful advance began again, zigzagging through a wild sea of ice. The weather, too, was wild. Every step, every yard gained on the mountain cost us such an effort that it left us trembling. I was seriously worried: if we had to go on struggling over this sort of ground for long, we should never win through. The others were no more optimistic than I was.

If only these heavy day-time snow-falls would stop, the snow would then freeze at night, and over this firmer ground we should be able to make reasonable progress. But every afternoon there was a storm bringing with it twelve to eighteen inches of snow daily. So that every day our work began all over again. We hoped that our tracks would at least leave a foundation for future use. This was our last remaining hope—would it, too, prove illusory?

Through the snowflakes I could see Schatz's grey shadow battling through the powder snow as he went ahead to relieve me. The wind continued to blow, we could not see more than fifty feet, and the angle of the slope was horribly steep. There was not the vestige of a site on which we could pitch the tent. In any case it would be preferable to have Camp III higher up: the aneroid registered 21,650 feet, though later on we found out that we were only at 21,000 feet. It seemed to us an enormous height.

It snowed without a stop, and snow-clearing was a terribly exhausting job. But anyway we were on the move. We really were making progress towards the summit, and it gave me tremendous satisfaction. We stowed the tent, equipment and food beneath a serac shaped like a crescent moon. To mark the cache for the others following later, we hollowed out a niche in the wall and stuck in a red flask, jamming it well in.

'They'll be able to spot that from a good way off,' I said to Schatz, and he agreed.

Once again I noticed how much easier it was going down. Lachenal and Rébuffat went first now and had already disappeared into the mist. The snow fell thicker than ever. I was in front of Schatz and I let myself drop over a very awkward little wall of ice. Unfortunately I had not made sure of the length of the rope between us, so Schatz felt a strong pull which he was not at all expecting, and he shot down the slope. He hurtled past me, yelling. By good luck the thick snow which we had been cursing slowed him up and then stopped him, deadening his fall. Getting up with great difficulty, he came back towards me—rather stunned, and swaying in a drunken sort of way, but not hurt. He now went ahead and I held him on a short rope as we retraced our tracks in the storm. Lachenal and Rébuffat waited for us before crossing the couloir. They were worried about Schatz's unsteady balance and they kept very close to him, following his movements with a watchful eye. For the second time we crossed the terminal shoot of the great couloir without any incident. In the days to come many parties had to cross and recross this dangerous place, but all were spared by the avalanches.

It grew warmer, and we continued to sink in as much as ever; we failed to spot Camp II, which was hidden in the clouds. We went by guess-work, though here and there we came upon the tracks of our ascent, which were now barely visible. The wind grew stronger, the snow stuck to our glasses and lashed our faces; we tightened the hoods of our anoraks and went along bent double beneath the squalls. A glissade, a few footprints, a large crevasse—we thought we must be quite close to the camp. We bore to the right and saw, a few paces off, a tent covered with snow: in actual fact we only spotted it because some of the fabric was showing. What were we to do? We could not all spend the night here, there just was not room. And if we went down we should be available to carry more loads up.

We went on again. It was getting late, and as we descended towards the plateau visibility decreased further. There was a thick mist, but by keeping in single file we were able to steer an approximately straight course. We knew that near Camp I we had to cross a very crevassed section. There was only one way through and this was marked with cairns, but we just could not find the first. Rébuffat thought we should go lower down on the left; Lachenal, higher on the right. As for me, I thought we were on the right route. But on no account did I want the party to separate. Finally we decided to try Rébuffat's way, though we were not altogether convinced. Actually, by bearing to the left we did reach the great line of seracs which ought to lead us straight to Camp I.

The mist grew thicker and thicker. We were going along between two crevasses which suddenly converged: impossible to advance a step further. Back we had to go and turn the whole crevassed section by traversing right round it. All at once we felt absolutely exhausted—this last petty difficulty on the glacier took the stuffing out of us. We knew we could not be far from the camp, so we bawled 'Hallo! Hallo!'

In a few seconds we heard, faint but distinct 'Over here!'

'I told you we ought to have gone to the right,' snapped Lachenal.

Soon a shadow appeared—it was Terray. He explained that there was not room for all of us at the camp; there was very little equipment, and the food would have to be saved up for the higher camps. I decided at once that Lachenal, Rébuffat and myself would take advantage of the last of the daylight to go down to Base Camp, while Schatz, who had not yet recovered from his fall, would remain here to recuperate a bit.

Terray described his night's bivouac, while Lachenal listened disapprovingly. We then told our story and described the serac under which we had dumped the equipment.

'Early tomorrow morning I'll go up with Pansy and Aila,' said Terray, 'and at the same time Ajeeba will go up and down between Base Camp and Camp I.' Ajeeba, who was extremely strong, had become a specialist on this particular job: twice a day he made this journey, bringing up hundreds of pounds of supplies to Camp I. It was unrewarding and unspectacular work but it had to be done and was of the utmost value. Individual efforts like these would give the Expedition its chance of success.

So, leaving Schatz, Terray, Pansy and Aila, we made off down the slopes with Ajeeba. We glissaded down the screes, braking as best we could, dashed along the ledges, and in a few minutes had descended 1000 feet or more. Then, reaching the névé, we found to our great joy not merely one tent pitched at Base Camp, but several. Ichack and Oudot had just arrived with the Sherpas and a number of porters. There were sleeping-bags for all and food in plenty. There was even one of the big green tents which would be much appreciated by the porters, for it was still snowing.

Victory was in sight! Contact had been established between the rearguard and the advance party.

# 10

## *The Sickle*

It was now the evening of the 24th, and Sarki had left with the all-important order of the day on the morning of the 23rd. Ichac told me that he had met our messenger careering down the gullies of the Miristi Khola, when he himself was coming up, as planned, to meet us. He and Oudot were delighted to learn that we had established camps up to nearly 21,700 feet[1] in such record time. That evening at Base Camp there was a general feeling of gaiety, and how delightful it was to relax in optimism and creature comfort! We had a delicious meal: chicken in aspic and a bottle of rum. (Terray was later to complain bitterly that we might have waited for him for this feast!) But in the end our physical exhaustion—as well as these other excesses—got the better of us.

We rose late next morning; we were pretty stiff after all our exertions, but in the warm sun soon began to show signs of life. I decided to go and wash, and even to shave. It was wonderful to feel clean again and to move about at ease in camp boots. I was able to see things more clearly, and plans for the coming struggle were beginning to take shape. This was uppermost in all our minds—as was quite clear from the way the others, field-glasses in hand, discussed the problems of the assault. As for myself, I had taken my decisions; but, there was the question of supplies to be dealt with. I had every confidence in Noyelle, who had prepared the 'mobilization' at Tukucha a good time in advance, and after a long series of calculations I felt reassured. There was no danger on that score—all our strength could be concentrated in the spearhead of the attack. So I decided to leave that afternoon with Rébuffat for Camp I, without hurrying, and to take a number of loads with us, we were determined not to come down again unless victorious. I wrote my last letter to Lucien Devies.

---

[1] At this time we still thought that we had been up to 21,700 feet, the height registered by our altimeters.

108

Base Camp,
May 25th, 1950

My dear Devies,

A final note before the attack. Everything is going well. Base Camp is three to four days from Tukucha and this doesn't help matters. The change-over from a strong reconnaissance to a full-scale attack might have proved extremely difficult at this distance from our starting point. Yesterday I went up to 21,700 feet. The route lies entirely over snow and ice. Objective dangers are comparatively small. Camps are situated thus: Base Camp on the right bank of the North Annapurna glacier at 14,500 feet. Camp I, also on the right bank, on the edge of a large plateau very like the upper Argentiere plateau, at 16,750 feet. Camp II on a glacier that descends directly from the summit of Annapurna, on a little plateau at 19,350 feet. In due course I expect to pitch Camp III at about 21,700 feet, Camp IV at about 24,600 on what we call the 'Sickle' glacier. (You will see this at once on Matha's drawings and sketch-map.) We may set up a Camp V—it all depends on the lie of the land.

The weather is fine in the mornings and bad in the evenings. It snows a lot, which is a fearful nuisance, for we sink in terribly. Everybody's fit. In a few minutes I am going up to Camp I. During the next few days we shall make the final assault. We are all very hopeful. Conditions are difficult high up, but if we get to the top we shall be so overjoyed we'll forget all that. I haven't time for more as there's a lot to be done, as you can imagine. Matha will explain the situation in more detail.

Yours ever,
MAURICE

While I was writing, the porters and the Sherpas had finished striking camp under Couzy's directions. After our meal the weather became very cloudy, and by 3.30 it was snowing. I thought of Terray who had left Camp I early that morning with two high-altitude units, plus twenty pounds of food, intending to carry on up to Camp III and spend the night there. When we left at about 5 o'clock it was snowing hard, but nevertheless we went up rapidly and reached Camp I by nightfall. Quickly we pitched one of the valley tents in which we all three slept. Rébuffat complained again of his sunburn, and of his lips, which were very sore.

The alarm watch rang at 6.30. 'Sherpas , , Sherpas!' But they were in no hurry and preparations dragged on. Through the glasses we picked out three black dots on the mountain a bit above and to the left of the highest point we ourselves had reached. 'No doubt that's Camp III,' we thought. We left at about 10 o'clock for Camp II: Rébuffat and Dawathondup on one rope—this Sherpa had been passed on to us by Ichac with various warning injunctions[2]—and Lachenal, Angdawa and I on another. It was appallingly hot on the

[2]On the way up, between Tukucha and the Base Camp, this particular Sherpa had consumed an excessive amount of chang and methylated spirits.

great plateau, and Lachenal suffered terribly. He plodded along in a daze, streaming with sweat, and when anyone spoke to him he looked up with dull and anguished eyes, and took advantage of the least excuse to flop down. Rébuffat had stomach pains which got worse and worse so that in the end we had to take it in turns to carry his sack. Progress was most difficult. At the end Lachenal was practically dragging himself along, and the last hundred yards to Camp II were a drawn-out agony for him. He had stuck a bit of elastoplast on to his terribly burnt lips, which gave them a slight protection. It was the only light coloured patch on his brown face, and it looked very odd.

At Camp II we found Terray, Pansy and Aila who had just come down. Terray was highly excited: 'There's no time to lose,' he said. 'Yesterday I went up to 22,000 feet and I couldn't find the equipment you left—so I suppose it must have been completely buried under the snow. At the point we got to there was no sign of a platform. So Pansy and Aila and I made one with our axes, but it's far from level, and right in the middle of a slope. The three of us spent the night in this tiny shelter with avalanches coming down all round us.'

To make his account more realistic he imitated the sound of the snow cascading down a few yards away from him, or perhaps even only a few inches. Then he laughed and went on:

'The Sherpas weren't very happy and neither was I! After such a night we weren't fit for anything but coming down, so here we are. I'm going back to Camp I to recuperate.'

'Right,' I said, 'I think it's the best thing to do. Couzy and Schatz are coming up with Ichac and Oudot to Camp I, so you'll be able to rest in comfort. Also this will mean you can make an extra journey up, with a load—these damned loads are always on my mind.'

'I left our stuff at 22,000 feet,' Terray went on, 'probably further to the left than the point you reached. Our place is in the middle of a slope, fifty yards to the right of a line of seracs.' He did up his sack, hailed the Sherpas, threw them each a loop of rope, and then, bidding us farewell in his deep voice; off he went.

We were now alone at Camp II. Neither Lachenal's nor Rébuffat's morale was very high, for they were not feeling too good. Moreover Terray's remarks about deep snow had not exactly encouraged them—they had already had a taste of it on the first trip. I realized that I must not push them too hard next day if I wanted to be able to count on them later. There were two Sherpas available, as well as equipment and the food that we had brought up. Why should I not go on, and try to establish Camp III, and even perhaps Camp IV, while the other two were resting? If I were to stay above Camp II for more than a day, then they, along with Schatz and Couzy, who would have arrived by then, would in their turn be able to carry stuff up to the higher camps. In view of the way things were going, and the fact that it was already May 26th, the four Sahibs would have to move up a stage—from Camp II to Camp III—and continue their slow progression, without any further descent, from camp to camp, up to the very top. Meanwhile Terray would come up again, fighting fit, and it should be possible for me to do another carry; in this way all the camps would be established in the least possible time.

For once it was fine in the afternoon. While the other two slept soundly in their tents, I went over all the equipment and got things ready for next morning.

At dawn I began to chivy Dawathondup and Angdawa. We had to get off early so as to take advantage of the hardness of the snow after the night frost, and the sun had not yet touched the camp when we left. I retraced Terray's descending tracks up towards the terminal shoot of the couloir. I had the camera and hoped to be able to get some pictures. In the couloir I made Dawathondup go first to see if he could cut steps reasonably well, but when we reached the pitch with the fixed rope there was no further question: the Sahib had to do his stuff. This reminded me of the story Terray had told me the night before: at this same point he had been on the rope with Pansy and Aila, Pansy leading. As they got near to the wall a look of terror spread over Pansy's face and he just dug his ice-axe firmly in the snow. Terray, the 'strong man' as the Sherpas called him, said: 'Carry on, Pansy, your turn.' And Pansy answered with a broad grin, 'No thank you, for Sahib only!'

Terray found it useless to press the point!

Dawathondup felt the same way as Pansy, but this time I wanted to take a few shots with the cine-camera so I pushed Angdawa into the lead. He was shaking with fright as he passed in front of me, but proceeded to lead up, since the Bara Sahib had willed it so. I held him firmly on the end of the rope and while he grappled with the pitch I manipulated the camera as best I could, lying awkwardly on the ice ledge, hardly able to lift my head on account of the overhang. Angdawa's efforts soon came to an end and in spite of the security of the rope I had not the heart to ask him to go on, so I took his place and went ahead. It was considerably easier with the fixed line, and in a few seconds I had hoisted myself up to the little stance on

111

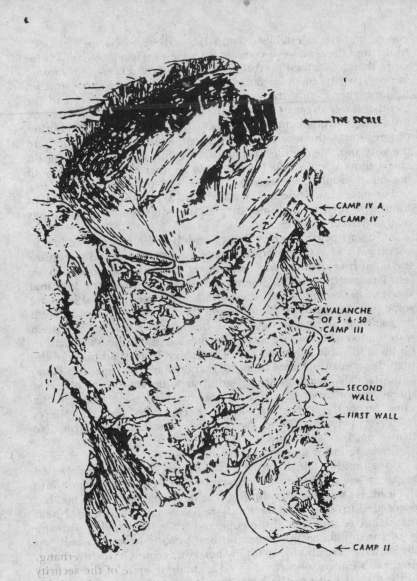

Routes between Camps II and IVA. The Camps are shown as black dots.

ANNAPURANA SEEN FROM CAMP I

the right, twenty-five feet above. There I fixed a belay and brought up Dawathondup, who found the going pretty difficult—the idea of climbing up ice had never entered his head. I felt that the prestige of the Sahibs was rising rapidly! Dawathondup arrived, puffing like a grampus, his face screwed up with effort. I showed him how to bring Angdawa up on the rope, while I took a shot of the proceedings. It all went off very well.

We sorted ourselves out and went on. But while we had been busy, time had slipped by; the sun was now directly overhead and beating down so fiercely on the slopes that we were wallowing in slush. It was most exhausting work and by now Terray's tracks were barely visible. Anyway, as they now went off to the left and I wanted to pick up the equipment we had dumped on the first trip, I continued straight up. Soon afterwards I recognized the serac shaped like a crescent moon. I poked round with my ice-axe for a while and finally located some compact objects: the stuff was there. We cleared away the snow, and sure enough we found the tent, quite complete, with the food and equipment which Lachenal, Rébuffat and myself had taken up three days before. We lifted the lot, and tried to rejoin Terray's tracks over on the left. They were fifty yards away, but it took us nearly an hour to reach them, for we had to make a regular trough, sinking in up to our waists in the snow. At last we reached the track at the foot of a very steep wall of bare and shining ice. The steps cut by Terray had already almost melted away and I had to re-cut the whole pitch. To make it easier for the Sherpas I drove in a big ice-piton at the top of the wall and fixed a long nylon line to it. Then I went up a few steps higher so as to be able to belay them well. I saw my Sherpas, one after the other, make wonderful pendulums, yell as they found themselves on their backsides, and then roar with laughter at the whole business.

We were now above the whole area of alternate ice walls and snow slopes. Lifting my head and looking upwards, I saw an even snow slope in the middle of which I could pick out Terray's tracks. On the left was the great central couloir, very steep and looking as if it were waiting to swallow up anything and everything that fell from the upper slopes. The air was luminous, and the light was tinged with the most delicate blue. On the other side of the couloir, ridges of bare ice refracted the light like prisms and sparkled with rainbow hues. The weather was still set fine—not a single cloud—and the air was dry. I felt in splendid form, and as if, somehow, I had found a perfect balance within myself—was this, I wondered, the essence of happiness?

But after all we had still a long way to go. Like ants getting over an enormous obstacle we climbed up without appearing to make any progress. The slope was very steep, and also the snow began to ball up under our feet, which made me keep an extra watchful eye on the Sherpas. Every other yard I stopped to get my breath: behind me I could feel the two Sherpas oppressed by the tremendous effort required. From time to time I looked up to gauge the distance we had to go. Suddenly I spotted a patch of bright yellow—undoubtedly Terray's tent. After an eternity of ploughing through the thick, treacherous snow we at last reached his highest point. The food and equipment were buried in the snow, but they were carefully wrapped in a *pied d'éléphant*—a nylon bag into which you put both legs, to protect them from the cold. I was very pleased to have got so far, but the site puzzled me. There could be no question of re-establishing Camp III on the slope itself. To the right there was a deep drop, to the left a cataract of seracs, on the far side of which ran the central couloir, and fifty yards above us a very broken-up area began. Looking at the seracs on the left I noticed that the crevasses between them were all blocked with fresh snow. Why not . . . ? An idea had come into my head: why not put the camp right there in a crevasse? Given the height, and the lie of the ground, it would be completely blocked up. Moreover the neighbouring seracs would form a splendid protection against avalanches. And so 'Why not?' became 'Let's go and have a look.'

With my two Sherpas I traversed across and reached the edge of the blocked-in crevasse. Well belayed, I ventured on it—my first steps were very cautious. I drove my ice-axe in right up to the hilt and found that the snow was well consolidated. I went forward now with more confidence and made a little platform on which I turned round, taking a few steps in each direction, then I started dancing about and finally jumping. It held! Once the hard crust had been removed, here and there, and the surface levelled, it would make an ideal site—there would easily be room for two tents facing each other. Without losing a minute the two Sherpas pitched the tents and prepared tea. That was all for the day: we had achieved our object of establishing a permanent Camp III. The others would not be able to see the site from below, and no doubt they would be wondering where we had got to.

While the Sherpas fixed up our bivouac I pushed on a little towards the central couloir at the far end of our crevasse, as we should have to go that way next day. For I had made up my mind that we must endeavour to establish Camp IV the following day. I had plenty of time to look at the surrounding peaks, to observe the remarkable Cauliflower Ridge with its bizarre formation, to admire the distant Dhaulagiri, and to let my mind and my eyes wander over the desert land of Tibet, hardly more than a dozen miles away from us.

A cold and violent wind got up, but no disquieting clouds appeared—it would be fine tomorrow for sure. With this optimistic prophecy I went inside the tent—a nice tent all to myself, with two air mattresses and two sleeping-bags. I was waited upon like a king by the Sherpas. They brought me tea and then I dealt round aspirin and sleeping-tablets and the whole chemist's shop that Oudot insisted on. It was not long before I dozed off.

In the morning we had to be very brisk. I took down one tent, packed up as much food as possible, shared out the loads and, after a quick breakfast, we started. I took the lead and made a détour towards the central couloir. We skirted along the foot of the serac that protected our camp and climbed up a sort of gable of bare ice which the Sherpas did not much appreciate. It was impossible to go any higher and we had to resign ourselves to crossing the couloir. It was, however, relatively narrow at this height, as if it had been squeezed in by the batteries of seracs on either side. It could scarcely have been more than a couple of hundred feet across. If one of us went over quickly while the others kept a look-out, they would be able to give warning of any avalanche; and in my opinion it was reasonably safe. Leaving Dawathondup on the left bank, I began to cross. The slope was exceedingly steep, falling straight down beneath my feet, and we could not get a grip on the snow, which had been hardened by successive avalanches. First, with the blade of my axe I had to cut little steps for the points of my crampons; then when I moved I stuck the pick into the ice above me as an anchor, and held on to it with both hands. I went as quickly as I could; a glance up every now and then had its uses, if only for one's morale. Looking down, on the other hand, was not to be recommended, for the sight of those colossal precipices might have shaken even the most confident climber. The traverse was quickly completed and I allowed myself a few moments to get my breath before bringing over the Sherpas.

'Dawathondup!'

'Yes, sir,' he replied in a voice which sounded rather queer. He smelt danger, the old fox! Without wasting a minute and in spite of his load he came over like a whirlwind to reach safety. Angdawa followed, but he was younger and did not move so well, and took much longer than Dawathondup. Whew! Here we were, safe and sound across that terrible couloir! From my present position I could see just what had been threatening us. The couloir ran up for about 1000 feet to merge into a very steep snow slope—a gathering-ground for avalanches. Above was the rock wall and then the Sickle glacier from which a few dozen tons of superfluous ice split off from time to time.

Our situation was critical; before me stretched a broken-up area lying at a very steep angle. From here onwards the route, as planned from Camp I, consisted in slanting up to the left and then back to the right as far as the top of the central couloir at the point where the great bergschrund, separating this couloir from the steep snow slope above, was blocked with snow and where, in all probability, there would be a way across. But straight ahead of me were enormous seracs. I could either skirt round them by descending slightly and then traversing to the left, or else I could climb up the true right-hand edge of the couloir and reach the upper slopes that way. I chose the latter alternative, since there was practically no danger of avalanches at this early hour. Moreover, by going rapidly up on the extreme edge of the couloir we gained the necessary hundred yards or so. We then bore over to the left and once more sank into deep snow with which we were unfortunately all too familiar. But at any rate we were out of danger.

After a few minutes' rest we started off again; we had to keep traversing to the left and gaining height at every possible opportunity. But the slope was steep and I had only limited confidence in my Sherpas' balance. They were not accustomed to such difficult ground and if one of them had slipped we should all three have shot out into space; so I kept a watchful eye on them. The first traverses were accomplished without incident. I did my best to pack the snow at each step in order to make a safe and comfortable track. One stretch over bare ice needed particular attention. Three blows of the axe and the ice chips flew—there was just room for two points of my crampons and on I went. But Dawathondup thought differently and began to enlarge the steps behind me, but desperately slowly. At last he arrived—I took his rope and belayed Angdawa who in his turn started off. He did not seem very confident—he lifted his left foot, failed to fix his crampon points properly into the ice, the toe of his boot slipped, he banged his knee, lost his balance and there he was sliding away down the slope. Luckily I had been watching him like a hawk: the loop of rope tightened round my axe, the rope stretched taut and then held fast. Angdawa got off with a fright—and in future he would have confidence in the rope. We continued over this soft snow lying on hard ice. The setting was wonderful—everything was a transparent blue, even our shadows, and there was not a cloud in the sky. On our left was the Sickle Ridge, quite close, apparently almost within reach, dripping bare ice and shining in the sun: a real Diamond Mountain.

My two Sherpas were exhausted and Dawathondup was very near to regretting those escapades which had made it necessary for him to come up such a height in so short a time. (From Choya, about 8000 feet, he had come up without a day's break to 23,000 feet.) We had some difficulty in climbing over a serac by a tricky piece of step-cutting during which I had my turn of being very frightened: after having cut three good steps, and a good hold for the left hand, I suddenly heard a dull sound; the ice made a cracking noise as if the whole serac were about to collapse. I held my breath but nothing happened: no doubt it was the ice settling deep down. So I was able to go on. After half an hour of cutting I came out on to the upper slopes and could distinctly see the great bergschrund running horizontally right round the sloping plateau, and the enormous wall of the Sickle.

'It's your turn, Dawathondup.'

I pointed out the line we had to follow, which was now rather easier. There was a fairly steep snow slope, then a hundred yards or so of moderately steep ice up which we should have to cut steps, another snow slope, and then we should be at the bergschrund.

This time I decided to take it easy; I let the others go ahead to do the work and took my place at the end of the rope. But the Sherpas lacked our technique and were very slow. Dawathondup cut too many steps too close together and much too big. All the same, we gained ground. Soon we came to the gaping bergschrund, very deep, but so long that the depth was not noticeable. There was no break in it for more than half a mile, except at the cone of avalanche snow. Certainly the place was not safe, but we had no option but to pass that way.

I took the lead again, climbed up the rib leading to the avalanche cone and began to go straight up it. Dawathondup belayed me from below and this was no sinecure—I slipped down as fast as I climbed up. The snow was soft and my worst fear was that it might collapse just where it bridged the bergschrund. When I reached the top of the avalanche cone I stretched out my axe as high up as I could to drive it into the slope. There was a dull sound—ice! I swung my axe and it stuck in—I was saved; with some difficulty I pulled myself up on it out of the snow which was sliding down everywhere and swishing between my legs. I tried to get my crampons on to the wall and just managed it; quickly I cut a few steps and at last reached an area which was less trying to the nerves. It was now the Sherpas' turn and I held them firmly. They had no principles to prevent them from pulling on the rope and they did so vigorously—my arms were nearly pulled out of their sockets. My little party was now assembled on the upper plateau. A great wave of content flowed through me: the technical difficulties seemed to be over. We did not know whether we should find good snow higher up, or an ice slope, but at any rate there would be no walls or couloirs.

'Let's get on. We must really put our backs into it.' This time we went right over to the left towards the Sickle, plainly visible from here. The glacier, which lay on a bed of reddish coloured rocks, stopped dead at the edge of space, and the great cliff, a huge drop of nearly 700 feet, plunged vertically down towards us—a most impressive sight.

Fortunately the handle of the Sickle offered a more accessible route and it was there we should have to go. Once again, ploughing through snow up to our waists and stopping at every step to get our breath, we approached the wall and after an hour of this exhausting going got to the foot of it. We had gone a long way since morning, and debated whether it was wise to increase still further the distance between Camps III and IV. I thought not; we should have to be capable of doing this lap in one day without undue fatigue, and I decided to establish the camp where we were. There was hardly any suitable site; the whole place seemed to be swept by avalanches. There was just one small serac which would give protection to a few square yards below. It made an ideal wind screen and our tents would be completely sheltered from avalanches. The three of us began to cut away at the ice with a will to make a comfortable platform. Soon the camp was in order—tent pitched and food stored away—and we could allow ourselves a good rest.

The Sherpas had frightful headaches. I looked at the altimeter which showed 24,600 feet, and thought the figure higher than it should have been. Aneroid barometers tend to exaggerate height and, reckoning from the summit, and the position of the other camps, I judged that we were at about 23,500 feet. I gave Dawathondup and Angdawa aspirin, and offered them some food, but they made it clear that they could not touch a thing. I was forced to consume a tin of tunny-fish before their eyes and the very sight of it made them feel sick. Looking all about me, I felt an exhilarating sense of domination, and complete confidence in our victory. I was almost at the height of the Great Barrier. Beneath me I could see the Cauliflower Ridge which had taunted us for so long, and then far down, right at the bottom, the plateau with Camp II where we could not even pick out the black dots of the other members of the Expedition.

'Off we go.' My two Sherpas needed no pressing—for once they were ready immediately. We shut the tent carefully, hoping we should find it again in good order in spite of the cascades of snow, and then plunged downwards. The return journey was made without incident and incomparably faster than our climb up. We descended the walls face inwards and the Sherpas went very well, safeguarded by myself. About an hour and a half later we reached Camp III, and found our friends in occupation.

I was delighted to be able to tell them that Annapurna was practically in the bag! The quick descent had rather gone to my head. The four others were lying in the two tents and hardly bothered to get up when we arrived. What could be the matter?

Couzy and Schatz, coming up the day before from Camp I, had picked up Lachenal and Rébuffat on their way. After a night's rest at Camp II they had left in the morning and come up here. As usual the snow had held them up a lot. Couzy, still insufficiently acclimatized, suffered from bad headaches, Schatz, was morose, Rébuffat felt he was not fit to go any further, and Lachenal had no appetite. I vainly tried to rouse them, telling them that we were practically there. I could see they had not yet found their form again, but I judged that the night's rest would do them all good. As for myself, there was no point in my waiting any longer. There was no room for me, and anyway we should have to make another carry. I hoped that, with Terray's convoy, we should be able to bring up everything necessary to equip the route, and that the next journey up would lead to victory.

But time was getting on—I was dismayed to see the days go by: it was already May 28th and the monsoon, according to the latest reports, would reach us about June 5th. That gave us barely a week to bring everything to a successful conclusion.

This time the Sherpas went much quicker; they had greatly benefited by the lessons learned during the last few days and their technique had improved. At the overhanging pitch they grasped the fixed line without hesitation, let themselves slide down rapidly and upon arrival gave an easy wave of the hand to indicate that the rope was free for the next man. My job was made much easier and I was well pleased to see the plateau on which Camp II stood getting quickly closer.

But for some time Dawathondup had been complaining of a strange pain which he found it difficult to locate precisely. He indicated the whole of that part of his anatomy between his chest and thighs. Was it excess of methylated spirits, altitude, or simply a kind of prudent precaution in view of the operations ahead, which looked like horribly hard work? He groaned continuously and Angdawa had to support him, but it was impossible to make out what this sly old fellow was about. As we reached camp, snow began to fall. We were welcomed by shouts from Terray.

# 11

## Camp II

The minute I arrived, Terray gave me some boiling hot tea. I was not allowed to get a word in: he forced me to eat, indeed, practically stuffed the food down my throat. In the other tents, the Sherpas were very busy looking after Dawathondup, who was putting up a continuously good performance as an invalid. And as for me, after this very substantial meal I was not in the least worried by the fact that I was tired; this seemed a perfectly natural result of our exertions. At last Terray allowed me to speak and I gave him particulars of the present position of the camps.

'By now most of the equipment is already on the spot. We've got to do one more carry to establish Camp V, which will be the taking-off point for the final attack; we've got it all taped. This time there's a very good chance.'

Terray had apparently completely recovered down at Camp I, from which he had just come up, but he still looked worried.

'Yes, everything will be all right if only the weather holds. The weather reports on the wireless are very bad: the monsoon has reached Calcutta, and it will be here in a few days.'

'Anyway, I'm feeling in splendid form,' I said, 'I'm certain, from the way I've been going at 23,000 feet, that I'll do fine at 26,000, and without oxygen, too.'

But Terray was not so optimistic.

'If we have to plough along as we've been doing so far, it will be a labour of Hercules and we shall end by running into trouble.'

He asked me what I thought of the condition of the climbers up at Camp III, and I had to admit it was not promising. The four I had left up there had struck me as being in a poor way, both in their physical condition and in their morale.

'On the other hand, Lionel, I'm not in the least anxious about us two,' I said. 'What's more, the route is now equipped right up to the glacier. With the four Sherpas we've got here, you and I can now go steadily on up to the top.'

'We'll have to go all out,' replied Terray, enunciating the phrase as though he had just invented it.

'Listen, I'm absolutely certain now: unless there is some unforseeable catastrophe, we'll succeed. Even admitting that the four at Camp III remain in poor form, which I don't think likely— particularly the ones who are better acclimatized—we ought to be able to make it. I suggest that we stay here all tomorrow to give ourselves a rest. We'll have plenty of time to make our preparations, and the day after tomorrow we'll be as fresh as paint and able to go on up from camp to camp. Then of the four who come down here tomorrow, the two strongest, after resting a day, will go up again to back us up. The other two, who will have had the advantage of an extra day's rest, will have plenty of time to follow on a camp behind. Both these parties will bring up more equipment, and help the first summit party to come down.'

'There's not a minute to lose,' Terray replied obstinately. 'Your plan is all very fine, but it makes me waste time. What will I be doing all day tomorrow? I'm already rested. It'll be better if I go on up and so gain a stage that might well turn the scales . . .'

'I don't deny that, but if you go tomorrow we shan't be together any more; we'll be out of step, and for the moment we're the only two who are really fit—and two men are needed for the work above 23,000 feet. I'm positive that together we'd bring if off.'

'Let's be practical, Maurice. However you look at it, we lose a day that way. It can't be helped if I'm not in the first party to reach the summit—I'll be in the second, that's all. But if only one party gets there, it may be because of the load that I'm going to carry up.'

I hardly knew what to do. Terray's selflessness did not surprise me—I had appreciated it for years—but at this moment it seemed to me that his heroism had in it a certain disregard for reality. Terray thought only of doing his duty. But I could not help wondering if there might not be an element of selfishness in my wish to have him as a partner the day after tomorrow. With Terray's example of utter disinterestedness before me, this notion worried me and made me hesitate.

'Well, I suppose I must say yes,' I said, regretfully 'on the face of it, you're right, but I am sure a chance like this will never occur again.'

Terray seemed uncertain. Then I had an idea.

'If you insist on going up tomorrow, Lionel, why don't you go up just to Camp III, with a high-altitude unit which the others can then take on further up, and come back here yourself the same evening?

We'll stay a day longer so that you've time to recuperate and then we can start. We'll both go up with lightly-loaded Sherpas who will then be able to take turns at making the tracks, leading for short spells. As we go up we can strike Camp IV, and establish Camp V if necessary, and then we'll carry right on to the top.'

I had seized on this solution, for I was positive that it would enlist Terray's support, anxious and impatient as he was to ensure the continuity of the load-carrying.

'All right, if that's what you want,' he said to my deep relief.

We spent a very cheerful evening. I appreciated the great comfort to Camp II with its valley tents, electric lighting, reserve containers, camp boots, and water in plenty. It had been entirely re-organized by Terray after an avalanche had blown down the tents: it was in a well-sheltered position behind a crevasse wide enough to swallow up even the largest avalanches.

We were warm in our sleeping-bags, while outside the snow was falling thick and fast. By the dim light of the hanging lamp I could barely see the smoke curling up from our cigarettes, and Terray's face was hidden in the shadows. We kept coming back to our plan of attack, and wondered how soon Noyelle would arrive from Tukucha with our main supply of food and equipment. But we were tired, and Terray, economical as ever, soon put out the light. In a few minutes we sank into oblivion.

In the dark somebody knocked against me, I heard a steady muttering—a hand brushed my face and the light went on. 'Time to be up,' said Terray.

He put his boots on and went out to wake his Sherpas. All through the expedition he remained faithful to his tactics of the early start. And he was certainly right, for the snow is far better during the first hours of daylight. But it needed resolution, and only he seemed to have it. I shut my eyes again and reflected with deep satisfaction that while others were sweating their guts out I should be warm and snug and pampered by the Sherpas. At the first streaks of dawn I heard a deep: 'Good-bye, then, Maurice.'

'Good luck!'

Terray closed the tent carefully. He was an invaluable chap. I know no one in France who comes nearer to being the ideal member of an expedition.

The hours went by and the sun lit up my tent and warmed it. The camp was silent as the grave. My two Sherpas were recuperating too. But it was getting late and from my sleeping-bag I called out.

'Angdawa! *Khana! Khana!*'

I heard muffled sounds, then: 'Yes, sir!' and I guessed that preparations were somehow getting under way.

With depressing slowness I extricated myself from my bedding, took my frozen boots, and began tapping them before putting them on. I put on my eiderdown jacket, my cap and glasses, and was then ready to go outside. The weather was magnificent but the valley down below was filled with a splendid sea of clouds. Above, everything was perfectly clear. There had been a heavy fall of snow during the night and I thought that Terray would be finding the going very bad. Looking through the glasses I followed his tracks and soon picked up his party just at the first ice wall. He and his Sherpas were battling their way up and must have been breathless with the struggle. I examined the neighbourhood of Camp III and saw two black specks leave it and come *down*. But they ought all to have been continuing *up* to Camp IV; I was afraid that their physical condition must have taken the heart out of them.

Heavy clouds appeared in the Miristi Khola Valley, and their unusual colour bothered me; I had gloomy forebodings about the outcome of the day. Could the clouds be the precursors of the monsoon?

Dawathondup was feeling worse and worse and I decided to send him down in the first party returning to Camp I. For the moment he lay in his sleeping-bag, moaning and holding his stomach with both hands.

Snow began to fall again; I went into my tent and lay on my air mattress day-dreaming. Before long I heard shouts. I thought it was sure to be Lachenal and shouted back. There was such a maze of tracks on the plateau that a sound signal might well be useful. A few minutes later he arrived, with Couzy.

'No use going on,' said Lachenal, 'my stomach was all inside out.'

'And I had the most appalling headaches,' said Couzy. 'Even with aspirin and sleeping-tablets I couldn't sleep a wink.'

'If only you could have heard him.' Lachenal began again. 'He moaned all night, and said he felt as if his skull was splitting.'

'It's the altitude,' I said. 'You were perfectly right to come down. What about the others? Will they go up again with Lionel?'

'We weren't feeling enterprising up there,' explained Lachenal, 'particularly after all the snow that fell during the night. I can't really tell you, but I think they were waiting for Lionel before deciding.'

We went inside the tent. Lachenal visibly relished the comfort it offered. Couzy's headache had disappeared as he came down. It commonly happens—as soon as you descend a few hundred yards all the ills due to altitude disappear. While the two of them were changing and getting dry, I went off to find out from Angdawa what there was for lunch. There must be no hesitation about killing the fatted calf to raise my friends' morale! In spite of their exertions they had scarcely eaten a thing since the day before yesterday.

We managed a very substantial meal, and, to my great satisfaction, Lachenal and Couzy did full justice to it; then we lay down and chatted in a more cheerful frame of mind. As we were taking it easy like this, Angdawa poked his panic-stricken little face through the opening of the tent and cried out:

'Bara Sahib! Other Sahibs come!'

Then, after a moment's silence:

'Bara Sahib, hear!'

And indeed I heard someone calling.

As it was still snowing steadily I quickly put on my gaiters and anorak and went out. I could not see more than ten yards. From time to time I distinctly heard shouts. It was certainly a Sahib, for the Sherpas could make themselves understood over great distances. The voice did not come from the direction of Camp III, but from a point much nearer the Cauliflower Ridge. There were two possibilities: either it was someone coming from Camp III who had gone off to the left and who now found himself among the crevasses, or else it was someone from Camp I who had gone up too high. Anyway they were in no danger, because there is never any mistaking a cry of 'Help!' in the mountains. I gave an answering shout, and in spite of the distance the man heard; he appeared to move to the left—he had understood. His shouts came nearer and I was able to give directions.

'Keep left, always to the left, beside the big crevasse.'

I went on repeating this until he answered that he had understood.

A quarter of an hour later a reeling white ghost appeared; I had difficulty in recognizing it as Schatz.

'Where's Rébuffat?'

'I came down alone.'

'Alone? You're crazy! In this weather and over the ground?' I felt the blood rushing to my face.

'But my dear chap,' said Schatz, 'I couldn't do anything else. I felt completely done up at Camp III. I was quite incapable of helping

Lionel tomorrow, and just a useless mouth to feed, so I decided to come down.'

I was really angry. It was, I think, the first time since the beginning of the Expedition that I had been roused like this.

'And so, in a place like this, you, practically a sick man, go and run useless risks! Just imagine, a simple slip, like the other day—and suppose Angdawa hadn't heard your shouts . . .'

However, it was over and done with. The thing now was to help Schatz forget the strain of his lone descent. Hot tea and a good meal brought the colour back to his face. And then he, too, became infected by the pervasive optimism of the camp and began to see the future in a rosier light.

'Did Lionel reach Camp III all right?' I asked him.

'The deep snow had slowed him up a lot. When Gaston and I were coming down we ran into him in the mist. He was in such tremendous form that we went back with him.'

'How was it that Gaston didn't come down with you afterwards?'

'I'll explain: we talked it all over. Lionel said that Camp IV ought, properly, to be organized by the four who had slept at Camp III the night before—Couzy, Lachenal, Rébuffat and myself. Even though two had gone down, the job ought to be done.'

'So you decided to go up with him?'

'Exactly.'

As usual Terray had put efficiency before everything else. He considered it his plain duty to do so. But Schatz went on:

'As I was so tired, I told Lionel that rather than conk out next day on the slope, it seemed far better for me to go down to recuperate. Later, I could make a rope with Couzy.'

'So tomorrow Lionel and Gaston will be going right up?'

'Yes, if it's fine enough.'

Would they really be able to go on? Perhaps they were now to be given the real, longed-for chance.

Outside, the Sherpas were talking excitedly. What was going on now? I put my head out and saw Ajeeba, who had just come up from Camp I, followed by a number of porters. Behind him was a coolie whom Ichac had dubbed 'the Chinee'. Later we learned that his real name was Pandy. He had come up to Camp II easily, in spite of the technical difficulties; he was a sort of honorary Sherpa. To celebrate this promotion, we made him a present of a magnificent nylon waistcoat which he wore with great pride. Ajeeba handed me two notes which I read aloud in the tent:

126

Marcel Ichac to Maurice Herzog

Angtharkay arrived 12.10. There are twenty-two loads at Base Camp.

Available to carry loads between Base Camp and Camp I—the Chinee, and a young gigolo brought up by Angtharkay. Angtharkay is going down again to Base Camp to meet Noyelle and his fifteen coolies and try to keep some of them on, to ferry loads. Send Ajeeba back as soon as possible with a list of things urgently required (high-altitude tents?).

Do you need us to convoy Sherpas between Camps II and III, and if so, when?

MARCEL ICHAC

Splendid news! With Noyelle coming up, we were certain now of being revictualled and supported by the main bulk of our equipment. There was great rejoicing in the camp.

The second note was a message in which Noyelle acknowledged receipt of my order of the day and announced his arrival in force. This note was dispatched from Tukucha on the 25th, the day after Sarki's arrival there. Good old Sarki! He had taken barely thirty-six hours to cover a distance which normally took four or five days; he had deserved well of the Expedition, and at the proper time the leader would know how to show his gratitude.

These happy events called for the opening of a bottle of rum. But there was no time to lose. Ajeeba would have to go down again immediately to get on with the load-carrying. I wrote a note at once to the Sahibs at the lower camps.

Herzog to Noyelle, Matha and all other Sahibs

Congratulations to Noyelle for the speed with which he's got going. It means a lot to us all. Yesterday Camp IV was established at 23,500 feet on the upper part of the handle of the Sickle. At this moment Terray, Rébuffat and two Sherpas are at Camp III (21,650 feet).

Our immediate objective is to pitch Camp V before the final assault which will be carried out by parties in succession.

*For Matha:* Urgent: Sarki, Ajeeba, Phutharkay and the Chinee to come up tomorrow very early with an extra valley tent and two lots of bedding (mattresses and sleeping-bag), plus a petrol stove and a quart of petrol (a large Coleman), also refills for the cine-camera (I have taken a certain number which I'm sending back), also some more medical supplies: sleeping-tablets, aspirin—the equivalent of ten tubes, ten tubes of *rosat* cream, tubes of anti-frostbite ointment (8), five tubes of anti-sunburn cream; *Tschamba-Fii*,[1] four pairs of Tricouni gaiters and one extra high-altitude unit.

Complete the loads with food: put in some *saucisson* and a bottle of cognac.

[1] Astringent anti-sunburn lotion

From Lachenal's sack get stockings, socks (three pairs), camp boots, a shirt and pair of pants.

We'll be calling you on the walkie-talkie at 8 o'clock this evening.

Couzy and Schatz go down tomorrow and will give further instructions.

*Important:* send all this off very early, as I shall be waiting to go up with Sarki, Phutharkay and Biscante to Camp III. Given good weather, we have high hopes.

MAURICE HERZOG

Ajeeba and the Chinee had brought up a high-altitude unit, food and a walkie-talkie. In the evening, at 8 o'clock as arranged, we intended to try to establish communication—at long last. This would make things much easier.

I was well satisfied with the way Noyelle was doing his job—he was showing the stuff he was made of. Without him there would have been no hope of getting up before the monsoon. I went off to have a look at Dawathondup whom I wished to send down as soon as possible. I found a very sick man—he looked almost at death's door—and I had not the heart to send him down in weather like this. He would have to go tomorrow.

Ajeeba did not waste a minute. This time he had no load and he disappeared rapidly with his great ungainly strides, followed by the Chinee trotting along behind him. In a few minutes they had vanished into the mist.

I set up the walkie-talkie. From time to time I pressed the button. 'Hallo, Maurice speaking. Can you hear me, Matha?'

All I heard was crackling. After a while I made out some wild Indian music—it almost set me dancing a jig up there, at nearly 20,000 feet, in the heart of the Himalaya.

'Hallo, Herzog speaking. Are you receiving me, Matha?'

Still no answer.

At 8.15, in accordance with our previous arrangements, I shut off. This matter of wireless communication on expeditions ought to be perfected. It was the only oversight I had to regret, but it was a big one. I went back into the tent, a little depressed by this setback, and found the others nearly asleep.

Next morning was fine, the light was brilliant and the sun was already beating down on the tent. I felt well rested and it was not long before I was up and having a look outside. The snow crystals sparkled in the sun like so many diamonds: it must have been a cold night. Our plan was simple: we would have to wait for the convoy from Camp I, which I hoped would not be long in arriving, and then set off immediately with fresh loads for Camp III. Couzy and Schatz were still not very fit: while Couzy preferred to remain where he was to recuperate, Schatz was definitely in favour of going lower down, and he decided to descend to Camp I. He would escort Dawathondup who was still, after three days, in the same state. Lachenal was a different man—I saw this by the way he got out of his sleeping-bag, went off to see what the Sherpas were doing, and looked up for signs of Terray. His morale seemed much better: would his physical fitness come back too? If so we should both be able to leave, and constitute the second party.

'What on earth can Ajeeba be doing?' I said impatiently. 'I particularly asked them at Camp I to send him off early so that we ourselves should have time to leave Camp II today.' We took it in turns to look through the glasses.

'Look, Biscante! You can spot Rébuffat and Terray moving along with their Sherpas.'

'They're going very slowly.'

'The snow's deep and it's making it difficult for them.'

Bluish mist—a very good sign—rose up from the depths of the Miristi Khola before being dispersed by the sun. We took some photographs of ourselves and of the mountains round us.

'Midday, and still no Ajeeba!'

We embarked on a great discussion about Chamonix guides, and Lachenal aired his views on his profession. The hours went by, and while Schatz got ready to go down with Dawathondup, it became obvious to me that it was too late for us to go up to Camp III that day.

'Salaam, Bara Sahib!'

'Salaam!'

It was six o'clock when Angtharkay, Phutharkay and Sarki arrived and I was very glad indeed to see them: they had brought up heavy loads with equipment, food, and most welcome this—a second valley tent for Camp II. Before the light went we had a look through the glasses at Camp IV, but we saw no movement. No doubt the party had already settled in for the night—the lack of activity was a good sign. Tomorrow they would go on to establish Camp V.

Angtharkay was wreathed in smiles; he, too, seemed pleased to see us. His little trip to Muktinath had been a great joy to him and he was still feeling the thrill of it. Now that I had him with me I felt much less anxious; with his great Himalayan experience, Angtharkay knew what to do and what not to do, and he had no hesitation about

129

taking the initiative; his authority over the Sherpas lifted a weight off my shoulders. Angtharkay undid the loads and handed me a note from Ichac, Noyelle and Oudot:

30.5.50

(1) Impossible to get the Sherpas off first thing this morning, since we didn't get your note until late yesterday and the Sherpas and equipment were at Base Camp.

(2) We are sending you Angtharkay, Sarki and Phutharkay. They are bringing up everything you asked for (complete); fix up about the bedding with the Sherpas.

(3) Tomorrow we'll send up a food convoy, perhaps accompanied by one of us, to Camp II.

(4) Leave any messages at Camp II.

(5) If you require one of us to escort Sherpas carrying food to Camp III, let us know.

(6) Wireless R.T.: heard nothing. Try again at 17 hrs. 19 hrs. 20 hrs. We've got a big receiver set.

(7) We are in the midst of temporary disturbances caused by the monsoon. The monsoon itself is advancing over Calcutta. It is ahead of time.

(8) G.B. has gone down to Base Camp. Send us news. A runner will leave here tomorrow. G.B. will go back to Tukucha.

(9) What are you doing about the return journey? The coolie situation will be critical: it takes eight days between giving the order here and the arrival of a first batch—only twenty at a time. Good hunting!

F.D.N., ICHAC, OUDOT

P.S. from Ichac: For taking cine-shots in colour: when the light is full strength you can go up to F.11.

It was too late for a wireless message at 17 hrs., but I would try at 19 hrs., this time, I hoped, with more success. The news about the monsoon was worrying: it would be heart-breaking to be stopped by its sudden arrival now we were nearing our goal. If it had already begun in the region of Calcutta it would be only a few days before it reached us here. I tried to establish wireless communication with Camp I, but with no success. To give the people at Camp I the latest news, I decided to answer their note at the last possible moment before leaving.

The sunset was magnificent; the precipices of the Nilgiris and of Annapurna turned from gold to orange, and orange to purple; the sky was pure and clear; it was very cold; all excellent signs. Were these last days of fine weather to be our final chance? The Nilgiris were now in shadow and the upper rocks of Annapurna had turned to old rose; when the rest of the mountain was already plunged in darkness one last point—the summit—held the light for a few seconds longer.

We passed an uneventful night: there were few avalanches since there had been no snow during the day. At 6 o'clock we jumped out of our sleeping-bags; the weather was perfect. Lachenal struck me as being in excellent form—he seemed to have got over his bad patch and to be making a splendid comeback.

'So you've got your socks and your shirt.' I said, while he was packing his rucksack. This extra little bit of comfort had put him in high good humour. We were both convinced that this journey up would bring us victory.

While the Sherpas made up the loads, I quickly wrote a note for Camp I:

31.5.50

#### To all Sahibs

I am about to leave for Camp III with Biscante. We intend to push on right to the top, weather permitting. Schatz and Couzy will form the third contingent. Will Matha dispatch the following telegram to Devics:

'Attacking Annapurna stop difficult route over snow and ice but allowing rapid progress stop objective dangers from avalanches and seracs slight stop Camp I/16,750; II/19 350; III/21,650; IV/23,500 established stop hoping for victory stop health and morale of all perfect Maurice Herzog.'

*Food:* a small quantity has been taken up. Couzy at Camp II will give directions for dispatch up to Camp III.

*Wireless:* have been able to hear very little. Look into it with Schatz who has gone down.

*Monsoon:* keep me well posted.

*Return:* an advance guard will go to Tukucha and see to recruiting coolies.

*Cinema:* I'll do my utmost to take a cine-camera to the summit.

M. HERZOG

That we were all optimistic was apparent in our preparations. I noticed that each of us paid great attention to the contents of his own little medical supply and to the spare films for cameras and cine camera. Surreptitiously I put the little French flag, made specially by Schatz, into my sack as well as the pennants which I was so anxious to take up. Everything was ready.

We left the camp and, having gone round the big crevasse, made straight for the great avalanche cone. The snow held well and it was neither too cold nor too hot, but just right. Our morale went rocketing up.

'Maurice, what's happening?'

'They're coming down!'

It was only too true. To our great disappointment we made out four black specks coming down the track towards us.

131

# 12

## *The Assault*

Why had they given up? We could not understand it. Lachenal, who was moving at a fair pace and appeared to be going much more easily than during the last few days, was the first up the avalanche cone and across the couloir. It was the third time I had been over this route and I knew it well by now, but again I found it both difficult and dangerous. On the little platform beneath the ice wall where we had left a fixed rope, we came upon Terray and Rébuffat.

'What's happened?' I asked Terray.

'We'd have been crazy to go on.' He seemed disheartened. 'What with the wind and this hellish snow it took us more than seven hours yesterday to get from Camp III to Camp IV.'

'Did you find the tent?'

'Yes, but we had to straighten the poles, which had been bent over by snow slides. We got the other tent up in a tearing wind. Gaston felt his feet beginning to freeze.'

'I thought I'd had it,' put in Gaston. 'Luckily Lionel rubbed me and flogged me with an end of rope, and at last got the blood circulating again.'

'This morning,' Terray went on, 'the cold was worse than in Canada and the wind even stronger than the previous day. I worked it out like this: if yesterday, when we were quite fit, we only covered just over 1000 feet in seven hours, we wouldn't have a hope of climbing the last 1000 feet under present conditions. I know we must do all we can, up to the limit of what's possible, but I'm beginning to have doubts about our success.'

Although Lachenal and I protested vigorously, the other two did not seem to be affected by our enthusiasm. Terray, for all his strength, had only just managed to cope with the snow (which covered the tracks afresh every day), with the slopes which had to be mastered yard by yard, and with the deterioration of mind and body brought on by altitude. But he did not care to dwell on all these obstacles—he had no wish to undermine our solid morale.

'We're going up,' I said without the least hesitation. 'When we come down it'll mean the top's been reached—it's all or nothing.'

132

And I felt that Lachenal was as determined as myself. The other two wished us good luck, but I read doubt in their faces. Now it was up to us.

We set to on the slope; Sarki, Angtharkay, Lachenal and myself took it in turns to go ahead to improve the tracks fortunately left by Terray and Rébuffat on their way down. The going wasn't too bad, but all the same Angtharkay was amazed at the difficulty of the ground. Pansy had already told him that neither on Kanchenjunga nor on Everest had they ever coped with such difficult terrain. It was the first time these Sherpas had done any climbing on ice and been obliged to get up vertical walls. But all went well, we pushed on steadily, and found the going much easier than the previous times, which showed just how vital acclimatization is on Himalayan expeditions. It was now burningly hot, and by the time we reached Camp III we were sweating profusely. What a truly magnificent camp this was, lost in the very heart of the mountains in a tiny snow-blocked crevasse! How snug and comfortable it managed to appear!

We had to conserve our strength: there would be no going further today. Most of the time we just lay in our sacks, and the Sherpas handed us our meals through the entrance of the other tent. The weather was set fine. This time everything was in our favour and we would get to the top.

It took the Sherpas ages to make tea because of the decreased heating power of the stoves at this height. A few cigarettes, followed by the ration of pills, which both Sahibs and Sherpas obediently swallowed, and before dark everybody at Camp III was already asleep.

In the morning we waited placidly for the sun, since the day's programme consisted of going only as far as Camp IV, which would take us barely four hours. But we should also have to move that camp again and re-pitch it right on the Sickle glacier. We each set about getting our things ready, and I took a few cine shots. Down below, the plateau on which Camp II was pitched appeared to have become a regular village. Big valley tents and high-altitude tents stood side by side and it looked altogether like an advanced Base Camp.

'Lionel and Gaston must be resting now,' said Lachenal.

We decided to move off, taking advantage of the relatively good state of the snow, and we reached the site of Camp IV more rapidly than we had expected. On the way I took some cine shots, in particular of the bergschrund by the plateau on which the camp was situated. The weather was still very fine. Angtharkay and Sarki had gone splendidly, one of them on Lachenal's rope, the other on mine. It was still early and we should therefore be able to move Camp IV right up on to the Sickle glacier. We were pleased about this, for beyond this camp there would be no further technical difficulties to keep us back. We quickly took down one tent, which we ourselves would be carrying, as well as food and equipment, etc.

'In less than an hour we ought to be up the big ice slope leading to the edge of the Sickle,' I said to Lachenal, 'it's not all that long.' Angtharkay and Sarki would come back to the present camp where we were leaving the other tent. The following morning they would have to dismantle it and carry it up to the new Camp IV. From there we would start out for the next one—Camp V.

Laden like donkeys, we sank up to our waists in new snow on the first few yards of the great ice slope. But presently there was less, and very soon only a thin layer of unconsolidated snow lying on ice. The angle was comparable with that of the steepest Alpine slopes. Now and again we cut a few steps, but most of the time we just went straight up on our crampons—though cramponing at this height was not exactly restful and we puffed away like steam-engines.

The Sherpas were not at all happy. They were not expert on this sort of ground, but as they were afraid of getting left behind they made all possible speed. After a couple of hundred yards of this exhausting work we came to the edge of the Sickle. Lachenal, who was leading, had a look round up there, and I did the same down below. Our choice fell upon an inviting site at the base of a serac just where we had emerged from the ice slope. It was an ideal place, protected from the wind both by the serac itself and by a little ice ridge which formed a natural screen. Lachenal was delighted:

'Once we've fixed things up we'll be as snug as in my own little chalet at Chamonix.'

We set to work at once and the tent was soon in position. As it was already late afternoon I packed Angtharkay and Sarki off to the lower camp, none too pleased at the prospect of going down such a difficult slope. But I knew that Angtharkay would not hesitate to cut extra steps and, if necessary, to make a staircase the whole way.

'Good night, sir!'

We shook hands warmly and our two Sherpas disappeared down the slope. Meanwhile we arranged our shelter. Mist closed round us and an icy wind got up, stinging our faces with blown snow. Neither of us had much appetite, but we forced ourselves to eat, and when the tea was ready I set out in a row the collection of pills that Oudot

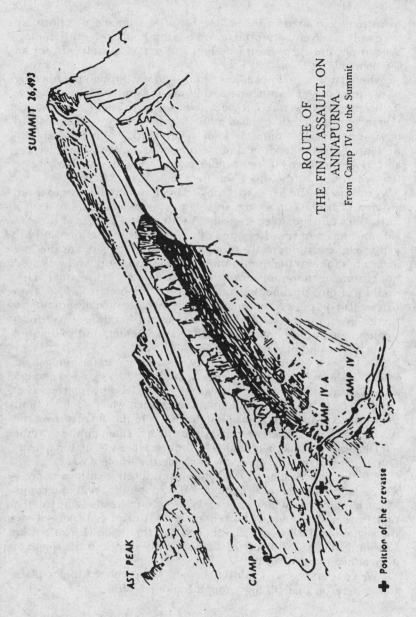

SUMMIT 26,493

AST PEAK

CAMP V

CAMP IV A

CAMP IV

✚ Position of the crevasse

ROUTE OF
THE FINAL ASSAULT ON
ANNAPURNA
From Camp IV to the Summit

135

had strictly enjoined us to swallow. For all Lachenal's assertions, we were only relatively comfortable. We put our boots into our sleeping-bags to prevent them from freezing, and settled ourselves in for an excellent night.

When dawn came I poked my head anxiously through the opening of the tent: the sun was rising and it was fine and cold. It looked as if the monsoon would not be arriving that day and I felt much relieved, for the latest news had rather worried me. We were embarked upon a race against time. As soon as Angtharkay and Sarki arrived we shared out the loads and made up our sacks. We were shivering and could not leave our serac quick enough. We set out, leaving one tent where it was; the other was for Camp V.

A traverse to the left across the Sickle glacier enabled us to avoid an area of broken-up seracs. In this way we reached the base of a wide valley of large, steep snow fields with a few obstacles in the way. No word was spoken—every one of us was tense with effort, and the loads weighed us down. We thought of what lay ahead. For me, the main question was the monsoon: it was now June 2nd, and we could not reasonably hope for more than four days of fine weather. That would just give us time, but there was not a moment to lose. Now that we had only this great snow field before us, we held the advantage: there were no technical obstacles—or at least hardly any. Not for a single moment did either Lachenal or myself entertain the slightest doubt about our victory.

We stopped frequently for sweets to suck, or for the nougat for which we always had a great craving. At our backs, the sight was enough to make anyone giddy: the plateau of Camp II was a mere pocket handkerchief, and the great Annapurna glacier, which took an hour to cross, was reduced to a small tongue of ice. In the distance, over the top of the Great Barrier, we could distinctly see Tibet; on the extreme left Dhaulagiri was partially hidden by the great rock wall of Annapurna. Our zigzagging upward tracks were visible the whole way.

The jagged ice ridge at the summit produced a curious effect—a snow-laden wind blew through it as if through the teeth of a comb. Mist straggled right across the sky over our heads. One of the buttresses of Annapurna towered above us, in rose-red rock—it was the shape of a bird's beak and looked like the Bec d'Oiseau on the Grépon in the Mont Blanc massif; a thin rib of rock in the shape of a spear-head ran up to it.

'We're pretty sure,' I told Lachenal, 'to be able to find a place somewhere on that rib big enough for our "coffin".'

Lachenal agreed: 'We'll make ourselves safe by using as many pitons as necessary, and anyhow we shall be on dry ground.'

With dogged perseverance he and I took it in turns to make the trail. The two Sherpas got terribly winded and we kept stopping to regain our breath. Two or three times we made long traverses to avoid the seracs and one particularly long crevasse. Often we sank in and each step seemed an eternity. Although we progressed upwards the rib always appeared to remain just as far off.

'Enough to dishearten anyone,' complained Lachenal.

Gradually the difficulties lessened, the snow became firmer and we did not sink in so deeply. We had the feeling that we were climbing on an enormous roof: the slope was even, and though it was at an angle of about forty degrees we were able to crampon up it. Every ten yards we halted, in cold so intense that our feet grew numb. But we could not afford any unnecessary delay: 'On to Camp V!' became for us a kind of refrain. The going became terribly exhausting, for the surface crust of the snow broke through beneath our crampons and again we sank in at each step.

With a final spurt of energy we gained the rib of rock.

'Oh hell!'

What a disappointment! Those fine, sound, clear-coloured rocks were plastered with ice—there were no ledges, no holds. We should have to pitch camp right on the slope.

The Sherpas joined us: we were at 24,600 feet and the height distressed them badly. They could not speak a word and made signs that their heads were bursting. But we all had to set to work. With our axes we made a level space, and to do this on such a steep slope we had to move great quantities of snow. Every thirty seconds I had to rest. I felt as though I were suffocating, my breathing was quite out of control, and my heart pounded away. Yet the Sherpas, who were not in such good trim as we were, managed to carry on for five minutes without a break.

An hour later the shelf was ready: it was close to the rib and we were able to tether the tent to two pitons which Lachenal drove into cracks in the rock.

I had a brief conversation with Angtharkay in our pidgin-English.

'Tomorrow morning Lachenal Sahib and Bara Sahib go to the summit of Annapurna.'

'Yes, sir.'

'You are the Sirdar and the most experienced of all the Sherpas. I should be very glad if you will come with us?'

'Thank you, sir.'

'We must share the victory! Will you come?'

At that moment I felt it my duty to take into consideration the Sherpas' very understandable feelings. After a pause Angtharkay replied. He was grateful for the choice of action I had given him, but he held back:

'Thank you very much, Bara Sahib, but my feet are beginning to freeze . . . '

'I see.'

'. . . and I prefer to go down to Camp IV.'

'Of course, Angtharkay, it's as you like. In that case go down at once because it is late.'

'Thank you, sir.'

In a second their sacks were packed and, just as they were setting off, they turned round and I could guess their anxiety at leaving us alone.

'Salaam, sir. Good luck!'

'Salaam—and be careful!'

A few minutes later two black dots were on their way down the slope we had just come up. How oddly their minds worked. Here were these men, proverbial for their trustworthiness and devotion, who quite certainly enjoyed going high on the mountains, and yet, when on the point of reaping the fruits of their labours, they prudently held back. But I don't doubt that our mentality struck them as even odder.

No word passed between Lachenal and myself, and our silence had something heavy and obsessive about it. This time we would not turn back.

It would be a grim night. The place was dangerous and the ground unstable. Under the action of the wind the snow slid down the length of the slope and piled up above our shelter. We hoped it would not weigh too much on the tent. The pitons driven into the limestone, the axes driven right into the snow, gave us only moral support and we had no illusions. We said nothing but we both feared that the edge of the platform would collapse and carry the tent away.

Our minds worked slowly during this last night before the final assault, I had great difficulty in concentrating, and I could not get up an interest in anything. Conversation languished. With great effort, and only because we urged each other on, we managed to make some tea on the stove and swallow our pills with military discipline. It was impossible to swallow any food.

A fierce wind sprang up and the nylon fabric of the tent flapped noisily. Several times we feared that the wind would blow the tent away, and at each gust we clung to the poles as a drowning man clings to a plank. It began to snow, and the storm howled and moaned around us. The air was fraught with terror, and in the end we became terrified too.

Every movement demanded a tremendous effort of will. There was no question of undressing. Pushing our boots to the bottom of our wonderful sleeping-bags we tucked ourselves in. Good old Pierre Allain! How we blessed him that night! And away flew our thoughts to the friend who had designed our marvellous equipment.

Lachenal settled himself on the outer side of the tent while I curled up against the slope. It wasn't pleasant for either of us. Lachenal, on the edge of the precarious platform, felt as though he were slipping off into space, while I was threatened with suffocation under the snow which slid down and piled up persistently on the roof of the tent.

'It's made of nylon, and it's elastic,' I said to Lachenal, 'otherwise the fabric would give way. Hell! I've forgotten to put my camera inside my sleeping-bag.'

I stretched out a hand for the precious object and slid it down beside me to the bottom of my sack, already cluttered up with my boots.

What a night! Lachenal slid further and further towards the edge, and I felt more and more suffocated. We looked at the time repeatedly. The situation was beginning to be alarming: I could no longer breathe. The weight of the snow was literally crushing me. Like a boxer on his guard I held both arms to my chest and so made a small space which allowed me to expand my lungs. The noise of the wind was ear-splitting, and every onslaught was accompanied by a high-pitched whistling. The tent poles bent over dangerously, while with the strength of desperation we tried to hold them in place. Why the tent was not blown down I don't know. Our very worst Alpine bivouacs were as nothing compared with this unequal and exhausting struggle.

We were worn out and utterly weary, but the storm saw to it that we were kept wide awake.

Rébuffat and Terray, sceptical about the success of our attempt, went down towards Camp II. When they arrived they found Couzy and Schatz, who gave them the latest news. Rébuffat and Terray were dropping with fatigue and so, no doubt, were Pansy and Aila, for

139

they disappeared into the Sherpas' tent and were seen no more that day. Couzy and Schatz, in excellent trim, were pleased to be on a rope together again. Early the following morning they left Camp II, and as arranged, they followed us up, one camp behind.

Terray gradually recovered. He felt that the final attack was imminent and set about his preparations with his usual meticulous care. Rébuffat was busy writing. Early in the afternoon sleet began to fall.

'Hallo, everybody!'

The white ghost who had just come in was Ichac!

'The others are coming up'.

Oudot and Noyelle then appeared, shaking the snow off inside the tent with the cheerful carelessness of people coming from outside. It was 5.30.

'It's *you*!' exclaimed Ichac. 'We were expecting to see Schatz and Couzy.'

'No—it's only us.'

And Terray went on to explain how they had had to retrace their steps the day before without having been able to establish Camp V because Rébuffat's feet showed signs of frostbite.

'We'll be off again tomorrow morning,' said Terray.

Outside the sleet had turned to snow. Oudot was impatient to find out to what extent oxygen would be of use. Displaying his usual authority, he insisted upon our liaison officer going round with a mask on. His face became a snout connected by a tube to cylinders of duralumin full of compressed oxygen. He might have been exploring the moon! Poor Noyelle, with his ridiculous hat pulled down over his nose and ears—he was the only one unable to appreciate the comic figure he cut.

After the tests everyone collected in the tent and Ichac took some flashlight photographs.

'I'm determined to establish a record for the highest flashlight shot.'

In fact this camp was not far off 20,000 feet high, and it was unlikely that many flashlights had been taken on Himalayan expeditions.

After dinner the sky cleared and the stars shone. The Great Barrier was clothed in a mantle of white and lit up by the moon. The latest news on the radio was alarming: the monsoon had reached the north of Bengal and, moreover, considerable disturbances were forecast from the west. The following morning—June 2nd—the sky was brilliant, it was going to be a glorious day. As usual Lionel had timed his departure for an early hour. He left camp with Rébuffat and two Sherpas at 6 o'clock, before the sun was up. (At Camp IV we were still sleeping soundly.) Ichac took some telephotos of them as they went up the avalanche cone.

Now the whole mountain was inhabited and as the hours went by activity increased. An onlooker would have seen an astonishing sight. At Camp II men were swarming round the settlement of tents. A little higher up Terray and Rébuffat with their two Sherpas, Pansy and Aila, were cutting fresh steps up the first slopes. Above, at Camp III, Schatz and Couzy, accompanied by Angdawa and Phutharkay, were preparing to cross the great couloir. And finally Lachenal and myself, with Angtharkay and Sarki, were once again ploughing through snow on the slope of the Sickle glacier.

During the afternoon clouds appeared along the bed of the Miristi Khola, and even on the plateau by Camp II. Through a rent in them Ichac was able to see, at the foot of the spear-shaped rib, a new black speck which he guessed must be Camp V. Would the final assault be made the following morning? That would be decided by the weather.

The mist grew thicker and calls for help were heard. Noyelle and Ichac went out to see who it was and found Angdawa and Phutharkay wandering in the mist. Having only one tent at Camp IV—the other was at Camp V—Couzy and Schatz had had to send their two Sherpas down.

The rest of the equipment for Camp IV was to be brought up the following day by the Rébuffat-Terray party who would strike Camp III and take it up with them. And the group at Camp II would move up the day after and re-establish Camp III.

At Camp IV morale was good, Rébuffat and Terray had just arrived and everyone was in good form. Terray meditated upon the unpredictable nature of conditions in the Himalaya: four days ago he and Rébuffat had climbed to Camp III with the greatest difficulty, taking seven hours to crawl up. This time they had successfully carried out an ambitious programme of which it would be hard to find the equivalent in the history of Himalayan climbing: leaving Camp II at dawn they had succeeded in reaching Camp III at about 11 o'clock in the morning; they had struck this camp and then carried everything on up to Camp IV, in this way gaining one precious day. Although there were only four of them they carried two high-altitude units as well as 22 lb. of food. Rébuffat, like Lachenal, had made a magnificent come-back.

There were two people who were mighty pleased to see them, and these were Couzy and Schatz. Otherwise, the next day these two would have had to carry up a complete camp themselves and they had not found this prospect particularly attractive. Thanks to aspirin, sleeping tablets and other drugs, and thanks also to a sense of tremendous well-being caused partly by good physical condition and partly by the imminence of a happy outcome, everybody passed an excellent night.

# 13

## The Third of June

On the third of June, 1950, the first light of dawn found us still clinging to the tent poles at Camp V. Gradually the wind abated, and with daylight died away altogether. I made desperate attempts to push back the soft yet icy mass which stifled me, but every movement had become almost an act of heroism. My mental powers were numbed: thinking was an effort, and we did not exchange a single word.

What an abominable place it was! For all who reached it Camp V was to supply one of their most wretched experiences. We had only one thought—to get away from it. We should have waited for the first rays of the sun, but at half-past five we felt we could not stick it any longer.

'Let's go, Biscante.'

'Yes, let's go.'

Which of us would have the energy to make tea? Although our minds worked slowly we were quite able to envisage all the movements that would be necessary—and neither of us could face up to it. It could not be helped—we would just have to go without. It was quite hard enough work to get ourselves and our boots out of our sleeping-bags—and the boots were frozen stiff so that we got them on only with the greatest difficulty. Every movement made us terribly breathless. We felt as if we were being stifled. Our gaiters were stiff as a board, and though I succeeded in lacing mine up, Lachenal could not manage his.

'No need for the rope, eh Biscante?'

'No need,' replied Lachenal laconically.

That was two pounds saved. I pushed a tube of condensed milk, some nougat and a pair of socks into my sack; one never knew, the socks might come in useful—they might even do as Balaclavas. For the time being I put them with the first-aid equipment. The Foca was loaded with a black and white film, but I had a colour film in reserve. I pulled the cine-camera out from the bottom of my sleeping-bag, wound it up and tried letting it run blank. There was a little click, then it stopped and jammed.

'Bad luck after bringing it so far,' said Lachenal.

In spite of all the precautions Ichac had taken to lubricate it with special grease, the intense cold, even inside the sleeping-bag, had frozen it up. I left it at the camp, rather sadly: I had looked forward to taking it right to the top. I had used it up to 24,600 feet.

We went outside and put on our crampons, which we kept on all day. We wore as many clothes as possible and our sacks were very light. At six o'clock we started off. It was brilliantly fine but also very cold. Our super-lightweight crampons bit deep into the steep slopes of ice and hard snow up which lay the first stage of our climb.

Later the slope became slightly less steep and more uniform. Sometimes the hard crust bore our weight, but at other times we broke through it and sank into soft powder snow which made progress exhausting. We took it in turns to make the track, and often stopped without any word having passed between us. Each of us lived in a closed and private world of his own. I was suspicious of my mental processes; my mind was working very slowly and I was perfectly aware of the low state of my intelligence. It was easiest just to stick to one thought at a time—safest, too. The cold was penetrating; for all our special eiderdown clothing we felt as if we had nothing on. Whenever we halted, we stamped our feet hard. Lachenal went as far as to take off one boot which was a bit tight: he was in terror of frostbite.

'I don't want to be like Lambert,' he said. Raymond Lambert, a Geneva guide, had to have all his toes amputated after an eventful climb during which he got his feet frost-bitten.[1] While Lachenal rubbed himself hard, I looked at the summits all round us, already we overtopped them all except the distant Dhaulagiri. The complicated structure of these mountains, with which our many laborious reconnaissances had made us familiar, was now spread out plainly at our feet.

The going was incredibly exhausting, and every step was a struggle of mind over matter. We came out into the sunlight, and by way of marking the occasion made yet another halt. Lachenal continued to complain of his feet. 'I can't feel anything. I think I'm beginning to get frost-bite.' And once again he undid his boot.

I began to be seriously worried. I realized very well the risk we were running and I knew from experience how insidiously and quickly frost-bite can set in if one is not extremely careful. Nor was Lachenal

[1] In May 1952 Lambert, with the Sherpa Tensing, reached 28,215 feet on Mount Everest, possibly the highest point yet attained. [Translators' note.]

144

under any illusions. 'We're in danger of having frost-bitten feet. Do you think it's worth it?'

This was most disturbing. It was my responsibility as leader to think for the others. There was no doubt about frost-bite being a very real danger. Did Annapurna justify such risks? That was the question I asked myself, and it continued to worry me.

Lachenal had laced his boot up again, and once again we began to force our way through the snow. The whole of the Sickle glacier was now in view, bathed in light. We still had a long way to go to cross it, and then there was that rock band—would we find a gap in it?

My feet, like Lachenal's, were very cold, and I continued to wriggle my toes, even when we were moving. I could not feel them, but that was not unusual in the mountains, and if I kept on wriggling them it would keep the circulation going.

Lachenal appeared to me as a sort of spectre—he was alone in his world, I in mine. But—and this was odd enough—any effort was slightly *less* exhausting than lower down. Perhaps it was hope lending us wings. Even through dark glasses the snow was blinding and the sun beat straight on the ice. We looked down upon precipitous ridges which dropped away into space, and upon tiny glaciers far, far below. Familiar peaks soared arrow-like into the sky. Suddenly Lachenal grabbed me:

'If I go back, what will you do?'

A whole sequence of pictures flashed through my head: the days of marching in sweltering heat, the hard pitches we had overcome, the tremendous efforts we had all made to lay siege to the mountain, the daily heroism, of all my friends in establishing the camps. Now we were nearing our goal. In an hour or two, perhaps, a victory would be ours. Must we give up? No, that would be impossible. My whole being revolted against the idea. I had made up my mind irrevocably. Today we were consecrating an ideal, and no sacrifice was too great. My voice rang out clearly:

'I should go on by myself.'

I would go alone. If he wished to go down it was not for me to stop him. He must make his own choice freely.

'Then I'll follow you.'

The die was cast. I was no longer anxious, I shouldered my responsibility. Nothing could stop us now from getting to the top. The psychological atmosphere changed with these few words, and we went forward now as brothers.

I felt as though I were plunging into something new and quite abnormal. I had the strangest and most vivid impressions, such as I had never before known in the mountains. There was something unnatural in the way I saw Lachenal and everything round us. I smiled to myself at the paltriness of our efforts, for I could stand apart and watch myself making these efforts. But all sense of exertion was gone, as though there were no longer any gravity. This diaphanous landscape, this quintessence of purity—these were not the mountains I knew; they were the mountains of my dreams.

The snow, sprinkled over every rock and gleaming in the sun, was of a radiant beauty that touched me to the heart. I had never seen such complete transparency; I was living in a world of crystal. Sounds were indistinct, the atmosphere like cotton wool.

An astonishing happiness welled up in me, but I could not define it. Everything was so new, so utterly unprecedented. It was not in the least like anything I had known in the Alps, where one feels buoyed up by the presence of others—by people of whom one is vaguely aware, or even by the dwellings one can see in the far distance.

This was quite different. An enormous gulf was between me and the world. This was a different universe—withered, desert, lifeless; a fantastic universe where the presence of man was not foreseen, perhaps not desired. We were braving an interdict, overstepping a boundary, and yet we had no fear as we continued upwards. I thought of the famous ladder of St Theresa of Avila. Something clutched at my heart.

Did Lachenal share these feelings? The summit ridge drew nearer and we reached the foot of the ultimate rock band. The slope was steep and the snow interspersed with rocks.

'Couloir!'

A finger pointed. The whispered word from one to another indicated the key to the rocks—the last line of defence.

'What luck!'

The couloir up the rocks, though steep, was feasible.

The sky was always a deep sapphire blue. With a great effort we made over to the right, avoiding the rocks; we preferred to keep to the snow on account of our crampons and it was not long before we set foot in the couloir. It was fairly steep, and we had a minute's hesitation. Should we have enough strength left to overcome this final obstacle?

Fortunately the snow was hard, and by kicking steps we were able to manage, thanks to our crampons. A false move would have been fatal. There was no need to make handholds—our axes, driven in as far as possible, served us for an anchor.

Lachenal went splendidly. What a wonderful contrast to the early days! It was a hard struggle here, but he kept going. Lifting our eyes occasionally from the slope, we saw the couloir opening out on to—well, we didn't quite know, probably a ridge. But where was the top—left or right? Stopping at every step, leaning on our axes, we tried to recover our breath and to calm down our hearts, which were thumping as though they would burst. We knew we were there now, and that no difficulty could stop us. No need to exchange looks—each of us would have read the same determination in the other's eyes. A slight detour to the left, a few more steps—the summit ridge came gradually nearer—a few rocks to avoid. We dragged ourselves up. Could we possibly be there?

Yes!

A fierce and savage wind tore at us.

We were on top of Annapurna! 8,075 metres, 25,493 feet.

Our hearts overflowed with an unspeakable happiness.

'If only the others could know . . .'

If only everyone could know!

The summit was a corniced crest of ice, and the precipices on the far side, which plunged vertically down beneath us, were terrifying, unfathomable. There could be few other mountains in the world like this. Clouds floated half way down, concealing the gentle, fertile valley of Pokhara, 23,000 feet below. Above us there was nothing!

Our mission was accomplished. But at the same time we had accomplished something infinitely greater. How wonderful life would now become! What an inconceivable experience it is to attain one's ideal and, at the very same moment, to fulfil oneself. I was stirred to the depths of my being. Never had I felt happiness like this—so intense and yet so pure. That brown rock, the highest of them all, that ridge of ice—were these the goals of a lifetime? Or were they, rather, the limits of man's pride?

'Well, what about going down?'

Lachenal shook me. What were his own feelings? Did he simply think he had finished another climb, as in the Alps? Did he think one could just go down again like that, with nothing more to it?

'One minute, I must take some photographs.'

'Hurry up!'

I fumbled feverishly in my sack, pulled out the camera, took out the little French flag which was right at the bottom, and the pennants.

Useless gestures, no doubt, but something more than symbols—eloquent tokens of affection and goodwill. I tied the strips of material—stained by sweat and by the food in the sacks—to the shaft of my ice-axe, the only flag-staff at hand. Then I focused my camera on Lachenal.

'Now, will you take me?'

'Hand it over—hurry up!' said Lachenal.

He took several pictures and then handed me back the camera. I loaded a colour-film and we repeated the process to be certain of bringing back records to be cherished in the future.

'Are you mad?' asked Lachenal. 'We haven't a minute to lose: we must go down at once.'

And in fact a glance round showed me that the weather was no longer gloriously fine as it had been in the morning. Lachenal was becoming impatient.

'We must go down!'

He was right. His was the reaction of the mountaineer who knows his own domain. But I just could not accustom myself to the idea that we had won our victory. It seemed inconceivable that we should have trodden those summit snows.

It was impossible to build a cairn; there were no stones, and everything was frozen. Lachenal stamped his feet; he felt them freezing. I felt mine freezing too, but paid little attention. The highest mountain to be climbed by man lay under our feet! The names of our predecessors on these heights chased each other through my mind: Mummery, Mallory and Irvine, Bauer, Welzenbach, Tilman, Shipton. How many of them were dead—how many had found on these mountains what, to them, was the finest end of all?

My joy was touched with humility. It was not just one party that had climbed Annapurna today, but a whole expedition. I thought of all the others in the camps perched on the slopes at our feet, and I knew it was because of their efforts and their sacrifices that we had succeeded today. There are times when the most complex actions are suddenly summed up, distilled, and strike you with illuminating clarity: so it was with this irresistible upward surge which had landed us two here.

Pictures passed through my mind—the Chamonix valley, where I had spent the most marvellous moments of my childhood, Mont Blanc, which so tremendously impressed me! I was a child when I first saw 'the Mont Blanc people' coming home, and to me there was a queer look about them; a strange light shone in their eyes.

148

'Come on, straight down,' called Lachenal.

He had already done up his sack and started going down. I took out my pocket aneroid: 8,500 metres. I smiled. I swallowed a little condensed milk and left the tube behind—the only trace of our passage. I did up my sack, put on my gloves and my glasses, seized my ice-axe; one look round and I, too, hurried down the slope. Before disappearing into the couloir I gave one last look at the summit which would henceforth be all our joy and all our consolation.

Lachenal was already far below; he had reached the foot of the couloir. I hurried down in his tracks. I went as fast as I could, but it was dangerous going. At every step one had to take care that the snow did not break away beneath one's weight. Lachenal, going faster than I thought he was capable of, was now on the long traverse. It was my turn to cross the area of mixed rock and snow. At last I reached the foot of the rock-band. I had hurried and I was out of breath. I undid my sack. What had I been going to do? I could not say.

'My gloves!'

Before I had time to bend over, I saw them slide and roll. They went further and further straight down the slope. I remained where I was, quite stunned. I watched them rolling down slowly, with no appearance of stopping. The movement of those gloves was engraved in my sight as something ineluctable, irremediable, against which I was powerless. The consequences might be most serious. What was I to do?

'Quickly, down to Camp V.'

Rébuffat and Terray should be there. My concern dissolved like magic. I now had a fixed objective again: to reach the camp. Never for a minute did it occur to me to use as gloves the socks which I always carry in reserve for just such a mishap as this.

On I went, trying to catch up with Lachenal. It had been two o'clock when we reached the summit; we had started out at six in the morning; but I had to admit that I had lost all sense of time. I felt as if I were running, whereas in actual fact I was walking normally, perhaps rather slowly, and I had to keep stopping to get my breath. The sky was now covered with clouds, everything had become grey and dirty-looking. An icy wind sprang up, boding no good. We must push on! But where was Lachenal? I spotted him a couple of hundred yards away, looking as if he was never going to stop. And I had thought he was in indifferent form!

The clouds grew thicker and came right down over us; the wind blew stronger, but I did not suffer from the cold. Perhaps the descent had restored my circulation. Should I be able to find the tents in the mist? I watched the rib ending in the beak-like point which overlooked the camp. It was gradually swallowed up by the clouds, but I was able to make out the spearhead rib lower down. If the mist should thicken I would make straight for that rib and follow it down, and in this way I should be bound to come upon the tent.

Lachenal disappeared from time to time, and then the mist was so thick that I lost sight of him altogether. I kept going at the same speed, as fast as my breathing would allow.

The slope was now steeper; a few patches of bare ice followed the smooth stretches of snow. A good sign—I was nearing the camp. How difficult to find one's way in thick mist! I kept the course which I had set by the steepest angle of the slope. The ground was broken; with my crampons I went straight down walls of bare ice. There were some patches ahead—a few more steps. It was the camp all right, but there were *two* tents.

So Rébuffat and Terray had come up. What a mercy! I should be able to tell them that we had been successful, that we were returning from the top. How thrilled they would be!

I got there, dropping down from above. The platform had been extended, and the two tents were facing each other. I tripped over one of the guy-ropes of the first tent; there was movement inside—they had heard me. Rébuffat and Terray put their heads out.

'We've made it. We're back from Annapurna!'

# 14

## The Crevasse

Rébuffat and Terray received the great news with excitement and delight.

'But what about Biscante?' asked Terray anxiously.

'He won't be long. He was just in front of me! What a day—started out at six this morning—didn't stop . . . got up at last.'

Words failed me. I had so much to say. The sight of familiar faces dispelled the strange feeling that I had experienced since morning, and I became, once more, just a mountaineer.

Terray, who was speechless with delight, wrung my hands. Then the smile vanished from his face: 'Maurice—your hands!' There was an uneasy silence. I had forgotten that I had lost my gloves: my fingers were violet and white, and hard as wood. The other two stared at them in dismay—they realized the full seriousness of the injury. But, still blissfully floating on a sea of joy remote from reality, I leant over towards Terray and said confidentially, 'You're in such splendid form, and you've done so marvellously, it's absolutely tragic you didn't come up there with us!'

'What I did was for the Expedition, my dear Maurice, and anyway you've got up, and that's a victory for the whole lot of us.'

I nearly burst with happiness. How could I tell him all that his answer meant to me? The rapture I had felt on the summit, which might have seemed a purely personal, egotistical emotion, had been transformed by his words into a complete and perfect joy with no shadow upon it. His answer proved that this victory was not just one man's achievement, a matter for personal pride: no—and Terray was the first to understand this—it was a victory for us all, a victory for mankind itself.

'Hi! Help! Help!'

'Biscante!' exclaimed the others.

Still half intoxicated and remote from reality, I had heard nothing. Terray felt a chill at his heart, and his thoughts flew to his partner on so many unforgettable climbs; together they had so often skirted death, and won so many splendid victories. Putting his head out, and seeing Lachenal clinging to the slope a hundred yards lower down, he dressed in frantic haste.

Out he went. But the slope was bare now; Lachenal had disappeared. Terray was horribly startled, and could only utter unintelligible cries. It was a ghastly moment for him. A violent wind sent the mist tearing by. Under the stress of emotion Terray had not realized how it falsified distances.

'Biscante! Biscante!'

He had spotted him, through a rift in the mist, lying on the slope much lower down that he had thought. Terray set his teeth, and glissaded down like a madman. How would he stop? How would he be able to brake, without crampons, on the wind-hardened snow? But Terray was a first-class skier, and with a jump turn he stopped beside Lachenal, who was concussed after his tremendous fall. In a state of collapse, with no ice-axe, balaclava, or gloves, and only one crampon, he gazed vacantly round him.

'My feet are frost-bitten. Take me down . . . take me down, so that Oudot can see to me.'

'It can't be done,' explained Terray regretfully, 'Can't you see we're in the middle of a storm . . . It'll be dark soon.'

But Lachenal was obsessed by the fear of amputation. With a gesture of despair he tore the axe out of Terray's hands and tried to force his way down, but soon saw the futility of his action, and resolved to climb up to camp. While Terray cut steps without stopping, Lachenal, ravaged and exhausted as he was, dragged himself along on all fours.

Meanwhile I had gone into Rébuffat's tent. He was appalled at the sight of my hands and, as rather incoherently I told him what we had done, he took a piece of rope and began flicking my fingers. Then he took off my boots, with great difficulty, for my feet were swollen, and beat my feet and rubbed me. We soon heard Terray giving Lachenal the same treatment in the other tent.

For our comrades it was a tragic moment: Annapurna was conquered, and the first 'eight-thousander' had been climbed. Every one of us had been ready to sacrifice everything for this. Yet, as they looked at our feet and hands, what can Terray and Rébuffat have felt?

Outside the storm howled and the snow was still falling. The mist grew thicker and darkness came. As on the previous night we had to cling to the poles to prevent the tents being carried away by the wind. The only two air-mattresses were given to Lachenal and myself while Terray and Rébuffat both sat on ropes, rucksacks and provisions to keep themselves well off the snow. They rubbed, slapped and beat us with a rope; sometimes the blows fell on the living flesh, and howls arose from both tents. Rébuffat persevered: it was essential to continue, painful as it was. Gradually life returned to my feet as well as to my hands, and circulation started again. It was the same with Lachenal.

Now Terray summoned up the energy to prepare some hot drinks. He called to Rébuffat that he would pass him a mug, so two hands stretched out towards each other between the two tents and were instantly covered with snow. The liquid was boiling though at scarcely more than 60° Centigrade (140° Fahrenheit). I swallowed it greedily and felt infinitely better.

The night was absolute hell. Frightful onslaughts of wind battered us incessantly, while the never-ceasing snow piled up on the tents.

Now and again I heard voices from next door—it was Terray massaging Lachenal with admirable perseverance, only stopping to ply him with hot drinks. In our tent Rébuffat was quite worn out, but satisfied that warmth was returning to my limbs.

Lying half-unconscious I was scarcely aware of the passage of time. There were moments when I was able to see our situation in its true dramatic light, but the rest of the time I was plunged in an inexplicable stupor with no thought for the consequences of our victory.

As the night wore on the snow lay heavier on the tent, and once again I had the frightful feeling of being slowly and silently asphyxiated. Occasionally in a bout of revolt I tried, with all the strength of which I was capable, to push off with both forearms the mass that was crushing me. These fearful exertions left me gasping for breath and I fell back into the same state as before. It was much worse than the previous night.

'Hi! Gaston! Gaston!'

I recognized Terray's voice.

'Time to be off!'

I heard the sounds without grasping their meaning. Was it light already? I was not in the least surprised that the other two had given up all thought of going to the top, and I did not at all grasp the measure of their sacrifice.

Outside the storm redoubled in violence. The tent shook and the fabric flapped alarmingly. It had usually been fine in the mornings: did this mean the monsoon was upon us? We knew it was not far off—could this be its first onslaught?

'Gaston! Are you ready?' Terray asked again.

'One minute,' answered Rébuffat. He did not have an easy job: he had to put my boots on and do everything to get me ready: I let myself be handled like a baby. In the other tent Terray finished dressing Lachenal, whose feet were still swollen and would not fit into his boots. So Terray gave him his own, which were bigger. To get Lachenal's on to his own feet he had to make some slits in them. As a precaution he put a sleeping bag and some food into his sack and shouted to us to do the same. Were his words lost in the storm? Or were we too intent on leaving this place to listen to his instructions?

Lachenal and Terray were already outside.

'We're going down!' they shouted.

Then Rébuffat tied me on to the rope, and we went out. There were only two ice-axes for the four of us, so Rébuffat and Terray took them as a matter of course. For a moment, as we left the two tents of Camp V, I felt childishly ashamed at abandoning all our good equipment.

Already the first rope seemed a long way down below us. We were blinded by the squalls of snow and we could not hear each other a yard away. We had both put on our *cagoules*, for it was very cold. The snow was apt to slide and the rope often came in useful.

Ahead of us the other two were losing no time. Lachenal went first and, safeguarded by Terray, he forced the pace in his anxiety to get down. There were no tracks to show us the way, but it was engraved on all our minds—straight down the slope for 400 yards then raverse to the left for 150 to 200 yards to get to Camp IV. The snow was thinning and the wind less violent. Was it going to clear? We hardly dared to hope so. A wall of seracs brought us up short.

'It's to the left,' I said, 'I remember perfectly.'

Somebody else thought it was to the right. We started going down again. The wind had dropped completely, but the snow fell in big flakes. The mist was thick, and, not to lose each other, we walked in line: I was third and I could barely see Lachenal, who was first. It was impossible to recognize any of the pitches. We were all experienced enough mountaineers to know that even on familiar ground it is easy to make mistakes in such weather—distances are deceptive, one cannot tell whether one is going up or down. We kept colliding with hummocks which we had taken for hollows. The mist, the falling snowflakes, the carpet of snow, all merged into the same whitish tone and confused our vision. The towering outlines of the seracs took on fantastic shapes and seemed to move slowly round us.

Our situation was not desperate, we were certainly not lost. We would have to go lower down: the traverse must begin further on—I remembered the serac which served as a milestone. The snow stuck to our *cagoules*, and turned us into white phantoms noiselessly flitting against a background equally white. We began to sink in dreadfully, and there is nothing worse for bodies already on the verge of exhaustion.

Were we too high or too low? No one could tell. Perhaps we had better try slanting over the left! The snow was in a bad state, but we did not seem to realize the danger. We were forced to admit that we were not on the right route, so we retraced our steps and climbed up above the serac which overhung us—no doubt, we reflected, we should be on the right level now. With Rébuffat leading, we went back over the way which had cost us such an effort. I followed him jerkily, saying nothing, and determined to go on to the end. If Rébuffat had fallen I could never have held him.

We went doggedly on from one serac to another. Each time we thought we had recognized the right route, and each time there was a fresh disappointment. If only the mist would lift, if only the snow would stop for a second! On the slope it seemed to be growing deeper every minute. Only Terray and Rébuffat were capable of breaking the trail and they relieved each other at regular intervals, without a word and without a second's hesitation.

I admired this determination of Rébuffat's for which he is so justly famed. He did not intend to die! With the strength of desperation and at the price of superhuman effort he forged ahead. The slowness of his progress would have dismayed even the most obstinate climber, but he would not give up, and in the end the mountain yielded in face of his perseverance.

Terray, when his turn came, charged madly ahead. He was like a force of nature: at all costs he would break down these prison walls that penned us in. His physical strength was exceptional, his will-power no less remarkable. Lachenal gave him considerable trouble. Perhaps he was not quite in his right mind. He said it was no use going on; we must dig a hole in the snow and wait for fine weather. He swore at Terray and called him a madman. Nobody but Terray would have been capable of dealing with him—he just tugged sharply on the rope and Lachenal was forced to follow.

We were well and truly lost.

The weather did not seem likely to improve. A minute ago we had still had ideas about which way to go—now we had none. This way or that . . . We went on at random to allow for the chance of a miracle which appeared increasingly unlikely. The instinct of self-preservation in the two fit members of the party alternated with a hopelessness which made them completely irresponsible. Each in turn did the silliest things: Terray traversed the steep and avalanchy slopes with one crampon badly adjusted. He and Rébuffat performed incredible feats of balance without the least slip.

Camp IV was certainly on the left, on the edge of the Sickle. On that point we were all agreed. But it was very hard to find. The wall of ice that gave it such magnificent protection was now our enemy, for it hid the tents from us. In mist like this we should have to be right on top of them before we spotted them.

Perhaps if we called, someone would hear us? Lachenal gave the signal, but snow absorbs sound, and his shout seemed to carry only a few yards. All four of us called out together. 'One . . . two . . . three . . . Help!'

We got the impression that our united shout carried a long way, so we began again: 'One . . . two . . . three . . . Help!' Not a sound in reply!

Now and again Terray took off his boots and rubbed his feet; the sight of our frost-bitten limbs had made him aware of the danger and he had the strength of mind to do something about it. Like Lachenal, he was haunted by the idea of amputation. For me, it was too late: my feet and hands, already affected from yesterday, were beginning to freeze up again.

We had eaten nothing since the day before, and we had been on the go the whole time, but man's resources of energy in face of death are inexhaustible. When the end seems imminent, there still remain reserves, though it needs tremendous will-power to call them up.

Time passed, but we had no idea of it. Night was approaching, and we were terrified, though none of us uttered a complaint. Rébuffat and I found a way we thought we remembered, but were brought to a halt by the extreme steepness of the slope—the mist turned it into a vertical wall. We were to find, next day, that at that moment we had been almost on top of the camp, and that the wall was the very one that sheltered the tents which would have been our salvation.

'We must find a crevasse.'

'We can't stay here all night!'

'A hole—it's the only thing.'

'We'll all die in it.'

Night had suddenly fallen and it was essential to come to a decision without wasting another minute; if we remained on the slope, we should be dead before morning. We should have to bivouac. What the conditions would be like, we could guess, for we all knew what it meant to bivouac above 23,000 feet.

With his axe Terray began to dig a hole. Lachenal went over to a snow-filled crevasse a few yards further on, then suddenly let out a yell and disappeared before our eyes. We stood helpless: would we, or rather would Terray and Rébuffat, have enough strength for all the manoeuvres with the rope that would be needed to get him out? The crevasse was completely blocked up save for the one little hole where Lachenal had fallen through.

'Hi! Lachenal!' called Terray.

A voice, muffled by many thicknesses of ice and snow, came up to us. It was impossible to make out what it was saying.

'Hi! Lachenal!'

Terray jerked the rope violently; this time we could hear.

'I'm here!'

'Anything broken?'

'No! It'll do for the night! Come along.'

This shelter was heaven-sent. None of us would have had the strength to dig a hole big enough to protect the lot of us from the wind. Without hesitation Terray let himself drop into the crevasse, and a loud 'Come on!' told us he had arrived safely. In my turn I let myself go: it was a proper toboggan slide. I shot down a sort of twisting tunnel, very steep, and about 30 feet long. I came out at great speed into the opening beyond and was literally hurled to the bottom of the crevasse. We let Rébuffat know he could come by giving a tug on the rope.

The intense cold of this minute grotto shrivelled us up, the enclosing walls of ice were damp and the floor a carpet of fresh snow; by huddling together there was just room for the four of us. Icicles hung from the ceiling and we broke some of them off to make more head room and kept little bits to suck—it was a long time since we had had anything to drink.

That was our shelter for the night. At least we should be protected from the wind, and the temperature would remain fairly even, though the damp was extremely unpleasant. We settled ourselves in the dark as best we could. As always in a bivouac, we took off our boots; without this precaution the constriction would cause immediate frost-bite. Terray unrolled the sleeping-bag which he had had the foresight to bring, and settled himself in relative comfort. We put on everything warm that we had, and to avoid contact with the snow I sat on the cine-camera. We huddled close up to each other, in our search for a hypothetical position in which the warmth of all bodies could be combined without loss, but we could not keep still for a second.

We did not open our mouths—signs were less of an effort than words. Every man withdrew into himself and took refuge in his own inner world. Terray massaged Lachenal's feet; Rébuffat felt his feet freezing, too, but he had sufficient strength to rub them himself. I remained motionless, unseeing. My feet and hands went on freezing, but what could be done? I attempted to forget suffering, to forget the passing of time, trying not to feel the devouring and numbing cold which insidiously gained upon us.

Terray shared his sleeping-bag with Lachenal, putting his feet and hands inside the precious eiderdown. At the same time he went on rubbing.

'Anyhow the frost-bite won't spread further,' he was thinking.

None of us could make a movement without upsetting the others, and the positions we had taken up with such care were continually being altered so that we had to start all over again. This kept us busy. Rébuffat persevered with his rubbing and complained of his feet; like Terray he was thinking: 'We mustn't look beyond tomorrow— afterwards we'll see.' But he was not blind to the fact that 'afterwards' was one big question mark.

Terray generously tried to give me part of his sleeping-bag. He had understood the seriousness of my condition, and knew why it was that I said nothing and remained quite passive; he realized that I had abandoned all hope for myself. He massaged me for nearly two hours: his feet, too, might have frozen, but he did not appear to give the matter a thought. I found new courage simply in contemplating his unselfishness; he was doing so much to help me that it would have been ungrateful of me not to go on struggling to live. Though my heart was like a lump of ice itself, I was astonished to feel no pain. Everything material about me seemed to have dropped away. I seemed to be quite clear in my thoughts and yet I floated in a kind of peaceful happiness. There was still a breath of life in me, but it dwindled steadily as the hours went by. Terray's massage no longer had any effect upon me. 'All was over', I thought. 'Was not this cavern the most beautiful grave I could hope for Death caused me no grief, no regret—I smiled at the thought.

After hours of torpor, a voice numbled, 'Daylight!' This made some impression on the others. I only felt surprised—I had not thought that daylight would penetrate so far down.

'Too early to start,' said Rébuffat.

A ghastly light spread through our grotto and we could just vaguely make out the shapes of each other's heads. A queer noise from a long way off came down to us—a sort of prolonged hiss. The noise increased. Suddenly I was buried, blinded, smothered beneath an avalanche of new snow. The icy snow spread over the cavern, finding its way through every gap in our clothing. I ducked my head between my knees and covered myself with both arms. The snow flowed on and on. There was a silence. We were not completely buried, but there was snow everywhere. We got up, taking care not to bang our heads against the ceiling of ice, and tried to shake ourselves. We were all in our stockinged feet in the snow. The first thing to do was to find our boots.

Rébuffat and Terray began to search, and realized at once that they were blind. Yesterday they had taken off their glasses to lead us down, and now they were paying for it. Lachenal was the first to lay hands upon a pair of boots. He tried to put them on, but they were Rébuffat's. Rébuffat attempted to climb up the shoot down which we had come yesterday, and which the avalanche had followed in its turn.

'Hi, Gaston! What's the weather like?' called up Terray.

'Can't see a thing. It's blowing hard.'

We were still groping for our things. Terray found his boots and put them on awkwardly, unable to see what he was doing. Lachenal helped him, but he was all on edge and fearfully impatient, in striking contrast to my immobility. Terray then went up the icy channel, puffing and blowing, and at last reached the outer world. He was met by terrible gusts of wind that cut right through him and lashed his face.

'Bad weather,' he said to himself, 'this time it's the end. We're lost . . . we'll never come through.'

At the bottom of the crevasse there were still two of us looking for our boots. Lachenal poked fiercely with an ice-axe. I was calmer and tried to proceed more rationally. We extracted crampons and an axe in turn from the snow, but still no boots.

Well—so this cavern was to be our last resting-place! There was very little room—we were bent double and got in each other's way. Lachenal decided to go out without his boots. He called out frantically, hauled himself up on the rope, trying to get a hold or to wriggle his way up, digging his toes into the snow walls. Terray from outside pulled as hard as he could: I watched him go; he gathered speed and disappeared.

When he emerged from the opening he saw the sky was clear and blue, and he began to run like a madman, shrieking, 'It's fine, it's fine!'

I set to work again to search the cave. The boots *had* to be found, or Lachenal and I were done for. On all fours, with nothing on my hands or feet, I raked the snow, stirring it round this way and that, hoping every second to come upon something hard. I was no longer capable of thinking—I reacted like an animal fighting for its life.

I found one boot! The other was tied to it—a pair! Having ransacked the whole cave I at last found the other pair. But inspite of all my efforts I could not find the camera, and gave up in despair. There was no question of putting my boots on—my hands were like lumps of wood and I could hold nothing in my fingers: my feet were very swollen—I should never be able to get boots on them. I twisted the rope round the boots as well as I could and called up the shoot:

'Lionel . . . boots!'

There was no answer, but he must have heard, for with a jerk the precious boots shot up. Soon after the rope came down again. My turn. I wound the rope round me; I could not pull it tight so I made a whole series of little knots. Their combined strength, I hoped, would be enough to hold me. I had no strength to shout again; I gave a great tug on the rope, and Terray understood.

At the first step I had to kick a niche in the hard snow for my toes. Further on I expected to be able to get up more easily by wedging myself across the tunnel. I wriggled up a few yards like this and then I tried to dig my hands and my feet into the wall. My hands were stiff and hard right up to the wrists and my feet had no feeling up to the ankles; the joints were inflexible and this hampered me greatly.

Somehow or other I succeeded in working my way up, while Terray pulled so hard he nearly choked me. I began to see more distinctly and so knew that I must be nearing the opening. Often I fell back, but I clung on and wedged myself in again as best I could. My heart was bursting, and I was forced to rest. A fresh wave of energy enabled me to crawl to the top. I pulled myself out by clutching Terray's legs; *he* was just about all in and I was in the last stages of exhaustion. Terray was close to me and I whispered:

'Lionel . . . I'm dying!'

He supported me and helped me away from the crevasse. Lachenal and Rébuffat were sitting in the snow a few yards away. The instant Lionel let go of me I sank down and dragged myself along on all fours.

The weather was perfect. Quantities of snow had fallen the day before and the mountains were resplendent. Never had I seen them look so beautiful—our last day would be magnificent.

Rébuffat and Terray were completely blind; as he came along with me Terray knocked into things and I had to direct him. Rébuffat, too, could not move a step without guidance. It was terrifying to be blind when there was danger all round. Lachenal's frozen feet affected his nervous system. His behaviour was disquieting—he was possessed by the most fantastic ideas:

'I tell you we must go down . . . down there . . .'

'You've nothing on your feet!'

'Don't worry about that.'

'You're off your head. The way is not there . . . it's to the left!'

He was already standing up; he wanted to go straight down to the bottom of the glacier. Terray held him back, made him sit down, and though he couldn't see, helped put his boots on.

Behind them I was living in my own private dream. I knew the end was near, but it was the end that all mountaineers wished for— an end in keeping with their ruling passion. I was consciously grateful to the mountains for being so beautiful for me that day, and as awed by their silence as if I had been in church. I was in no pain, and had no worry. My utter calmness was alarming. Terray came staggering towards me, and I told him: 'It's all over for me. Go on . . . you have a chance . . . you must take it . . . over to the left . . . that's the way.'

I felt better after telling him that. But Terray would have none of it: 'We'll help you. If we get away, so will you.'

At this moment Lachenal shouted: 'Help! Help!'

Obviously he didn't know what he was doing . . . Or did he? He was the only one of the four of us who could see Camp II down below. Perhaps his calls would be heard. They were shouts of despair, reminding me tragically of some climbers lost in the Mont Blanc massif whom I had endeavoured to save. Now it was our turn. The impression was vivid: we were lost.

I joined in with the others: 'One . . . two . . . three . . . *Help!*' 'One . . . two . . . three . . . *Help!*' We tried to shout all together, but without much success; our voices could not have carried more than ten feet. The noise I made was more of a whisper than a shout. Terray insisted that I should put my boots on, but my hands were dead. Neither

Rébuffat nor Terray, who were unable to see could help much, so I said to Lachenal: 'Come and help me put my boots on.'

'Don't be silly, we must go down!'

And off he went once again in the wrong direction, straight down. I was not in the least angry with him: he had been sorely tired by the altitude and by everything he had gone through.

Terray resolutely got out his knife, and with fumbling hands slit the uppers of my boots back and front. Split in two like this I could get them on, but it was not easy and I had to make several attempts. I lost heart—what was the use of it all anyway since I was going to stay where I was? But Terray pulled violently and finally he succeeded. He laced up my now gigantic boots, missing out half the hooks. I was ready now. But how was I going to walk with my stiff joints?

'To the left, Lionel!'

'You're crazy, Maurice,' said Lachenal, 'it's to the right, straight down.'

Terray did not know what to think of these conflicting views. He had not given up, like me: he was going to fight; but what, at the moment, could he do? The three of them discussed which way to go.

I remained sitting in the snow. Gradually my mind lost grip—why should I struggle? I would just let myself drift. I saw pictures of shady slopes, peaceful paths, there was a scent of resin. It was pleasant— I was going to die in my own mountains. My body had no feeling— everything was frozen.

'Aah . . . aah!'

Was it a groan or a call? I gathered my strength for one cry. 'They're coming!' The others heard me and shouted for joy. What a miraculous apparition! 'Schatz . . . It's Schatz!'

Barely 200 yards away Marcel Schatz, waist-deep in snow, was coming slowly towards us like a boat over the surface of the slope. I found this vision of a strong and invincible deliverer inexpressibly moving. I expected everything of him. The shock was violent, and quite shattered me. Death clutched at me and I gave myself up.

When I came to again the wish to live returned and I experienced a violent revulsion of feeling. All was not lost! As Schatz came nearer my eyes never left him for a second—twenty yards—ten yards—he came straight towards me. Why? Without a word he leant over me, held me close, hugged me, and his warm breath revived me.

I could not make the slightest movement—I was like marble. My heart was overwhelmed by such tremendous feelings and yet my eyes remained dry.

'Well done, Maurice. It's marvellous!'

# 15

## The Avalanche

I was clear-headed and delirious by turns, and had the queer feeling that my eyes were glazed. Schatz looked after me like a mother, and while the others were shouting with joy, he put his rope round me. The sky was blue—the deep blue of extreme altitude, so dark that one can almost see the stars—and we were bathed in the warm rays of the sun. Schatz spoke gently:

'We'll be moving now, Maurice, old man.'

I could not help obeying him with a good grace, and with his assistance I succeeded in getting up and standing in balance. He moved on gradually, pulling me after him. I seemed to make contact with the snow by means of two strange stilt-like objects—my legs. I could no longer see the others; I did not dare to turn round for fear of losing my balance, and I was dazzled by the reflection of the sun's rays.

Having walked about a couple of hundred yards, and skirted round an ice wall, without any sort of warning, we came upon a tent. We had bivouacked 200 yards from the camp. Couzy got up as I appeared, and without speaking held me close and embraced me. Terray threw himself down in the tent and took off his boots. His feet, too, were frost-bitten; he massaged them and beat them unmercifully.

The will to live stirred again in me. I tried to take in the situation; there was not much that we could do—but we should have to do whatever was possible. Our only hope lay in Oudot; only he could save our feet and hands by the proper treatment. I heartily agreed to Schatz's suggestion that we should go down immediately to the lower Camp IV which the Sherpas had re-established. Terray wanted to remain in the tent, and as he flailed his feet with the energy of despair he cried out:

'Come and fetch me tomorrow if necessary. I want to be whole, or dead!'

Rébuffat's feet were affected, too, but he preferred to go down to Oudot immediately. He started the descent with Lachenal and Couzy, while Schatz continued to look after me, for which I was deeply grateful. He took the rope and propelled me gently along the track.

The slope suddenly became very steep, and the thin layer of snow adhering to the surface of the ice gave no foothold; I slipped several times, but Schatz, holding me on a tight rope, was able to check me.

Below there was a broad track: no doubt the others had let themselves slide straight down towards the lower Camp IV, but they had started an avalanche which had swept the slope clear of snow, and this hardly made things easier for me. As soon as we drew in sight of the camp the Sherpas came up to meet us. In their eyes I read such kindliness and such pity that I began to realize my dreadful plight. They were busy clearing the tents which the avalanche had covered with snow. Lachenal was in a corner massaging his feet; from time to time Pansy comforted him, saying that the Doctor Sahib would cure him.

I hurried everyone up; we must get down—that was our first objective. As for the equipment, well it could not be helped; we simply must be off the mountain before the next onslaught of the monsoon. For those of us with frost-bitten limbs it was a matter of hours. I chose Aila and Sarki to escort Rébuffat, Lachenal and myself. I tried to make the two Sherpas understand that they must watch me very closely and hold me on a short rope. For some unknown reason, neither Lachenal nor Rébuffat wished to rope.

While we started down, Schatz, with Angtharkay and Pansy, went up to fetch Terray who had remained on the glacier above. Schatz was master of the situation—none of the others were capable of taking the slightest initiative. After a hard struggle, he found Terray:

'You can get ready in a minute,' he said.

'I'm beginning to feel my feet again,' replied Terray, now more amenable to reason.

'I'm going to have a look in the crevasse. Maurice couldn't find the camera and it's got all the shots he took high up.'

Terray made no reply; he had not really understood, and it was only several days later that we fully realized Schatz's heroism. He spent a long time searching the snow at the bottom of the cavern, while Terray began to get anxious; at last he returned triumphantly carrying the camera which contained the views taken from the summit. He also found my ice-axe and various other things, but no cine-camera, so our last film shots would stop at 23,000 feet.

Then the descent began. Angtharkay was magnificent, going first and cutting comfortable steps for Terray. Schatz, coming down last, carefully safeguarded the whole party.

Our first group was advancing slowly. The snow was soft and we sank in up to our knees. Lachenal grew worse: he frequently stopped and moaned about his feet. Rébuffat was a few yards behind me.

I was concerned at the abnormal heat, and feared that bad weather would put an end here and now to the epic of Annapurna. It is said that mountaineers have a sixth sense that warns them of danger— suddenly I became aware of danger through every pore of my body. There was a feeling in the atmosphere that could not be ignored. Yesterday it had snowed heavily, and the heat was now working on these great masses of snow which were on the point of sliding off. Nothing in Europe can give any idea of the force of these avalanches. They roll down over a distance of miles and are preceded by a blast that destroys everything in its path.

The glare was so terrific that without glasses it would have been impossible to keep one's eyes open. By good luck we were fairly well spaced out, so that the risk was diminished. The Sherpas no longer remembered the different pitches, and often with great difficulty, I had to take the lead and be let down on the end of the rope to find the right way. I had no crampons and I could not grasp an axe. We lost height far too slowly for my liking, and it worried me to see my Sherpas going so slowly and carefully and at the same time so insecurely. In actual fact they went very well, but I was so impatient I could no longer judge their performance fairly.

Lachenal was a long way behind us and every time I turned round he was sitting down in the track. He, too, was affected by snow-blindness, though not as badly as Terray and Rébuffat, and found difficulty in seeing his way. Rébuffat went ahead by guess-work, with agony in his face, but he kept on. We crossed the couloir without incident, and I congratulated myself that we had passed the danger zone.

The sun was at its height, the weather brilliant and the colours magnificent. Never had the mountains appeared to me so majestic as in this moment of extreme danger.

All at once a crack appeared in the snow under the feet of the Sherpas, and grew longer and wider. A mad notion flashed into my head—to climb up the slope at speed and reach solid ground. Then I was lifted up by a super-human force, and as the Sherpas disappeared before my eyes, I went head over heels. I could not see what was happening. My head hit the ice. In spite of my efforts I could no longer breathe, and a violent blow on my left thigh caused me acute pain. I turned round and round like a puppet. In a flash I saw the blinding light of the sun through the snow which was pouring past my eyes. The rope joining me to Sarki and Aila curled round my neck—the Sherpas shooting down the slope beneath would shortly strangle me, and the pain was unbearable. Again and again I crashed into solid ice as I went hurtling from one serac to another, and the snow crushed me down. The rope tightened round my neck and brought me to a stop. Before I had recovered my wits I began to pass water, violently and uncontrollably.

I opened my eyes, to find myself hanging head downwards, with the rope round my neck and my left leg, in a sort of hatchway of blue ice. I put out my elbows towards the walls in an attempt to stop the unbearable pendulum motion which sent me from one side to the other, and caught a glimpse of the final slopes of the couloir beneath me. My breathing steadied, and I blessed the rope which had stood the strain of the shock.

I simply *had* to try to get myself out. My feet and hands were numb, but I was able to make use of some little nicks in the wall. There was room for at least the edges of my boots. By frenzied, jerky movements I succeeded in freeing my left leg from the rope, and then managed to right myself and to climb up a yard or two. After every move I stopped, convinced that I had come to the end of my physical strength, and that in a second I should have to let go.

One more desperate effort, and I gained a few inches—I pulled on the rope and felt something give at the other end—no doubt the bodies of the Sherpas. I called, but hardly a whisper issued from my lips. There was a death-like silence. Where was Gaston?

Conscious of a shadow, as from a passing cloud, I looked up instinctively; and lo and behold! two scared black faces were framed against the circle of blue sky. Aila and Sarki! They were safe and sound, and at once set to work to rescue me. I was incapable of giving them the slightest advice. Aila disappeared, leaving Sarki alone at the edge of the hole; they began to pull on the rope, slowly, so as not to hurt me, and I was hauled up with a power and steadiness that gave me fresh courage. At last I was out. I collapsed on the snow.

The rope had caught over a ridge of ice and we had been suspended on either side; by good luck the weight of the two Sherpas and my own had balanced. If we had not been checked like this we should have hurtled down another 1500 feet. There was chaos all around us. Where was Rébuffat? I was mortally anxious, for he was unroped. Looking up I caught sight of him less than a hundred yards away:

'Anything broken?' he called out to me.

I was greatly relieved, but I had no strength to reply. Lying flat, and semi-conscious, I gazed at the wreckage about me with unseeing eyes. We had been carried down for about 500 feet. It was not a healthy place to linger in —suppose another avalanche should fall! I instructed the Sherpas:

'Now—Doctor Sahib. Quick, very quick!'

By gestures I tried to make them understand that they must hold me very firmly. In doing this I found that my left arm was practically useless. I could not move it at all; the elbow had seized up—was it broken? We should see later. Now, we must push on to Oudot.

Rébuffat started down to join us, moving slowly; he had to place his feet by feel alone, and seeing him walk like this made my heart ache; he, too, had fallen, and he must have struck something with his jaw, for blood was oozing from the corners of his mouth. Like me, he had lost his glasses and we were forced to shut our eyes. Aila had an old spare pair which did very well for me, and without a second's hesitation Sarki gave his own to Rébuffat.

We had to get down at once. The Sherpas helped me up, and I advanced as best I could, reeling about in the most alarming fashion, but they realized now that they must hold me from behind. I skirted round the avalanche to our old track which started again a little further on.

We now came to the first wall. How on earth should we get down? Again, I asked the Sherpas to hold me firmly:

'*Hold me well because. . .*'

And I showed them my hands.

'Yes, sir,' they replied together like good pupils. I came to the piton; the fixed rope attached to it hung down the wall and I had to hold on to it—there was no other way. It was terrible; my wooden feet kept slipping on the ice wall, and I could not grasp the thin line in my hands. Without letting go I endeavoured to wind it round them, but they were swollen and the skin broke in several places. Great strips of it came away and stuck to the rope and the flesh was laid bare. Yet I had to go on down; I could not give up half way.

'Aila! *Pay attention! . . .'Pay attention!*'

To save my hands I now let the rope slide over my good forearm and lowered myself like this in jerks. On reaching the bottom I fell about three feet, and the rope wrenched my forearm and wrists. The jolt was severe and affected my feet. I heard a queer crack and supposed I must have broken something—no doubt it was the frost-bite that prevented me from feeling any pain.

Rébuffat and the Sherpas came down and we went on, but it all seemed to take an unconsciously long time, and the plateau of Camp II seemed a long way off. I was just about at the limit of my strength. Every minute I felt like giving up; and why, anyway, should I go on when for me everything was over? My conscience was quite easy: everyone was safe, and the others would all get down. Far away below I could see the tents. Just one more hour—I gave myself one more hour and then, wherever I was, I would lie down in the snow. I would let myself go, peacefully. I would be through with it all, and could sleep content.

Setting this limit somehow cheered me on. I kept slipping, and on the steep slope the Sherpas could hardly hold me—it was miraculous that they did. The track stopped above a drop—the second and bigger of the walls we had equipped with a fixed rope. I tried to make up my mind, but I could not begin to see how I was going to get down. I pulled off the glove I had on one hand, and the red silk scarf that hid the other, which was covered in blood. This time everything was at stake—and my fingers could just look after themselves. I placed Sarki and Aila on the stance from which I had been accustomed to belay them, and where the two of them would be able to take the strain of my rope by standing firmly braced against each other. I tried to take hold of the fixed rope; both my hands were bleeding, but I had no pity to spare for myself and I took the rope between my thumb and forefinger, and started off. At the first move I was faced at once with a painful decision: if I let go, we should all fall to the bottom; if I held on, what would remain of my hands? I decided to hold on.

Every inch was a torture I was resolved to ignore. The sight of my hands made me feel sick; the flesh was laid bare and red, and the rope was covered with blood. I tried not to tear the strips right off: other accidents had taught me that one must preserve these bits to hasten the healing process later on. I tried to save my hands by braking with my stomach, my shoulders, and every other possible point of contact. When would this agony come to an end?

I came down to the nose of ice which I myself had cut away with my axe on the ascent. I felt about with my legs—it was all hard. There was no snow beneath. I was not yet down. In panic I called up to the Sherpas:

'Quick . . . Aila . . . Sarki . . . !'

They let my rope out more quickly and the friction on the fixed rope increased.

My hands were in a ghastly state. It felt as though all the flesh was being torn off. At last I was aware of something beneath my feet—the ledge. I had made it! I had to go along it now, always held by the rope; only three yards, but they were the trickiest of all. It was over. I collapsed, up to the waist in snow, and no longer conscious of time.

When I half-opened my eyes Rébuffat and the Sherpas were beside me, and I could distinctly see black dots moving about near the tents of Camp II. Sarki spoke to me, and pointed out two Sherpas coming up to meet us. They were still a long way off, but all the same it cheered me up.

I had to rouse myself; things were getting worse and worse. The frost-bite seemed to be gaining ground—up to my calves and my elbows. Sarki put my glasses on for me again, although the weather had turned grey. He put one glove on as best he could; but my left hand was in such a frightful state that it made him sick to look at it, and he tried to hide it in my red scarf.

The fantastic descent continued and I was sure that every step would be my last. Through the swirling mist I sometimes caught glimpses of the two Sherpas coming up. They had already reached the base of the avalanche cone, and when, from the little platform I had just reached, I saw them stop there, it sapped all my courage.

Snow began to fall, and we now had to make a long traverse over very unsafe ground where it was difficult to safeguard anyone: then fifty yards further, we came to the avalanche cone. I recognized Phutharkay and Angdawa mounting rapidly towards us. Evidently they expected bad news, and Angdawa must have been thinking of his two brothers, Aila and Pansy. The former was with us all right—he could see him in the flesh—but what about Pansy? Even at this distance they started up a conversation, and by the time we reached them they knew everything. I heaved a deep sigh of relief. I felt now as if I had laid down a burden so heavy that I had nearly given way beneath it. Phutharkay was beside me, smiling affectionately. How can anyone call such people 'primitive', or say that the rigours of their existence take away all sense of pity? The Sherpas rushed towards me, put down their sacks, uncorked their flasks. Ah, just to drink a few mouthfuls! Nothing more. It had all been such a long time . . .

Phutharkay lowered his eyes to my hands and lifted them again, almost with embarrassment. With infinite sorrow, he whispered: 'Poor Bara Sahib—Ah . . . '

These reinforcements gave me a fresh access of courage, and Camp II was near. Phutharkay supported me, and Angdawa

169

safeguarded us both. Phutharkay was smaller than I, and I hung on round his neck and leant on his shoulders, gripping him close. This contact comforted me and his warmth gave me strength. I staggered down with little jerky steps, leaning more and more on Phutharkay. Would I ever have the strength to make it even with his help. Summoning what seemed my very last ounce of energy, I begged Phutharkay to give me yet more help. He took my glasses off and I could see better then. Just a few more steps. . .the very last . . .

At Camp II Marcel Ichac had been following our movements for the past two days, noting down the sequence of events, minute by minute. Here are some extracts from his log:

*Saturday, June 3rd*[1] (1)—Camp II:
Oudot and Noyelle left at 9 o'clock;[2] at 10 o'clock Noyelle arrived back. Something to do with the oxygen? Possibly the mask didn't allow a sufficient flow? Oudot and the three Sherpas are going very slowly up the funnel.
Meanwhile I am playing hide and seek with the clouds looking through the telescope of the theodolite, and also watching the parties above the seracs of the Sickle through field-glasses. There are four of them; Lionel and Rébuffat, and behind them Couzy and Schatz. No sign of Maurice. He must be on the final slopes which are less steep, and so invisible from here. The wind is blowing the powder snow violently. But he can't be far from the summit now, perhaps even . . .

*Sunday, June 4th*
A dull day. Snow fell during the night—sleet, then fine snow with a strong north wind. Annapurna is hidden in the mist. Tired and anxious. What's happening to the others? By midday eight inches of powder snow. Continual avalanches, visibility nil.
Heard voices about 4 o'clock and in the mist, which continues for about a hundred yards below the camp, four forms appeared—Oudot and his three Sherpas. Obviously sinking in up to their waists. Nothing to do but to get boiling water ready for them. They arrived at 7 o'clock: that morning Oudot had remained in his tent. Towards 1 o'clock the bad weather got worse and Ajeeba had come to him and said: 'It's the monsoon! If we stay here we're done for.'

*Monday, June 5th*
Will today end better than it has begun? What alarms there have been—for us, anyway! At one time I thought Oudot and myself were the sole survivors of the party of eight who left Le Bourget on March 30th!
At 6 o'clock thought I heard someone calling and went outside: the sun was rising through threatening clouds. Nothing to be seen. Got back into my sleeping-bag; immediately heard two distinct shouts and through the field-glasses saw two men on a patch of ice at the height of Camp IV, but well over to the left. They kept on

[1]The day Lachenal and I left Camp V and were going up towards the summit.
[2]Oudot and Noyelle were intending to go up to Camp III to pitch tents to replace those taken on by Gaston and Lionel to Camp IV. For Oudot this ascent was to be a vitally important experiment in the use of oxygen.

170

shouting and signalling with their arms. Who could they be—Oudot thought Schatz and Couzy. Their immobility—particularly one of them—was most alarming. Frost-bitten feet no doubt. What did they want? Normally it takes six hours to get up so far in fine weather. But in powder snow and with the monsoon striking repeatedly . . . They're still shouting . . . things are getting urgent. Where are the other eight? Higher up near the summit? Their position must be pretty precarious at Camp IV, but what can they be waiting for to descend to Camp III?

*8 o'clock:* Oudot is preparing a rescue party. He has no ice-pitons, etc. Noyelle is going down to Camp I with Ajeeba to bring up reinforcements (equipment and Dawathondup). Up here the Sherpas are uneasy. Three of them belong to the same family: Pansy, Aila and Angdawa.

*8.30:* Shouting continues. On the off-chance I'am tracing out the letters 'VU' in the snow. A few minutes later a man moves quickly towards the seracs which must shelter Camp IV. He's stopped 300 yards away from it—on the same level—is making signs and has now gone back again. The others are getting up, apparently without difficulty, and are traversing across to Camp IV. Not two of them but four.
So there are four, plus the one who went to meet them, plus his companion or companions. The position of Camp IV near the funnel of the Sickle is more sheltered, and from there one can get down quickly to Camp III or Camp II. The avalanches have now stopped.

*9.30:* Saw Noyelle arrive at Camp I.

*10 o'clock:* At last—three men have appeared in the funnel of the Sickle coming down towards Camp III (one Sahib, two Sherpas?) Miraculously the weather is holding, with a west wind. Annapurna is completely clear—if only it lasts!

*11 o'clock:* Two men, unroped and therefore Sahibs, appear and come quickly down the former party's track. At the pace they're going, they should be here by evening. At last we'll know everything!

*11.15:* A man has appeared exactly at the spot where we saw one this morning, going *towards* Camp V. He has stopped and is evidently looking up. His appearance is comforting in one way, for he is certainly not alone at Camp IV. So that he and his probable companion make two plus those coming down—three and two—seven in all. Seven out of ten. It looks, then, as if one party must still be somewhere higher up.

*12.20:* I'm watching the group of four crossing a very steep slope above Camp III. Behind them is one man alone, lagging a bit. Now, very high up, another man has just left Camp IV and is quickly descending: perhaps one of those I saw a short time ago? Suddenly a cloud of snow—like a volcano—appears to spurt out beneath the feet of the four near Camp III. They are knocked down and go rolling over and over. Then the avalanche passes on, leaving three figures stretched out on the snow; the lowest, who has been swept down 150 feet,[3] is now climbing up the slope again, now two more—ah, thank God! they have separated and revealed a fourth. So they are safe.
Our Sherpas have realized what's happened. Angdawa and Phutharkay have gone off to meet them with ice-axes and glasses which they have lost. The others are continuing to descend. At 3 o'clock they meet the two Sherpas at the top of the avalanche cone. At last we shall know everything . . .

[3]In fact it was 500 feet.

171

We were now quite near the tents of Camp II and Ichac, Noyelle and Oudot rushed up to meet us. I was in a fever to tell them the good news.

'We're back from Annapurna.' I shouted. 'We got to the top yesterday, Lachenal and I.' Then, after a pause: 'My feet and hands are frost-bitten.'

They all helped me; Ichac held something out to me, and Noyelle supported me, while Oudot was examining my injuries.

My responsibility was now at an end. We had succeeded, and I knew that the others would all be with us in a few minutes.

We were saved! We had conquered Annapurna, and we had retreated in order. It was now for the others to take the initiative, above all Oudot, in whom lay our only hope. I would put myself entirely in their hands; I would trust myself to their devotion. Henceforth only one thing would count—the victory that we had brought back, that would remain for ever with us as an ecstatic happiness and a miraculous consolation. The others must organize our retreat and bring us back as best they could to the soil of France.

My friends all rallied round—they took off my gloves and my *cagoule* and settled me into a tent already prepared to receive us. I found this simplification intensely comforting: I appreciated my new existence which, though it would be short-lived, was for the moment so easy and pleasant. In spite of the threatening weather the others were not long in arriving: Rébuffat was the first—his toes were frost-bitten, which made it difficult to walk and he looked ghastly, with a trickle of blood from his lips, and signs of suffering writ large on his face. They undressed him, and put him in a tent to await treatment.

Lachenal was still a long way off. Blind, exhausted, with his frost-bitten feet, how could he manage to follow such a rough and dangerous track? In fact, he got over the little crevasse by letting himself slide down on his bottom. Couzy caught up with him on his way down and, although desperately weary himself, gave him invaluable assistance.

Lionel Terray followed closely behind them, held on a rope by Schatz, who was still in fine fettle. The little group drew nearer to the camp. The first man to arrive was Terray, and Marcel Ichac went up towards the great cone to meet them. Terray's appearance was pitiful. He was blind, and clung to Angtharkay as he walked. He had a huge beard and his face was distorted by pain into a dreadful grin. This 'strong man', this elemental force of nature who could barely drag himself along, cried out:

'But I'am still all right. If I could see properly, I'd come down by myself.'

When he reached camp Oudot and Noyelle were aghast. Once so strong, he was now helpless and exhausted. His appearance moved them almost to tears.

Immediately after, Schatz and Couzy arrived, and then Lachenal, practically carried by two Sherpas. From a distance it looked as though he was pedalling along in the air, for he threw his legs out in front in a most disordered way. His head lolled backwards and was covered with a bandage. His features were lined with fatigue and spoke of suffering and sacrifice. He could not have gone on for another hour. Like myself, he had set a limit which had helped him to hold on until now. And yet Biscante, at such a moment, still had the spirit to say to Ichac:

'Want to see how a Chamonix guide comes down from the Himalaya?'

Ichac's only reply was to hold out to him a piece of sugar soaked in adrenalin.

It was painful to watch Terray groping for the tent six inches from his nose: he held both hands out in front of him feeling for obstacles. He was helped in, and he lay down; then Lachenal, too, was laid on an air mattress.

# 16

## The Retreat

Everyone was now off the mountain and assembled at Camp II. But in what a state! It was Oudot's turn to take the initiative, and he made a rapid tour of inspection. Faced with the appalling sight that we presented, his countenance reflected, now the consternation of the friend, now the surgeon's impersonal severity.

He examined me first. My limbs were numb up to well beyond the ankles and wrists. My hands were in a frightful condition; there was practically no skin left, the little that remained was black, and long strips dangled down. My fingers were both swollen and distorted. My feet were scarcely any better: the entire soles were brown and violet, and completely without feeling. The arm which was hurting me, and which I was afraid might be broken, did not appear to be seriously injured, and my neck was all right.

I was anxious to have Oudot's first impression.

'What do you think of it all?' I asked him, ready to hear the worst.

'It's pretty serious. You'll probably lose part of your feet and hands. At present I can't say more than that.'

'Do you think you'll be able to save something?'

'Yes, I'm sure of it. I'll do all I can.'

This was not encouraging, and I was convinced that my feet and hands would have to be amputated.

Oudot took my blood pressure and seemed rather concerned. There was no pressure in the right arm, and the needle did not respond at all on my left arm. On my legs the needle oscillated slightly, indicating a restricted flow of blood. After putting a dressing over my eyes to prevent the onset of ophthalmia, he said:

'I'm going to see Lachenal. I'll come back in a moment and give you some injections. I used them during the war and it's the only treatment that's any use with frost-bite. See you presently.'

Lachenal's condition was slightly less serious. His hands were not affected, and the black discoloration of his feet did not extend beyond the toes, but the sinister colour reappeared on his heels. He would very likely lose his toes, but that would probably not prevent him from climbing, and from continuing to practise his profession as a guide.

Rébuffat's condition was much less serious. His feet were pink except for two small grey patches on his toes. Ichac massaged him with Dolpyc for two hours and this appeared to relieve his; him eyes were still painful, but that was only a matter of two or three days. Terray was unscathed: like Rébuffat he was suffering from ophthalmia—most painful, but only a temporary affliction. Couzy was very weak, and would have to be considered out of action. That was the balance sheet.

Night fell gradually. Oudot made his preparations, requisitioned Ichac and Schatz as nurses, and Camp II was turned into a hospital. In cold and discomfort, and to the accompaniment of continual avalanches, these men fought, late into the night, to save their friends. Armed with torches, they passed from tent to tent, bending over the wounded and giving them emergency treatment, at this minute camp, perched 20,000 feet up on the flanks of one of the highest mountains in the world.

Oudot made ready to give me arterial injections. The lamp shone feebly and in the semi-darkness Ichac sterilized the syringes as best he could with ether. Before starting operations, Oudot explained:

'I am going to inject novocaine into your femoral and brachial arteries.'

As I could not see a thing with the bandage over my eyes, he touched with his finger the places where he would insert the needle: both groins and in the bends of my elbows.

'It's going to hurt. Perhaps I shan't get the right place first shot. But in any case you mustn't move, particularly when I have got into the artery.'

I was not at all reassured by these preparations; I had always had a horror of injections. But it would have to be done, it was the only thing possible.

'Go ahead,' I said to Oudot, 'but warn me when you are going to stab.'

Anyhow, perhaps it would not hurt all that much in my present condition. I heard the murmur of voices—Oudot asking if something was ready, and Ichac answering: 'Here you are. Got it?'

Oudot ran his fingers over my skin. I felt an acute pain in the groin and my legs began to tremble; I tried to control myself. He had to try again, for the artery rolled away from the needle. Another

175

stab, and my whole body was seized with convulsions, I stiffened when I should have relaxed, and felt all my nerves in revolt.

'Gently!' I could not help myself.

Oudot began again: my blood was extremely thick and clotted in the needle.

'Your blood is black—it's like black pudding,' he said in amazement.

'That's got it!' This time he had succeeded in spite of my howls which, I knew very well, made the operation all the more difficult to perform. The needle was now in position:

'Don't move!' Oudot shouted at me. Then to Ichac:

'Hand it over!'

Ichac passed him the syringe. I felt the needle moving in my flesh and the liquid began to flow into the artery. I should never, until then, have believed so much pain to be possible. I tried to brace myself to the utmost to keep myself from trembling: it simply had to be successful! The liquid went on flowing in.

'Can you feel any warmth?' asked Oudot, brusquely, while he was changing the syringe. Again the liquid went in; I gritted my teeth.

'Does it feel warm?'

Oudot was insistent—the point was evidently crucial; yet still I felt nothing. Several times the syringe was emptied, filled up, and emptied again.

'Now, do you feel anything?'

'I seem to feel a little warmth, but it's not definite.'

Was it auto-suggestion? The needle was withdrawn abruptly, and while Ichac sterilized the instruments, I had a few moments' respite.

'It's excruciating, the way it hurts,' I said, just as if Oudot needed telling!

'Yes, I know, but we must go on.'

The performance was repeated on the other leg. My nerves were all to pieces, and to brace myself like this took all my strength. In went the needle and I howled and sobbed miserably, but tried in vain to keep still. I could see nothing because of the bandage. If only I could have seen the faces of my friends it might perhaps have helped me. But I was in the dark—a terrible darkness—with nowhere to look for consolation but within myself. It was late and we had all had more than enough. Then for that day it was over and the first-aid party moved on to Lachenal's tent. Perhaps he would have more courage in face of physical pain.

It seemed to me, when I vaguely became aware of the end of the session, that things had gone more quickly for him. Terray slept in Lachenal's tent and Couzy and Ichac slept beside Rébuffat, who was delirious and moaned about his feet all night. Oudot came and lay down next to me. If anything were to happen, he would be there.

Next day plans were completed for the evacuation of the entire camp: the three injured men would be taken down on sledges, two would be able to walk, with assistance, and four were all right. There were miles of glacier to cover, rock barriers to get down, interminable moraines and scree slopes to skirt round or to traverse, a river to cross, and a pass of over 13,000 feet to negotiate—and all this in the monsoon!

It was now June 6th, and Ichac was worried; he remembered the Tilman expedition to Nanda Devi, which was held up for three weeks by rivers swollen by the torrential monsoon rains. Should we have time to reach the Gandaki Valley where the easier gradient would put fewer obstacles in our way? In a week's time we must be clear of the mountains. Soon Couzy would be fit again, Terray cured of his ophthalmia and Rébuffat able to walk. But there were two serious casualties who would have to be carried on the porters' backs under the most appalling conditions, as far as the main valley.

'I can't believe it,' remarked Ichac, 'it's actually fine today.'

The medical supplies urgently demanded by Oudot had arrived from Camp I. He began his rounds with me, and was pleased because the injections had been effective and warmth had returned as far as my insteps. He put fresh dressings on my hands, and though I felt no real pain, there was, nevertheless, some sort of feeling in my fingers. Again I put my question:

'What shall I have left?'

'I can't exactly say. Things have not completely settled down yet and I hope to be able to gain an inch or so. I think you'll be able to use your hands. Of course,' and he hesitated for a moment, 'you'll lose one or two joints of each finger, but if there's enough of the thumbs left, you'll have a pinch hold, and that's of prime importance.'

It was grim news, but still, only yesterday I had feared that the consequences would be far worse. For me this meant goodbye to a great many plans, and it also implied a new kind of life, perhaps even a new conception of existence. But I had neither the strength nor the wish to look into the future.

I appreciated Oudot's courage and was grateful to him for not being afraid to tell me the extent of the amputations which he foresaw would be necessary. He treated me as a man and as a friend, with courage and frankness which I shall never forget.

The injections, which had already done so much good, had to be repeated. This time the session would be even worse and I was terrified at the prospect. I am ashamed to say that the thought of this treatment daunted me—and yet so many people have had to endure it. This time it was to be an injection not of novocaine but acetylcholine, of which a few ampoules had been brought up from Camp I. Terray joined me in the tent and stood close beside me. He, too, could see nothing under his bandage, and he had to be guided if he wanted to move about at all. I pictured his face, and touched his features with my forearms while Ichac and Oudot prepared the needles, ether and ampoules. I whispered to Lionel what a fearful ordeal I found it all, and begged him to stay close.

'Oudot will warn me before inserting the needle; I mustn't budge then, and you must hold me as tight as you can in your arms.'

I hoped that Terray's presence would help me bear the agony. Oudot began with my legs; as on the day before, it was too awful for words. I howled and cried and sobbed in Terray's arms while he held me tight with all his strength. I felt as if my foot was burning—as if it had been suddenly plunged into boiling oil. Professionally, Oudot was in the seventh heaven and everybody shared his delight in my suffering, which was proof of the success of the treatment. This gave me courage and at last, after the fourth syringeful, the necessary 100 c.c. had been injected.

'Now for the arms,' announced Oudot.

This session seemed to go on for ever and I was utterly worn out, but there was distinctly more feeling in my right arm. Oudot stormed away—the needles were either too thick or too small, too thin or too long; never just right, and each time it meant a fresh stab. I began to howl like a dog again.

'Hold me tighter,' I gasped between sobs to Terray, who was already holding me as tightly as he could. I tried hard not to tremble, but Oudot was not satisfied:

'Don't move, *nom d'une pipe!* We'll go on as long as we must. It's *got* to succeed.'

'Sorry, I'm doing all I can: I'll bear it, never fear.'

I held out my arm for a fresh attempt. When Oudot did find the artery, then it was the needle that got blocked—the too-thick blood clotted inside. From the bend of the elbow Oudot gradually tried higher and higher up towards the shoulder so as not always to stab in the same place. Twice he touched a nerve: I did not cry but sobbed spasmodically. What an eternity of suffering! I could do nothing. Oudot stopped for a moment. 'We'll manage all right,' Ichac assured me.

'Stick it, Maurice!' Terray whispered, 'It'll soon be over; it's dreadful, I know, but I'm here beside you.'

Yes, he was there. Without him I could never have borne it all. This man whom we thought hard because he was strong, who made himself out to be a tough peasant, showed a tenderness and affection towards me that I have never seen equalled. I hid my face against him and he put his arms round my neck.

'Come on! Get on with it!'

'Too small and too fine,' shouted Oudot.

He began to lose patience. All this fuss with the instruments exasperated me, and I wondered if they would have succeeded 'first go' in a nursing home.

After several hours, and goodness knows how many attempts, the injection was successfully made. In spite of frightful pain I remained still as the syringe was emptied. Deftly Oudot replaced it with another without removing the needle from the artery. With the second syringeful, I felt the warmth spreading, and Oudot was exultant. But this warmth became unbearable. I howled and clung to Terray in desperation, holding my arm out stiff, without, so I hoped, moving it a fraction of an inch. Then I felt the needle being withdrawn and cotton wool applied.

'Right arm finished! Now for the left!'

Oudot could not find the artery, and this puzzled him. I told him that when I was young I had seriously damaged this arm, and that explained everything: that was why there had been no blood pressure, and why he could feel no pulse. The position of the artery was not normal, and it was not possible to make an injection in the bend of the elbow; it would have to be done at the shoulder—much more difficult. I thought of what it had been like for the right arm! Suddenly, at the fifth or sixth attempt, Oudot shouted:

'I've got it!'

I kept absolutely still: syringeful after syringeful went in.

'I'll have to do a *stellaire.*'

I had no idea what this was. Oudot explained that it meant injecting novocaine into the nerve ganglion to dilate the arteries and make them easier to find, and improve the blood supply. A long needle was necessary, to stick into the neck in the region of the pleura. I was in despair. It was just too much. For hours and hours I had endured this agony—I should never have the strength for more. But Oudot lost no time, the needle was ready, and he began to explore my neck.

'This is a tricky bit of work. You have to insert the needle in a certain direction, then, when you come up against an obstacle you have to push to the left, and you're bound to be in the right spot.'

'Warn me before you stick it in.'

In the silence that followed I heard things being moved around.

'I'm going to insert the needle,' Oudot announced.

I braced myself immediately, and resolved to keep perfectly still. The needle went in—it must have been a tremendous length; it touched a very sensitive part and the pain made me cry out in Terray's arms. Oudot was now manoeuvring to get the needle into the ganglion, and I could feel it moving deep down. It was in! First shot! The liquid must have started flowing in, but I could not feel it.

'Will it take long.' I asked faintly.

'It's almost finished,' he replied holding his breath. 'Only another 20 c.c. to go in.'

I felt the awful needle being pulled out: it was over, and now I could relax. Oudot was very pleased: it had been almost a whole day's work, but he had managed to do everything he wanted. Never had I suffered so much in my life; but if my feet and hands were saved it was thanks to Oudot and his perseverance. Ichac helped him collect the instruments to take along to Lachenal's tent. For the time being he was satisfied with my general condition, but what effect this generalized frost-bite would have on my body in the next few days remained to be seen. The camp was becoming more and more like a hospital: everybody's thoughts and actions were dictated by the condition of the casualties, and everybody hung on the surgeon's lips. From now on his word was law.

That same day began the incredible work of transporting the injured, which ended only after a long and painful retreat, lasting five weeks, beneath torrential rain and over dangerously steep ground. This retreat, during which all the injured slowly recovered, will for ever remain an achievement of the highest order, and it reflects great honour upon all the members of the Expedition.

The sledge we had at our disposal was an extra-lightweight Dufour *luge* mounted on two skis for runners. Naturally, the Sherpas were not familiar with this contraption, so Oudot and Ichac decided to make the least injured of us, Rébuffat, the victim of the first tryout.

Schatz took charge of operations, with four Sherpas whom he placed in V formation round the sledge, and the procession started off about 2.30. Rébuffat was well wrapped up and firmly tied to the sledge in case it should tip over. As night fell the four Sherpas arrived back in camp, bringing a note from Schatz advising the use of six men for subsequent descents.

Meanwhile Oudot had given all his patients injections and the evening was spent in changing the dressings. Soon after nightfall the weather worsened, and again it snowed heavily. The others were alarmed and decided to get the rest of the casualties down before it became too late. As luck would have it next morning, when we woke up, it was fine. I was to be taken down first, and before I left Oudot inspected my feet and hands and changed the dressings. He was very satisfied and described my progress as 'spectacular'! I was dressed, put in a sleeping-bag and laid on the Dufour sledge, and Angtharkay directed the team of Sherpas. I could see nothing under my bandage, but I felt the air was warm and so knew it must be fine; I hated the thought of being transported without being able to see what was going on. I was very glad to hear that Ichac would accompany me down so that I should not be alone if I needed anything. In my heart I dreaded this descent, particularly the passage over the rock barriers. How would they manage? But the Sherpas were intelligent chaps and never had to be shown anything twice. Afterwards, when we were in camp, Ichac told me how much he had admired them: 'It would have been difficult to find a team like this in France,' he said; 'every one of them did his utmost and every move was perfectly co-ordinated.'

With a few jerks the sledge started off. I was weak and slightly deaf, but I recognized Oudot's voice in the climber's familiar *Bonne descente!* No doubt he was there behind us, waving a hand. Swaddled in all my clothes, I began to sweat; the sun must have been beating down. Sometimes my back skimmed the surface of the snow; now and again Ichac came close and said something, and it did me good to hear him and know he was there. Suddenly the slope steepened, and in spite of the straps holding me in position, I slipped forward. The Sherpas took up their positions in an inverted V in order to brake the sledge. We had reached the big rock band, and as far as I could remember the angle here was steep. I guessed that Ichac had driven his axe in to keep me in balance.

I heard a hollow echo—seracs—and the pace had to be forced now for there was danger of their collapsing. We came to the rocks—

and how these Sherpas managed, I shall never know. The wall was very steep yet I was carried on the sledge itself; Ichac told me later that if my eyes had not been blindfolded I should never have been able to stand the sight of such acrobatics and of such impossible positions. I heard sighs of relief—we must have reached the glacier at last. The sledge reverted to a horizontal position, and I was on the snow. A few minutes rest, and on we went at what seemed to me a breakneck pace; I pictured the Sherpas pulling on the ropes all round me and running in the snow, though no doubt this was only imagination. Then we slowed up—we had reached the moraine of Camp I.

I was left alone for a moment while the Sherpas put up a big valley tent into which they carried me a few minutes later. Ichac settled himself beside me—from now on we always shared the same tent and he watched over me, day and night, like a brother. The descent had taken two hours and twenty minutes and the Sherpas had been marvellous. What should we have done without them?

Ichac briefly explained what was going on. Being blind was most demoralizing: I felt I was nothing but a chattel to be carted about. I knew my ophthalmia was less serious than that of the others and I kept asking for the bandage to be taken off. But since I was nothing but a chattel I had no right to speak.

Although it had clouded over and had began to sleet, the Sherpas went up again to Camp II with Schatz and Noyelle to fetch Lachenal. About 3 o'clock snow started to fall. Time dragged as I lay in my tent alone with my thoughts. The silence was broken only by the persistent sound of cracking ice, which rather alarmed me: where had they placed the tent? Suppose a crevasse suddenly opened? I was ashamed of these childish fears—surely a mountaineer of many years' experience should know very well that a crevasse does not yawn open like that in a second!

Ichac, the only fit sahib, supervised the organization of Camp I. Towards the end of the afternoon, at about 5 o'clock, he saw, to his great surprise, Noyelle and Lachenal's convoy emerge through the mist, covered in snow. This time the Sherpas had taken only an hour-and-three-quarters to come down—they had had a terrific day and were worn out. This resulted in some complaints: there was not enough food, and part of their equipment had remained up at Camp III and Camp IV! This last point especially bothered them, for on Himalayan expeditions the normal practice is for the Sherpas to keep their personal equipment as a perquisite. They bitterly regretted these clothes, which had to be considered as lost, and Angtharkay even declared his intention of going up to Camp III again.

I summoned Angtharkay and warned him that I expressly forbade anyone to return higher than Camp II to fetch anything whatsoever. But at the same time I told him of my very great satisfaction at the magnificent behaviour of the Sherpas under his orders, and assured him that they were not to worry about the clothes, for they would all receive generous compensation. Angtharkay went off to give the others the good news.

There was tremendous activity all over the camp, where Lachenal was being made as comfortable as possible. Tents seemed to have sprung up as if by magic, and what looked like a little village was formed at the foot of the great wall of ice.

The next day, after a fine start, the clouds collected again towards 11 o'clock, and it was not long before snow began to fall. Oudot had not yet come down from Camp II. I could hear the avalanches rumbling down in ever closer succession, making an appalling row which wore my nerves thin. Ichac tried to make a joke of it.

'Here we are—that's the 3.37 goods! Now for the 4 o'clock express!' He succeeded in making me smile.

Through the telescope he saw, towards the end of the morning, the last tents of Camp II being taken down, and in the afternoon our M.O. arrived with his Sherpas, laden like donkeys. Before even putting down his sack he asked about the condition of his patients: any developments since yesterday?

There was marked improvement: Rébuffat could now walk and his ophthalmia was nearly cured. As for Lachenal, circulation had been restored to his feet, and warmth had returned, except to his toes, though the black patches on his heels would probably leave scars. Improvement was visible on my limbs, too, and Oudot was well pleased. He spoke with a frankness that touched me far more than he will ever know:

'I think that the fingers of your left hand will have to be amputated, but I hope to be able to save the end joints of your right hand fingers. If all goes well, you'll have passable hands. As for your feet, I'm afraid that all your toes will have to go, but that won't prevent you from walking. Of course to begin with it'll be difficult, but you'll adapt yourself all right, you'll see.'

I was aghast at the thought of what would have happened if Oudot had not given me the injections so promptly and efficiently. Perhaps they had not yet produced all their effect. More sessions would be necessary and I wondered whether I should be able to overcome the immense lassitude that came over me after all these painful ordeals. In any case I wanted to take every advantage of the respite, and celebrate our success with due ceremony. For the first time since our victory the whole Expedition was assembled together and the condition of the casualties was now such as to warrant a little festivity. We gathered round the one and only tin of chicken in aspic and we uncorked the one bottle of champagne. There were already a lot of us who wanted a drink of it but I was determined that the Sherpas should, somehow or other, join in the general rejoicing. I invited Angtharkay and we drank with him to our victory. Ichac put our thoughts into words:

'You've taken a lot of punishment, but our victory will remain.'

In spite of the circumstances, the general atmosphere in the tent was remarkably cheerful. We wrote a telegram to be sent off to Devies by the next mail-runner:

FRENCH HIMALAYAN EXPEDITION 1950 SUCCESSFUL STOP ANNAPURNA CLIMBED JUNE 3RD, 1950—HERZOG

Directly the festivities were over there were more injections—those in my legs were finished fairly quickly. Then Oudot tackled my arms and I knew by experience that these would be the most painful. For an hour all attempts were unsuccessful: the afternoon wore on and Oudot became exasperated.

'Don't move about like that!' he cried.

'Take no notice of the noise I make . . . carry on . . . do what you have to.'

Terray had come close to me. I was writhing in pain, and he held me tight.

'Stick it! Don't move, don't move, Maurice!'

'It's hopeless!' shouted Oudot. 'When I do succeed in finding the artery, the blood clots. We'll never manage it!'

He sounded in despair, but his words belied him: he had not the slightest intention of giving up, and neither had I, in spite of the pain. The rest of them were appalled as they listened to the cries coming from the tent where Oudot was in action. The Sherpas were silent. Were they praying for their Bara Sahib? I sobbed so convulsively that I could not stop, and was shaken by continual spasms.

Then, after a short rest, late in the evening at about 10 o'clock, the injection was successfully accomplished. Ichac passed the syringes to Oudot in the dark. There was blood all over the tent. Ichac and

Oudot went out, while Terray soothed me with infinite gentleness. Never had I felt so wretched. I was utterly worn out with suffering and fatigue, incapable of resistance. Terray still held me in his arms: 'It'll be all right, you'll see, later on.'

'Oh but, Lionel, everything's over for me, and I simply can't bear what they're doing to me any longer.'

'Life's not over,' he insisted, 'you'll see France again, and Chamonix.'

'Yes, Chamonix perhaps, but I'll never be able to climb again.'

It was out at last. I had told him, and I let myself go in despair. 'I'll never be able to climb again—I'll never do the Eiger now, Lionel, and I wanted to so much.'

Sobs choked me. My head was against Terray's and I felt his tears, for he was crying, too. He was the only one who could fully understand the tragedy that this represented for me, and I could see that to him, too, it appeared hopeless.

'No, of course, not the Eiger, but I'm sure you'll be able to go back to the mountains . . . ' and then, very hesitantly, he added: 'Not the same sort of climbs as before, of course.'

'It will never be the same again. But, Lionel, even if I can't do the sort of climbs I used to, if I could still do easy things, that would be a great deal. The mountains meant everything to me—I spent the best days of my life among them—I don't want to do spectacular climbs, or famous ones, but I want to be able to enjoy myself in the mountains, even if it's only on the standard routes.'

'You'll go back all right, you'll see,' said Lionel. 'I feel just the same way.'

'But mountains aren't the only thing; there are other things in life as well—what shall I do about all that?'

'I am sure you'll manage somehow.'

There was a silence; then: 'You ought to lie down now.'

He settled me with such affectionate care that he accomplished the impossible and left me comforted and soothed; then, after a last look to see that I was cosy, he went slowly out. What a friend I had found in Terray!

Next morning Oudot took off my bandage: it was wonderful to be able to see everything. I noted that the weather was fine, and I asked the date: the last few days had been one long night.

'Friday, June 9th,' Ichac told me.

At the moment Lachenal was being made ready to go down to Base Camp. He would travel in a *cacolet*—an awkward and primitive

185

contraption and I had never liked the look of it. Lachenal, on the contrary, who was accustomed to the thing and had himself carried many casualties down by this method, was perfectly ready to descend this way, though later on he was not quite so enthusiastic. Soon he started off with his Sherpas, escorted by Couzy and Noyelle: his legs dangled down most uncomfortably and made him groan. In the afternoon the Sherpas came up again followed by Couzy: the descent had taken two hours, and Rébuffat and Lachenal were none the worse for the journey.

While I rested the others made up the loads. The next day, before going off, Oudot examined me and his favourable impression was confirmed: the injections of acetylcholine, which had been abominably painful, had saved a part at least of my feet and hands. Ajeeba, Sarki, Phutharkay and Pandy the Chinee were going to take turns at carrying me in the *cacolet*. The route was well marked, there were no stones and the going was straightforward. But I was crushed up against the porter and horribly jolted at every step. I was afraid of falling and clung desperately to his neck with both arms though I tried to do all in my power not to hinder his movements. Whenever his step faltered I was perfectly aware of it. Several times both Ajeeba and Pandy slipped, and instinctively I tried to put my arm out, without realizing that it was useless. I was less anxious in the couloirs than on the steep rock slabs where the porter might fall, and I was afraid that my hands or my feet might knock against the rock.

'Sarki . . . *Pay attention!* . . . *Pay attention!* . . . ' Again and again I repeated this cry; it became an entreaty. At the awkward pitches they helped each other: one placed the carrier's feet in position, and another would push from behind to maintain his balance. After many difficulties we got over the rocky section and arrived in view of Base Camp.

It felt as if we had been all day on this journey, but in fact it was only two hours and a half, and there had not been the slightest hitch. It was now the turn of Base Camp to be the centre of an activity it had not hitherto known. Suddenly Ichac dashed into the tent where I had just been laid down and shouted:

'The coolies! The coolies are here!'

REBUFFAT SCHATZ TERRAY HERZOG NOYELLE PANSY SARKI AJEEBA AILA DAWATHONDUP
NOEL COUZY OUDOT ICHAC PHUTHARKAY ANGTHARKAY ANGDAWA

*Previous Page:*
At Tansing, April 11th
1950

*Right:* Angtharkay pays
off the porters

*Left:* Tukucha,
headquarters of
the expedition

*Above:* The Great Ice Lake on the Tilicho Pass,
with Ganga Purna in the background

*Below:* Village and valley of Manangbhot

*Left:* Chahar, where pilgrims make their last halt before arriving at the sacred springs of Muktinath

*Below:* Annapurna, showing the ice cliffs of the Sickle glacier and the couloir by which the summit was reached. The avalanche hides Camp II

*Facing page:* Rebuffat being taken down on a sledge from Camp II

*Left:* Between Camp I and base camp. Sarki (left) helps the porter who is carrying Herzog

*Right:* The return by the Miristi Khola in the monsoon

Through the paddy fields

*Previous page:* Herzog on the north - west spur of Annapurna

*Left:* Evening at Camp

*Below:* Sherpas at Camp II with the Cauliflower Ridge in the background

# 17

## *In the Woods of Lete*

These wild-looking creatures, most of whom we recognized, arrived in small groups. By a miracle they had kept the rendezvous we had fixed with them a fortnight before, and Ichac was overjoyed. Soon he got the wireless going; it was just about time for the weather report. A bulletin, specially broadcast in English for us, warned us of the approach of the monsoon proper:

'This is All India Radio, Delhi calling on 60.48.
You will now hear a special weather bulletin for the French Expedition to Nepal:
Monsoon extending over all eastern Himalaya will be reaching your area by June 10th.
Q.F.F. Gorakhpur 980 millibars.
I repeat: you have just heard a special bulletin . . . '

So the storms of the last few days, which had added such hazards to our enterprise, were nothing but forerunners of this enormous disturbance which spreads over Asia at this season every year. The rains, which are torrential over the rest of India, become a solid deluge within a few hours of reaching the mountains. Tomorrow the skies would open and the flood would be upon us; but we heard the news calmly enough now that we were clear of the mountain.

A coolie handed a scrap of paper through the door of the tent: it was a note from Schatz, who had gone on ahead to discover an easier crossing of the Miristi Khola gorges than we had made on the way up, and who now wrote that the volume of water had doubled in a single afternoon. So it became urgent to get away from this valley, which might easily become a vast trap, and though we said nothing we were all thinking of what had happened on Nanda Devi.

As forecast, the weather was bad next morning and rain fell ceaselessly. The Sherpas broke camp with feverish haste. We had given them orders to distribute to the coolies, before leaving, all the food we were unable to take down with us. The porters pounced gleefully on the tins and tubes which Sarki and Angtharkay threw into the air by handfuls. Here was unlooked-for baksheesh! Oudot, on the contrary, was beginning to run short of essential medical supplies. Bad luck lent a hand, too, for the needles had been dropped, and the syringes broke as he struggled with my arteries, which were practically impossible to find.

The situation was serious; there were only two ampoules of acetylcholine left. Lachenal had had his two injections and my arms and right leg were done, and there we had to stop; but I was unmoved by this news, which so distressed the others. I lay there like a dying man, in a state of extreme nervous excitement, knowing that these sessions were a terrible strain on my general condition.

While the last loads were leaving the camp under Angtharkay's supervision, Lachenal started down. After a few yards the coolies abandoned the stretcher and the sledge was tried, but with no success, Oudot sent for the *cacolet*.

'We *must* get away at all costs,' he said.

Before fixing him in it he gave Lachenal an injection of morphia. For me they found a wicker basket. The Sherpas hoisted me up and tucked my legs into a sleeping-bag covered by a *pied d'éléphant*. Everything was soaked. From the walls all round us came echoes of rumbling avalanches mingled with the continual noise of falling stones loosened by the rain. The porters' naked feet sank into the soggy ground of the moraine on which they were walking, and we sent boulders flying down as we went. We were like the ragged remnant retreating in a disorderly rout from the scene of some catastrophe.

The column, composed of the two invalids, and of Oudot, Terray Couzy, Ichac, Sarki and eight coolies, moved with painful slowness. Should we be able to reach the pre-arranged stopping-place before night? Judging by the time we had taken on the way up it *should* have been possible, even easy, but seeing the porters struggling beneath the weight of their burdens, and constantly sliding on the moraine where every step was a problem, we began to have our doubts. Time was getting on. The clouds lifted and the rain stopped for a while. We lacked torches and food: Angtharkay, unaware of our difficulties, had not made any provision for the party in the rear, so Sarki was sent on ahead with a message.

We were soon completely lost in the featureless country with neither colour nor horizon. The scree of the moraine had given place to enormous boulders surrounded with a prickly vegetation which hindered our movements still further. The porters showed great fortitude, and made no complaint. Night fell and three torches discovered among our baggage were brought into action. The Sahibs guided the coolies in the mist and the rain which had started up again harder than ever. It was past 8 o'clock when the porters and their burdens, anxious, exhausted and disheartened, halted after an acrobatic descent of a slippery chimney down which somehow or other we had managed to come.

Lachenal and myself were placed under shelter, the others judged that we were in no fit state to go any further that night. Terray decided to stay with us, while Couzy, Ichac and Oudot went off rapidly towards the camp. They had only just left us when they met Sarki and Phutharkay coming up—with nothing but a flask of coffee by way of supplies! They sent Sarki on up to us and took Phutharkay back with them to the tents, which they reached after an hour. They told Schatz and Noyelle that it was not possible to carry the two casualties over such dangerous ground at night, and described our wretched bivouac. Immediately Schatz offered to take us up food and equipment, and Dawathondup went with him. In our shelter the situation was not ideal, in spite of Terray's efforts to cheer things up. Lachenal was still under the influence of morphia, but I was serious that we had failed to reach the camp, which I knew to be so near.

When we were no longer expecting anyone, Schatz arrived; water streamed down his face as he raised his startled eyes to mine, and with a little smile announced triumphantly that he had brought up sleeping-bags, warm clothing and food. What more did we need? Soon a petrol primus was roaring away. None of us had eaten since the morning and the smell of the open tins of food made Terray's mouth water. Meanwhile Dawathondup had inflated the mattresses and, though the food did not tempt me, I enjoyed the comfort of a mattress. All night long it rained and I could not sleep. Deathly cold, my teeth chattering, I was haunted by anxiety and a shameful fear.

In the morning the weather improved. The formation of the clouds had changed, and they now tended to creep along the walls, and move upwards. When this happens in Chamonix it means fine weather. Getting back into my wicker basket was unpleasant. Lachenal, too, found little pleasure in returning to his *cacolet*. We were in a hurry to reach the camp and every few minutes I kept asking:

'Are we there?'

I always got the same answer, as though I were a child:

'Five minutes more!'

At last we saw the yellow roofs of the tents at the far end of a small flat space. The sky was clear when we reached the camp where Ichac, Noyelle and Oudot welcomed us. We were not yet at the end of our troubles; the bridge which Schatz had built would not hold out until the evening: already it was only a foot above the water, and would in any case have to be reinforced before the loads and the casualties could be taken across. None of the coolies would volunteer to carry us over, and even the Sherpas thought it dangerous. Finally Ajeeba made up his mind, and the others stood by to help him, at the start and at the finish. From my tent I heard Lachenal being taken across, then Ajeeba returned, I was hoisted on his back, and with a firm step he went towards the bridge. This consisted simply of four or five tree-trunks lashed together with liana and fixed somehow or other to either bank; the river went swirling by beneath, only just clearing the bridge, and spray wet the porters' feet, making them liable to slip. The feeling of helplessness was awful, I wanted to shut my eyes. But I had to look, and though he carried me with great care I whispered in Ajeeba's ear:

'*Slowly*, Ajeeba!'

Would he be able to keep his balance on this rickety, slippery foot-bridge? Oudot, who was watching the operation, tried not to show his anxiety; his expressionless smile was intended to be encouraging. The moment we set foot on the bridge I could feel the precariousness of our situation. Ajeeba calculated his moves and put each foot forward gingerly.

'*Slowly*, Ajeeba!'

The water raced by, forming eddies which made me dizzy to look at. The Sherpas on the other side were not far off now. I was afraid that my bearer would quicken his steps as we approached terrafirma. Again I murmured:

'*Slowly*, Ajeeba!'

A few inches more—and then helping hands brought us safely to the bank. I heaved a deep sigh of relief, but at the same time felt a strong desire to cry: the inevitable nervous reaction after such an ordeal. Ajeeba took me at once into a tent and settled me there while the rest of the party hastily crossed the river, which was rising visibly. The coolies queued up to cross, and two hours later everything had been taken over. The expedition would not be trapped in the Annapurna massif, though by the following morning the bridge would have gone—swept away by the rushing torrent.

Oudot began to examine us at once; he feared that the cold and damp of the previous night would have caused a deterioration in our condition. Lachenal's feet were very swollen and the improvement of the last few days was arrested. As for me, it was mainly my right hand which had suffered from our unfortunate bivouac. Oudot had assured me that the damage would not go beyond the end joints of my fingers. Now he said that at least two joints would have to go. All these emotions tried me sorely.

We all gathered together in one tent for lunch. Schatz, who the day before had gone off to reconnoitre the Miristi gorges, told us that there was not the slightest chance of our being able to follow these gorges direct to Baglung and the Gandaki Valley. This route would have avoided a long détour, but it was quite impracticable: gigantic walls fell sheer to the river's edge over a distance of several miles, so that almost immediately we should have been forced to climb up out of the gorge to the ridges above—in other words to take the same route by which we had come on April 27th.

We decided to dispatch Pansy as a special messenger to New Delhi to send off the telegrams we had written a few days ago.


I took little part in the conversation. When my attention was not needed I preferred to doze and not to think about the present. My strength was ebbing and I dreaded the next stages of the march. After examining me once again Oudot did not hide the fact that it was difficult, in view of the extensiveness of my injuries, to foretell the course things would take. With half-closed eyes I heard him explaining to Ichac how dry gangrene can turn into gas gangrene which necessitates immediate and extensive amputation. Ichac shuddered when Oudot told him that the toxins spreading from the affected parts to the living tissue become diffused over the whole body and produce general septicaemia. Or sometimes it concentrated in one organ, the liver for example, particularly after antibiotic injections such as penicillin.

Meanwhile Terray was adroitly constructing a chair in the shape of a hook, like those used for carrying in the Alps. He made it out of sticks fastened together with wire—it would enable the legs to be supported at the same level as the rest of the body, thus avoiding the wounded man's principal cause of suffering. The Sherpas copied Terray's model for me. The rain drummed ceaselessly on the tents, almost making us wonder whether the canvas would give way beneath the enormous bullet-like drops.

After a bad night I woke slowly and was told that the weather had improved. If only it would keep fine till evening! Today, they told me, we should have to go up from 12,000 to 15,000 feet over extremely steep slopes without any hope of a bivouac site before the Pass of

April 27th. At all events the chairs were satisfactory. Thanks to Terray's ingenuity both Lachenal and I were slightly less apprehensive about the next stages of our journey.

The coolies climbed up steadily, although there was no track and sometimes steps had to be cut in the earth, so steep was the slope. Noiselessly as ghosts, they laboured heroically through the mist to complete the allotted stage before nightfall. Shadows appeared and disappeared, outlines faded into the mist. This retreat would have seemed like a dream, and the men mere phantoms, had it not been for the jolting of my chair, which caused pain in every part of my body. I tried my best to keep drowsy and semi-conscious, and envied Lachenal who managed to go to sleep on the back of his porter.

A little before noon the main contingent had ascended the grassy gullies and reached the C.A.F. shoulder—the point at which Schatz had left a Club Alpin Français pennant on the way up. The coolies wanted to camp here, saying that higher up there would be no better site, but Ichac and Oudot turned deaf ears to this suggestion. They sent the casualties ahead and themselves walked with the Sherpas; the coolies were obliged to follow. The long, long traverse across to the Pass of April 27th had begun.

Visibility was down to ten yards, and the porters walked in single file. They kept warm while they were moving with their loads, but as soon as they stopped their teeth began to chatter; their only clothing was a small blanket. I tried to adjust myself to the swaying rhythm of my bearer, but he continually upset my calculations by hesitating, taking a longer or a shorter step, or, in certain awkward places, striding sideways. I could not stop trying to stretch out my arms in an endeavor to hold back or help on, or with the idea of protecting myself. Far away in the depths of its infernal gorges I heard the roar of the Miristi.

At the end of the afternoon we came upon the site of a shepherds' camp, the only one before the pass, which there was obviously no question of our reaching that evening. Prudence demanded that we should remain where we were for the night, and all that I asked was to be put down in a tent where I could lie still.

Dawn was sullen and we left in pouring rain, with visibility less than twenty yards. Today we had to continue the flanking movement and cross a whole series of streams, which would be no easy matter. It was a sad day for me. I felt quite definitely that my condition was getting worse: I was aware that I had no reserves and I was profoundly disheartened.

For some time Schatz had been trying to encourage me with the assurance that the ridge was not now very far off. There came a shout of triumph, but although Ichac was only a few yards away I could barely hear him:

'Maurice, you're on the Krishna side now!'

I was not particularly elated, although it was an important moment. As I passed in front of Ichac I saw him shooting with his cine-camera. It struck me as a crazy proceeding—surely it would not come out—there was no light, and this, as he had often enough told me himself, is essential for colour film.

We began to descend gradually to the pass. At each step the porters let themselves slide down the slope, feet foremost, and the violent jerking caused me unbearable pain. It was raining harder than ever. In the mist we tried to find the camp site, and while the others went on looking, the porters continued down to a gap marked by a *chorten*. I could not understand what was happening: it had been understood that we should stop at the pass. Those on ahead, forgetting about the others, no doubt thought that we should have time to reach the edge of the forest, which was more than two hours away. I protested. To go on was madness, and, moreover, I just did not feel capable of standing another couple of hours of this torture. I had no strength left and was ready to give up the ghost. I implored Ichac to stop everyone and go up again to the site which we had passed. Very unwillingly, those in front retraced their steps, while the Sherpas pitched the tents on the soaking ground.

We had now come to the last really hard day: we should have to descend for some 6000 feet to the Chadziou Khola and the shepherds' camping ground. How would all the porters manage, especially those who would have to carry the two casualties across the terribly steep slopes on this part of the route?

Right at the beginning, on leaving the gap marked with a *chorten*, one of the coolies slipped and rolled down for fifty yards or so. We feared he would disappear into the river 6000 feet below but he clung on and brought himself to a stop; for a moment he lay stretched out on the ground. The sack he had been carrying went bowling down the slope as well as a container, which burst open. The sack bounced, described a fine curve and disappeared into space. The man was only dazed; he picked himself up and came back towards us. He was a Tibetan from Tukucha, and one of the few who had consented to wear expedition boots!

I heard a frightful yell. I could not see what was happening, but

I could guess from the shouts: a huge stone had fallen above Lachenal in the couloir. Terray succeeded in diverting it from its course, but the rock had hit Lachenal's bearer. The man fell without being able to protect himself; his arms were caught in his *cagoule*, and the block hit him on the nose. His face was covered with blood and he had an enormous bruise.

Ichac, Rébuffat and Schatz went down the great grass couloir, the haunt of the marmots discovered by Rébuffat on the way up. They stopped at the first trees while the rest of the party came carefully down in their turn. To find out the owner of the sack that had fallen into the Chadziou Khola, they decided to check the loads as they were carried past on the porters' backs.

'I think it was mine,' said Schatz, 'and for once both my fountain pen and wallet were in it!'

Schatz was staring at a porter—he lifted up a sack that was concealing another and saw the name written plainly for all to see on the main pocket: 'M. Schatz.'

'There's no doubt,' said Ichac, proceeding by elimination, 'it must be Gaston's.'

Rébuffat was not pleased. This retreat had been an ordeal for him, too: and his frost-bitten feet were still giving him some trouble. I saw him sitting down disconsolately, thinking of what he had lost. Suddenly Ichac had an inspiration.

'Gaston, look what you're sitting on!'

He shot up like a jack-in-the-box and read on the sack 'G. Rébuffat'. The lost sack turned out to be the only one which belonged to no one: it contained spare clothes.

We were now in the forest, which was extraordinarily thick and tangled; we felt as if we were walking through submarine scenery in a damp unhealthy jungle, expecting at any moment to meet hideous monsters. It was here that, on the way up, we had seen those giant rhododendrons of such magnificent shades of red. We entered the 'triumphal way', a natural archway of flowers, which we had noticed on the outward journey. The coolies in front had stopped here—and why not? There was a general halt and soon fires were crackling. Oudot was of the opinion that the hardest part of this stage still lay ahead, and he wanted to go on at all costs. He gave me fresh injections of morphia and spartocamphor—these were the more painful because I had grown so thin, and I lost consciousness for a few moments. I felt the eyes of the Sherpas and coolies upon me. What a sight I must have been! There was a new expression in their eyes, which I had not seen before. Was it pity, or grief, or a kindly indifference? Before we left, they arranged on my knees a garland of the most beautiful flowers they could find. This gesture touched me deeply, and from now on during the whole course of our long retreat, whenever it was possible, the Sherpas never once forgot to put flowers beside me.

Now began the descent through the dead trees of the dense jungle. The Sherpas went ahead, and with great sweeps of their *kukris* cut away the branches and bamboos that barred the way. The ground was soaking and everyone kept slipping—there was scarcely a man who did not fall that day. Couzy, Ichac, Oudot, Schatz and Terray went on to reconnoitre the route; Noyelle according to plan, was always one march ahead, and Rébuffat stayed with Lachenal and myself. The injections Oudot had given me were very effective: I was completely worn out, but I felt less pain, and most of the time I dozed with my eyes half shut. Lachenal followed immediately behind me. The last bit before the river was particularly steep, and I would never have given myself one chance in a thousand of coming through alive. The slope was practically vertical and the minute track crossed it at an angle; the coolies had to cling to the trees growing alongside.

My bearer was in trouble; he could move neither backwards nor forwards. Finally he pressed himself up against the wall and went along sideways step by step. The hook-shaped chair in which I was stowed hung right over the precipice. Now and again the Sherpas dug their ice-axes into the wet ground and clung to them desperately the better to help my bearer. I was painfully aware of the slightest jolt. With bulging eyes I looked under my feet at the swirling Chadziou Khola into which I was in danger of falling at every step. If the porter slipped there would not be a chance—perhaps he would be able to stop himself, but who could stop me? I no longer had the strength to fight my fears, and I knew now what fear really was. Lachenal also was petrified by fright. Fortunately for him, his arms were free and occasionally he was able to help himself. Every step was a reprieve, for it brought us nearer our goal. Before we arrived there was one last ordeal. For about five yards the track, which was already sketchy, disappeared entirely. A little ledge ran across a slab of rock and the feet had to be shuffled along it. My bearer carried on with great courage—my admiration for these men who unhesitatingly tackled such dangerous work was unbounded. He moved along sideways, clinging to the smallest holds and letting the other porters guide his feet into the next steps.

At long last we reached the Chadziou Khola, swollen by the

monsoon rains. Lachenal followed me over this dangerous crossing, and for all his fear, seemed completely master of himself, whilst I was a mere human wreck. Standing shoulder to shoulder and holding each other up, the porters succeeded in bracing themselves against the force of the current. We climbed up a hundred yards through strongly scented jungle and then, in the distance, I saw the shepherds' camp.

The porters halted before making this final effort, but after a few minutes I asked my bearer to get to the camp as quickly as he could. At the foot of a cliff it seemed to me that he took the wrong direction—on the way out we had traversed across, but the Sherpas who accompanied us seemed to be quite sure of the route. On we went, and the way ran up such a steep grass slope that we had to adopt the technique we would have used for traversing on ice. The Sherpas persisted, and here we were, embarked on a regular climb. I called nervously to Ichac to intervene, saying that we were about to have a frightful fall, but the porters were obstinate. We were beneath a sort of cornice overhanging a practically vertical wall and the rock was rotten. Perched up on my bearer and sticking out a yard from the rock, I was able to gaze into the very depths of the gorge below me. The Sherpas were worried and told me that my bearer would not turn round—he must go on. I could not stand any more, and called for help—but still, I reflected, my luck had held during many a long day. After a few steps the going became easier and we got back on the grass and picked up the track which we ought to have followed from the beginning, and which Lachenal now took, profiting from our experience. We reached the camp just as the rain stopped.

As I went into my tent I longed for nothing but peace and quiet. I scarcely had the strength to speak, but I murmured to Oudot that the hard part was over now—there was a good path as far as Lete. I remembered a larchwood near the village and beautiful meadows dotted with granite boulders which reminded me of the Chamonix valley. During the long retreat I had thought of this idyllic little wood as a welcoming haven. I hoped we should make a long halt there, and my friends agreed. It was unnecessary for everyone to go up to Tukucha and back again to Lete. We would reorganize the whole expedition in this wood before beginning the long trek homewards through the valleys of Nepal to the Indian frontier.

'Where's my ice-axe?' I asked Schatz.

I set great store by it, as Lachenal had lost his, it was the only one to have been to the top of Annapurna. No one had seen it since we had left Base Camp. Schatz inspected all the Sherpas' axes, but it was not to be found. I felt this loss deeply. Though in itself it was of no importance, I had intended to present the axe to the French Alpine Club on my return. (It turned up two days later.)

The next day we had only a short march. As Oudot reckoned that we should reach the woods of Lete before midday, there was no need to hurry, and we might just as well enjoy the few rays of sun that had appeared as if by magic. The coolies started off and then we, too, left the shepherds' camp.

We arrived together at Choya and were enthusiastically received. The inhabitants rushed towards us and looked at the casualties with curiosity. Dawathondup's throat must have been dry with the thought of the pleasures of the outward journey, and Angtharkay volubly explained to Ichac and Oudot that this would be an excellent place to pitch camp—there was water, wood and food.

'Good place!' insisted our Sirdar. There was also good chang at Choya. But somehow the Sahibs did not seem to understand. *En route!* Unwillingly the party moved on, and soon we came to the banks of the Krishna Gandaki. Its clear, pure waters had become a dirty black flood, foaming and swirling and making an infernal row. We crossed over by a bridge without any incident, and after a short hour's walk at last reached the resting-place of which I had dreamed so long.

We chose a good-sized grassy site, bounded by three enormous granite boulders, and surrounded by the soft green of the larches— a cool and restful place. The wind played among the tall trees, and, closing my eyes, I fancied myself back in Chamonix, in the Prin Wood or at the Pendant. The tents were pitched where the Sherpas pleased. The sun was warm, and Oudot decided to make his examinations out of doors. One of my feet had begun to suppurate, and my hands were in an awful state. There was a most unpleasant nauseating smell; all the bandages were soaked with pus. Oudot broke into his last reserves of dressings—he knew that fresh equipment would be coming from Tukucha. For the first time he took his scissors and began 'trimming', or cutting away the dead and affected parts. My feet did not hurt too badly, but my hands were so sensitive that the slightest touch made me cry out in pain and I broke down—I could fight no longer. Oudot decided to stop. He painted the wounds with mercurochrome.

'Stay outside while I do Lachenal,' he said.

Lachenal's condition had improved. He had come through the ordeals of the retreat very well indeed, and his morale was high, now that we were down in the valley; his excellent appetite had not deserted him.

In the afternoon Ichac, Oudot and Schatz left for Tukucha, where they were welcomed by Noyelle and G. B. Rana. That evening, in the few tents still standing, they talked at length, but not very cheerfully, for their main topic was Lachenal's and my condition. Oudot was of the opinion that I would undoubtedly have to undergo an operation before we reached the Indian frontier, which would not be until the first fortnight of July.

The next day the dismantling of the camp was completed before a circle of coolies and children who squatted there hour after hour, keeping a look-out for tins or old tubes of milk. Noyelle saw to paying off the porters, and there was a grand distribution of rupees. In the afternoon Oudot finished his preparations and left to return to Lete and his patients.

Twenty-four hours later everything was ready for the others to leave the village which had given us such a kindly welcome and had been our headquarters for nearly two months. The coolies and the inhabitants paid their farewell respects to the Sahibs with a series of shouts. At 4 o'clock everyone was back at Lete.

The condition of the casualties—of myself in particular—was now distinctly alarming; Oudot on his return the day before, had pronounced the situation critical. He had been hard at it since morning, resuming the agonizing injections. I presented an increasingly distressing picture. I had lost three stone and become extremely thin. The fever got steadily worse—that evening my temperature was 105°!

'102°,' announced Ichac without batting an eyelid.

I was oblivious of everything now, most of the time unconscious, in a coma.

'Heavy doses of penicillin,' ordered Oudot.


Shadows appeared close by out of the mist. They leant over, then disappeared noiselessly. The silence awed me. I no longer suffered. My friends attended to me in silence. The job was finished, and my conscience was clear. Gathering together the last shreds of energy, in one last long prayer I implored death to come and deliver me. I had lost the will to live, and I was giving in—the ultimate humiliation for a man who, up till then, had always taken a pride in himself.

This was no time for questions nor for regrets. I looked death straight in the face, besought it with all my strength. Then abruptly

I had a vision of the life of men. Those who are leaving it for ever are never alone. Resting against the mountain, which was watching over me, I discovered horizons I had never seen. There at my feet, on those vast plains, millions of beings were following a destiny they had not chosen.

There is a supernatural power in those close to death. Strange intuitions identify one with the whole world. The mountain spoke with the wind as it whistled over the ridges or ruffled the foliage. All would end well. I should remain there, for ever, beneath a few stones and a cross.

They had given me my ice-axe. The breeze was gentle and sweetly scented. My friends departed, knowing that I was now safe. I watched them go their way, with slow, sad steps. The procession withdrew along the narrow path. They would regain the plains and the wide horizons. For me, silence.

# 18

## *Through the Paddy Fields*

I cried out as I felt a little stab of pain: Ichac had just given me his first injection, and was quite agitated. The rain poured down incessantly, giving us a melancholy send-off. Oudot had hesitated about giving the order, but it was now June 19th and high time we were off. Lachenal and I were laid on stretchers made for us by G. B. Rana, but before I sank back again into apathy I gave a last fond glance round the little wood.

The party began to move off, with Rébuffat, who had found a horse, prancing beside us. We forded a stream coming down from Dhaulagiri, the coolies standing shoulder to shoulder to brace themselves against the current. Ichac and Oudot undressed and crossed over with great dignity in their underpants. They had lost weight after all the events of the past weeks and their bodies were slim and youthful-looking.

When we came to Dana we felt that we had really left the mountains behind us. Here were fields of maize, banana trees, and heat, as we made our way down towards the main valleys. Even after all we had been through, we hated to feel that we were now leaving—for good, as well we realized—the scene of our great adventure.

One after the other, our coolies left us; in spite of all our offers even Pandy would come no further. The valley climate did not suit him, and great beads of sweat rolled down his body. There was also another reason—he had earned a lot of rupees and reckoned it was enough. He would not have known what to do with more money.

On the afternoon of the 20th, as we were going along an easy path, the sun, which we had not seen lately, came out for a few minutes, and we halted under some huge banyan trees for lunch. It was an ordeal for me: I revolted at the mere idea of food. Oudot had become my tormentor—he insisted on my taking nourishment, and the others all tried to get me to swallow something. Ichac and Terray tried every means: sometimes they reasoned with me, sometimes they cajoled, until at last they got angry and threatened:

'You won't last more than a few days at this rate.'

If only they would realize how cold this argument left me! When they had finished their vain appeals, Oudot turned up; he wasted no time in making a tactful approach, but simply commanded me to swallow what I was given:

'You must finish up those kidneys. I'll be back in a moment to see if you have. Surely you don't want to be forcibly fed.'

Sarki cut up the beastly kidneys with his dirty, sticky hands and stuck them on the end of his knife to feed me. For ages I chewed away like a child without being able to swallow. Oudot would be certain to come back! He was my bogeyman . . . There! That's one bit down! I felt that it would choke me and that I would bring it up again immediately. Hell! Still all that to swallow. Oudot came back, looking stern: 'You're not trying, Maurice!' Turning towards Sarki, he ordered him to carry on . . .

Every meal was like that.

Under the banyan trees the air was cool. Nice plump chickens ran about unsuspectingly. If I could have one of these, now, that would be a change from the tough mutton whose very smell nauseated me. A peasant was ready to sell us one on condition that we caught it ourselves. He had hardly finished speaking when G. B. Rana grabbed his gun and fired. The chicken was cut in half and ended its existence in a casserole. Angtharkay brought it to me in triumph, for it was quite an occasion if the Bara Sahib actually wanted to eat something.

My particular coolies, who came from Dana, were extraordinarily expert; four of them carried me as though I was a feather. Among them there was a one-eyed fellow of about fifty who was full of the kindliest attentions towards me. At every halt he would explain that there was not much further to go, and that they knew the paths. My confidence in their strength and ability gave me courage; if a single coolie had stumbled, either Lachenal or I might have been hurled down hundreds of feet. Sometimes the stretcher would be at an angle and I would have to make desperate efforts with knees and elbows to stop myself sliding. When I could not do so I called out, and a Sherpa would run up and hold me on. These alarms were nerve-racking and I asked for a Sherpa to remain constantly by my side. Sarki was detailed to do this and he stayed by me the whole time. He gave me fresh water and bananas, helped me to eat, and inflated my mattress at each halt to keep the stones on the path from sticking into me. I had grown so thin that the least irregularity hurt me.

One night we camped near Banduk at the foot of a huge waterfall.

The rain teemed down as I lay in my tent, but I scarcely heard the onslaughts of the monsoon as I tried to get to sleep. I was thinking of the nightmare descent, and it seemed to me to be physically impossible to bear such a prolonged agony. Though the smell from my dressings made everyone feel ill, no one uttered a complaint; but I often came very near to fainting myself.

Ichac slept by my side, and at last I dropped off too. In the middle of the night I woke with a start. It was pitch dark. An overpowering force made me sit up and a horrible fear held me in its grip. I had the dreadful feeling that I was about to die, and I was deafened by the sound of bells. Where was I? I cried out loud. The light went on, and to my enormous relief I realized that I was in the tent, and remembered I was part of the Expedition. Ichac was alarmed:

'What on earth's the matter?'

I tried to explain to him that appalling sensation of nothingness.

'Must have been a nightmare,' he said. But all the same he left the light on and talked gently until I had quietened down again.

First thing next morning I spoke to Oudot about it. He told me that morphia sometimes produces such reactions, and from then on I resolved never to take morphia again; I would rather bear the worst pain than pay that price for relief.

Near Beni we were told there was an epidemic of cholera, so we had to avoid the village by crossing the Gandaki by a bridge spanning the whole breadth of the swirling, unbridled torrent. But this bridge, which was 200 feet long and suspended 50 feet above the river, gave us a good deal of anxiety. It was made of two chains with bent rusty rods supporting some old worm-eaten planks, and its length caused disquieting oscillations which could become alarmingly violent. The *cacolet* would have to be used. Lachenal went first, and after a few yards he began to cry out. Some of the Sherpas helped Ajeeba, who was carrying him, by holding back the rods to prevent Lachenal's feet from being hurt. When my turn came I tried to bear it all with as much courage as I could muster, but though the Sherpas held back the rods and Ajeeba walked as carefully as he could, the swaying made me feel horribly sick. On the other side I joined Lachenal and the two of us howled in concert before the embarrassed coolies.

G. B. Rana intended to make his horse swim across. Several nylon ropes were tied together and from the opposite bank everyone hauled on the animal. The unhappy beast resisted heroically, for he smelt danger. He was thrown into the river willy-nilly and immediately disappeared beneath the water. From time to time his ears, a leg, or a flank appeared—surely he would be a corpse when he arrived. Not a bit of it! A few yards from the bank a head emerged and gradually the horse scrambled on to terra firma and advanced on us with Olympian calm.

It was late and we pitched camp near the river. But cholera was raging on this side too, and the next morning, after an unforgettable session of 'trimming', we hastened to leave this unhealthy district.

It was raining every day and when we had to find shelter that evening we cursed and swore. We wanted a house where we could all be together, where we should have more room to sort things out and where, too, we should no longer hear the exasperating noise of rain on the roofs of the tents. When we reached the straggling hamlet of Kusma we were in a quandary, for there was no suitable house and the 'authorities' whom we had approached conducted us to the gompa! We settled ourselves without ceremony, and soon, from the sacred place which we supposed to be no longer in use, there arose a cacophony of bawdy songs.

Some of the party saw to paying off the coolies who had to go back to Dana, and recruiting others to come on with us to Tansing. Schatz collected the equipment and checked the loads; Couzy, who had been unanimously elected cook, peered into all the open containers. Everything was uncertain: we did not know whether we should have enough coolies to enable us all to leave next day. We were told there were another five marches. Actually it took us over ten days.

Some fifty patients awaited the Doctor Sahib. They had all kinds of diseases, mostly inflammation or unaccountable fevers. It would have taken a long time to see all the patients, and required a lot of medical supplies, not to speak of endless patience on Oudot's part. He drew up a standard questionnaire:

(1) How old are you?
(2) Do you sleep well at night?
(3) Have you a good appetite?
(4) Where is the pain?
(5) Do you cough?

This questionnaire was given to Noyelle who translated it into English for G. B.'s benefit, with the help of a few words of Hindustani, and G. B. translated it into Gurkhali. The replies had to follow the reverse order, and after all these intermediaries they were often pretty queer. The Sherpas were doubled up with laughter. They could only understand part of the conversation—the last bit that began in Hindustani, went on into Gurkhali and then came back in Hindustani. By this stage it had suffered a farcical change!

Oudot had tremendous prestige. People came long distances to see him, for he had become a sort of god. We admired the touching simplicity of these creatures who put their health and sometimes their lives in the hands of a complete stranger. It was the first time they had been examined by a real doctor. When they were ill they consulted the village witch doctor, or so-called 'healer'. The great panacea was always the same—an ointment of cow-dung.

The patients were not always very tractable; they were bound by the dictates of their religion, and they did not like it when Oudot touched them. The hardest job was to examine the women, who were excessively modest and would not allow themselves to be touched on any account, still less undressed. On one occasion Oudot succeeded in getting all the finery off a Nepalese girl. When she was half undressed Sarki, who had been helping, discreetly lit the tent. Nothing would then persuade the girl to proceed further.

Medicine had to be dealt out to all of them. Whenever he could, Oudot gave them something relevant to their ailment; otherwise distributed inoffensive pills which had a mainly psychological effect. But there was no knowing what they might do with the thing. They would unhesitatingly swallow anti-sunburn ointment or the most solid of plasters, and cheerfully swap medicines given for particular illnesses. But they showed great courage in any surgical treatment.

One day an unfortunate youth came along with a double compound fracture of the wrist. The radius stuck out from a mass of pus, the arm was enormous, and the hand swollen out of all recognition. He was certainly in a bad way. Oudot—always by the same complicated process of interpretation—discovered that the accident had happened a fortnight ago. He told the parents that amputation of the arm was the only way of saving their son. They refused, and made it plain that all they wanted was a dressing. Well, it could not be helped. Oudot gave the patient morphia and then tried to get things back in place: he succeeded after a fashion and finally put the arm in plaster.

'What will happen?' I asked Oudot anxiously. There would be no one to change the dressing, and in a few days the wound would begin to suppurate again.

'There's nothing else to be done. He'll probably be dead in a fortnight.'

He said this with a fatalistic air which rather frightened me. Yet he was right. It was not possible to reason with these people as if we were in Europe—here we were still in the dark ages. I thought of all these unfortunate people who were a prey to epidemics against which they had no means of protecting themselves: no doctor, no vaccine. In countries like these death gets its own way easily and the process of selection is intensive. On our long homeward march we often met funeral processions, and it was not cheering for Lachenal and myself to see the biers, so like our own litters. The corpses were swathed in strangely coloured winding sheets and were preceded by horns whose notes re-echoed back and forth among the mountains. The families and friends of the deceased followed in silence, showing no undue sorrow. Death was but a period of transition and had no distressing implications. Were they not assured of reincarnation in other and more perfect shapes? The bodies were buried along the banks of the Krishna Gandaki, and the monsoon floods would carry them away down to the sacred Ganges.

Every day Oudot attended to the injured members of the Expedition. He was perpetually running after his medicine chest, which was invariably either right on ahead, and then we had to catch up with it, or else far in the rear, and we had to wait ages. But neither Lachenal nor I was ever in any hurry for the M.O. to get to work. Gradually the injection of large quantities of penicillin began to take effect; the fever abated and the fear of generalized septicaemia receded. I began to talk and to take an interest in what was going on around me. One day on a green sward at Putliket, Oudot started performing on me as usual.

'Don't make such a noise!' he begged me.

'Gently, Oudot, please!'

'I'm being as gentle as I can. Look out—does that hurt?'

I braced myself with all my strength to bear the pain, and clenched my teeth:

'It's all right, I didn't feel a thing.'

'Good!' said Oudot, and gave a great snip with his scissors.

'Ouch!'

I felt a shock all over me, and Oudot announced:

'The first amputation! The little finger!'

This gave me rather a twinge. A little finger may not be much use, but all the same I was attached to it! Tears were very near. Oudot picked up the joint between his finger and thumb and showed it to me.

'Perhaps you'd like to have it as a souvenir? It'll keep all right, you know! You don't seem very keen?'

'I certainly don't want it. There's no point in keeping a black and mouldy little finger.'

Throwing the 'souvenir' casually on to the lid of a container, Oudot said:

'Well, you're no sentimentalist.'

The line of demarcation between the living tissue and the dead was now clearly visible. Oudot worked with a *rugine*,[1] and every day one or two joints, either on my feet or my hands, were removed. All this was done without anaesthetics, in the open, how and when it was possible.

One day Oudot would operate in a native house, another by the side of the road, amidst the unavoidable dust; sometimes along the rice-swamps in spite of the damp and the leeches; or again in the middle of a field, in the rain, beneath the uncertain shelter of an umbrella held in the shaking hand of G. B. Rana's orderly. Without respite Oudot cleaned, cut and dressed.

While these sessions went on, and we casualties endured our tribulations in a nauseating stench—blood everywhere, pus dripping from the bandages and hundreds of flies sticking to our wounds—we were often, paradoxically, spectators of amusing incidents. Now, after the first rains, came the season for planting the rice. All available labour was busy in the rice-fields, and to find porters became the Expedition's worst headache. The others were very perturbed: we *had* to get out of these parts at all costs. Oudot begged G. B. Rana to use his authority and employ high-handed tactics to recruit coolies. He reminded him that we were under the protection of the Maharajah, who would not tolerate our being held up at the moment of leaving his country. G. B. did all he could, but his efforts had no success.

Gradually our attitude hardened. Although we had offered to supplement the ordinary pay, we soon saw that, unless we paid exorbitant prices, the further we penetrated into the densely cultivated areas the greater our difficulties would become, until we just should not be able to advance. For all their reluctance to act as slave-drivers, my friends were obliged to employ a system of 'voluntary' recruitment. The method was simple: we had to get men where they were to be found, take them by the seat of their pants and place them very

[1] A surgical instrument used for scraping bones and separating living and dead tissue.

gently underneath the loads and the stretchers. The men objected strongly at first, but it ended in smiles. They would get enough rupees to wipe away all regrets on the one side and all remorse on the other. The Sherpas tumbled to the operation perfectly, and I imagined that we were not the first Himalayan expedition to employ this method. They would stroll innocently about the villages sniffing the air, ready to pounce upon the first native whom they judged capable of carrying a load.

Under the lee of a house right in the centre of the little village of Garomboree, I lay exhausted after a session with the surgeon's knife during which I had undergone several amputations. I gazed blankly at the bustling activity of the stony main street. The Sherpas had gone coolie-hunting, and a porter belonging to the Suba of Tukucha who, the day before, had given me a superb sword of chased silver, had gone with them. He took our side and held forth louder than anyone. He had a stentorian voice, and the teeth of a savage, which terrified me: I was always afraid he would take a bite out of me. Suddenly Sarki, Angtharkay and Ajeeba shot out of a nearby alley pushing before them four bewildered rice-planters. In a twinkling all their tools had been taken away and after some 'friendly' propelling, hey presto, here they were! One after the other the 'volunteers' arrived at the scene of action as the enrolment went ahead.

We moved along in single file in the rain. As the day was drawing to a close and a strange and restful quiet reigned in the green countryside, the Sherpas spotted a fisherman, going home with his net well filled, walking slowly along ahead of us. Ajeeba nudged Phutharkay and Sarki, picked up a cudgel and advanced stealthily. There was a sudden scuffle: away went the captive's net and line and his bags of bits and pieces, and a few moments later he found himself at the right front end of my stretcher, marching in step with his new friends. Poor fisherman! The Sherpas softened their tone, explaining that he would have to go on as far as Tansing, but that he would have a handsome number of rupees by way of compensation. The fisherman cried, and begged, and if he had not been prevented would have knelt down and chanted a dirge. But as there was nothing to be done about it, he finished by smiling. 'Well, that's a good one on me!' he appeared to be thinking.

Every day during our retreat, such scenes were enacted, for every night a number of coolies deserted, preferring to forgo the rupees owing to them. The situation became critical. The Expedition wa scattered over several villages, and sometimes the front and the rear were separated by two days' march. Some groups were brought to a standstill in lonely places where it was impossible to find even the trace of a coolie.

On June 29th, at Darjing, twenty-five coolies were missing at the roll call—and the weather was appalling. A former Gurkha N.G.O., who sported a magnificent cap, had, for several days, been playing a queer and rather sinister role as he prowled round the Expedition without any discernible reason. His conversations with the coolies were always followed by desertions; he harangued them and made trouble. Ichac came to Oudot and myself and said:

'If this chap has such a bad influence on the coolies it may be that he has some authority.'

'Yes, but if he uses it in this way, we shall end up like Harrer,'[2] replied Oudot.

'Perhaps we could conciliate him and make good use of his influence,' suggested Ichac. 'Why not employ him—use him as a recruiting sergeant?'

So we engaged him at ten rupees a day. He was not exactly a desirable character. If he managed to enlist coolies by bringing pressure to bear on the Subas of the neighbourhood, he also possessed an immoderate liking for chang and for the pretty girls of Nepal. In the evening yelling mobs threw themselves into wild dances which went on until far into the night. The next morning our recruiting sergeant reported for duty, seedy-looking and with tired eyes; but he braced himself up and was soon off on the quest for volunteer porters.

For days on end, through the most fantastic country, we descended the high valleys of Nepal to reach the plains. After following the Krishna Gandaki for a whole week to Kusma, we had to abandon the route we had taken on the journey out: the waters of this great river were now so high that the crossings had become hazardous, if not impossible. So at Kusma we left the Gandaki and crossed a range of fairly high hills to rejoin the Andhi Khola Valley which runs parallel to the Gandaki, the banks of which were still negotiable. We rejoined our outward route again at Tansing.

The Expedition had turned into a limp and anaemic body

[2]Harrer was a member of a German expedition, who, during an extraordinary trip, crossed the Himalaya, followed the course of the Brahmaputra and finished by settling in Lhasa where it is said he was chief engineer and then commander-in-chief of the Tibetan army.

straggling without much spirit on a course the reason for which escaped us. We were buoyed up by a single wish: to get to India as quickly as possible. This interminable descent of the valleys of Nepal, in endless rain and in the damp heat of the monsoon, had a bad effect on us physically. The others had lost their energy and they dragged themselves miserably along the little walls of the rice-fields, plodding listlessly on and taking no interest in anything.

Couzy and Terray brought up the rear. When we got near to the frontier, Noyelle went on to Gorakhpur, with the object of making arrangements with the Indian railways for our return journey. In the centre of our formation were Oudot, Ichac, Lachenal, Rébuffat, Schatz and myself. Every day Lachenal was more restive; he could not endure the least delay and swore at the coolies. During halts we sometimes found ourselves side by side. He was reading the Expedition's only thriller—by small instalments, so as to savour it all the better; it was, I gathered, the story of a headless man—I never got further than that.

'What a lot of time we're wasting!'

'We'll have to be patient, Biscante; things aren't always easy. Think of the difficulty of recruiting volunteers!'

'What about G. B.! Don't you think he could bestir himself a bit?'

'The heat depresses everyone after all this hard going.'

'Oh, hell!' burst out Lachenal, his patience exhausted. 'I just *can't* stand all these chaps round us day in and day out, gesticulating, and bellowing a gibberish that you can't understand a single ruddy word of! You make signs to them to come near, and they put down their loads! You make signs that you want to drink, so they bring you bananas! Oh, for my house in Chamonix, my wife and the kids!'

'There's not much further to go now. After Tansing it's two days' march to India. It's no longer a question of days but of hours. All I ask for is a good nursing-home with a modern operating theatre, masses of medical supplies, dressings which are changed continually . . . and nice thick ones at that!'

The fact was that for some time our cotton wool had been getting scarce, though Oudot saved all the usable pieces. The surgical spirit had all gone and the needles had to be disinfected in my eau-de-Cologne.

'Thank God we've got our M.O.,' acknowledged Lachenal. 'I can't think what we'd ever have done without him. For one thing, you wouldn't be here now! But don't you think he could be a bit more gentle? God, how he hurts sometimes! You know, these surgeons, when they're on the job they don't worry about whether people are under an anaesthetic or not, they go on just the same—cut, snip, stab. Oh, what miserable wretches we are!'

And what a duet we set up! But how pleasant it was to complain!

# 19

## *Gorakhpur*

The party had become gradually accustomed to the nomadic life which we had been leading for the last few weeks. Sometimes we made our way along the slippery little walls running between the rice-fields, but the stretchers were too wide for this and had to be carried right through the fields. This reminded me of those medieval lords whom, as a child, I had pictured trampling down flourishing crops for their pleasure. Sometimes we proceeded in single file along tracks that took us right through the middle of strange maize-fields where the gigantic plants towered several feet above our heads.

During the halts the coolies would squat round us, taking it in turns for a puff at the same cigarette. Their religion forbade them to put their lips to tobacco, source of an impure pleasure; but they got round this difficulty by inserting the tip of the cigarette between thumb and forefinger, curled round to form a little bowl; putting their lips to this they inhaled without touching the tobacco, and so obtained an innocent delight.

As we approached Tansing the weather improved, and it was the sun now that made us suffer. The flies swarmed over my saturated bandages and there was nothing I could do about it. A Brahman came up and embarked on a long prayer; listlessly I answered, 'Atcha! Atcha!' As far as I could make out he said he was a sun worshipper: it was not quite the best moment for such a declaration, and I wished him and his sun to the devil!

He gesticulated continuously while he droned on. I got tired of him and my eyes strayed to the freshly rain-washed sky. Suddenly my attention was caught by an object—unless I was mistaken it was an umbrella that the Brahman carried under his arm. Immediately I began to take an intense interest in what he was saying, and after a few moments I got him to understand that his umbrella would be most useful to me, and we continued to converse under its restful shade as he held it over us, trotting along beside the stretcher.

Another two hours and we were at the end of our march. While Sarki fed me with an astonishing number of bananas I heard cries and protests: it was Angtharkay hastening the poor Brahman on his way with a few well-placed kicks. I asked our Sirdar what it was all about and he explained as best he could:

211

'Bara Sahib, he's a robber, not a porter! He wants to be paid four rupees for the march! And where is his load, I should like to know!'

My Brahman, seeing that I was inquiring about him, came up, jabbering incomprehensibly. Angtharkay went on:

'Bara Sahib, he says he worked as he went along, that it tired him greatly, and that it is only natural he should be compensated for his trouble.'

'Give him two rupees.'

He was bitterly disappointed.

We were nearing Tansing and there was now no danger of the porters deserting us; they all wished to go to the 'big town', and trotted along briskly.

'There's Pansy!'

'Can't be!'

Pansy, who had been gone a long while and about whom we were beginning to feel concerned, came up quite unruffled, with his usual pleasant grin, as though he had only been away a few moments. Everyone rushed to greet this splendid Sherpa who had just completed a nineteen days' march with only one halt, at Delhi. There he had stayed for forty-eight hours.

'Here's the post!'

'Any letters?'

It was almost unbelievable; for the first time we were going to get news from France. The letters were soon distributed and faces disappeared behind sheets of notepaper.

'My wife's not very well,' Ichac told me, 'the last letter was written some time ago. I wonder how she is.'

'I say, there's going to be another Himalayan expedition!'

This was surprising news.

'Well they must be feeling tough!'

'How many are going?'

'Where are they going?'

There was a cross-fire of questions and answers. Not everybody received good news; some of the party looked worried or anxious as they resumed the march.

In the distance a green hill appeared. Sarki pointed with his finger:

'Tansing, Bara Sahib, Tansing!'

Were we nearing the end?

Next day, after a heavy shower, though we had to go down a very muddy path full of potholes, the porters no longer walked, they flew. Tansing was only a few hundred yards away; already we were on the outskirts. Here again were the little stalls, the motley and inquisitive populace. We crossed the town and came out at last on a wide level place where we pitched our camp. Terray shifted the loads about eagerly and sang at the top of his voice—a good sign—the one and only song he knew: '*Au son joyeux des balalaikas.*' Everyone had taken fresh heart.

Just for a change Oudot did some operating that afternoon. During this session I lost my second big toe and the thumb of my right hand. It began to rain and I was taken into a tent, where for over an hour I listened in terror to Lachenal's cries as he underwent his first amputation. I was terribly upset by his sufferings, especially when I heard him protesting: 'No! No!' as though he could not resign himself to losing anything so precious.

Next day the 'authorities' were received at the camp. The Governor, who impressed me most favourably, seemed very well disposed towards us. Why should he not help us to recruit coolies? He promised to do so at once. It was now the morning of July 4th and in a few hours' time porters would be at our disposal—a great relief. Officially, G. B.'s assignment would come to an end in two days' time, at Butwal, but I wanted him to accompany us as far as Katmandu. There was no doubt he would be very useful to us there, but I was chiefly concerned with giving him a richly deserved reward. G. B. was agreeable, and promised to make the necessary application to the Maharajah. A few hours later he burst into the tent, his face wreathed in smiles, and announced that the Maharajah had given permission for him to go to the capital.

Before leaving for Butwal, our last stage, I wanted to spruce myself up a bit. I asked for a barber, for I had a beard like an ancient prophet. G. B.'s orderly undertook to go and fetch one, and he returned soon after accompanied by a Gurkha with a hang-dog air and revoltingly dirty. I was apprehensive as he approached, but I hugged the thought of his razor which would skim my cheeks so delicately. Water was brought and my Gurkha began to soap me. He used some primitive stuff which was not soapy, nor did it lather, and he rubbed my face with it vigorously. All ten fingers as well as his palms were energetically employed and the massage became painful.

'Bechtari, Bechtari!' I said, 'Gently!'

But the man seemed quite determined. Soon the beard was ready. He rummaged in his box and drew out an instrument which I did not at all like the look of. It was a small steel blade, very short, fixed between two bamboo sticks. The whole thing looked most peculiar.

The barber seized hold of my face roughly with his smelly hands and began to 'shave' me. The blade dragged the hairs and with his fingers he plucked them out one by one most conscientiously. I yelled blue murder, but he scolded me and took not the slightest notice of my protests.

Oudot poked his head into the tent with an almost triumphant expression:

'I'd rather have an amputation,' I shouted, 'than the attentions of this savage!'

After an hour my cheeks and chin were more or less presentable. Now for the moustache! I was most particular about its shape. He started and I could feel the blade, which really did cut this time. I pursed up my lip—there was nothing left at all! The session was over. My tormentor had the effrontery to demand an exorbitant fee. Marcel Ichac gave him three rupees in a lordly manner and told Sarki to send him packing.

Lachenal was sent on to Butwal in the first contingent, in charge of Rébuffat. I followed in the second. Everything around us was so green that I did not recognize the route by which we had come three months ago. Towards evening we topped a hill. Ichac was beside me:

'Look, Maurice!' he said.

He asked the Sherpas to place my stretcher so that I could look back at the country we were leaving. Everything breathed an indefinable melancholy at this twilight hour. Did this feeling come from the sight of these high valleys, of the vast mountains which we could see on the horizon, or from the memory of our almost incredible struggles up there; or was it because we could feel reality already changing imperceptibly into dream? Ichac and I gazed in silence.

In a few minutes we should be back in contact with the world outside. The wonderful adventure which linked us to these mountains would soon belong to the past. Already the porters were preparing to lift me up: the long procession must resume its way. With my forearms I tried to touch my face, which felt all wrinkled—and surely my hair must be quite white. My heart was full, and I looked away; jolting along in silence, we went in search of shelter for the night.

Before getting to Butwal next day we met Noyelle, who had returned from his mission to Gorakhpur:

'Hallo, boys!' he called out from a distance, directly he saw us, and it was not long before he was with us.

'How are you? Is it hot in India?'

'Terribly enervating—like a Turkish bath.'

Noyelle told us the carriers would be at Nautanwa station on July 6th—that was next day. There was no time to be lost. In a heavy storm and a deluge of rain we arrived at our old camp at Butwal, where we found Lachenal. The latter part of the day was given up to more operations, and often I nearly fainted.

All the loads were assembled. But the question was whether the lorries would be there next day to take us to the terminus of the Indian railway where we were due at 10 o'clock. I begged G.B. to do what he could. So off he went at once, in the middle of the night, through a stretch of thick and unhealthy jungle, to reach Bethari. On the morning of July 6th the lorries arrived! It was a triumph for G. B. and I congratulated him warmly. We paid off the porters and embarked for Nautanwa. The jungle was full of monkeys, who were not in the least alarmed by our presence. One of the lorries had a burst tyre, and the one I was in broke down. However, it all turned out all right, for out of the two crocks we made one sound one.

At last we came to Nautanwa and settled ourselves into the two palatial carriages reserved for us. By early afternoon all the loads were aboard and the train moved off towards Gorakhpur. All sorts of plans were brewing. Everyone wanted to get back to France without delay. All the members of the party, who for three months had shown exemplary courage and patience, were now ready to do anything to gain twenty-four hours. But the various individual wishes were hard to reconcile. As far as I was concerned, I intended to make every effort possible to keep the promise I had given at the start to visit the Maharajah of Nepal. Oudot would accompany me to Katmandu, and Ichac and Noyelle would come too. The others would go on to Delhi and wait there a few days. Lachenal, to avoid the heat, would go up to a hill station, such as Mussoorie.

While these plans were being debated, Oudot was busy at his job, scissors in hand, trimming feet and hands yet again in spite of the temperature—113° in the shade—and the swarms of mosquitoes. We were nearing Gorakhpur. Now for Lachenal, and look sharp! In another two hours the Expedition would split up, and for nearly a week he would be deprived of our M.O.'s care.

In the carriage we were shaken about like dice in a box and it was difficult for Oudot to operate: he took advantage of the stops to perform his amputations. Between stations everything was made ready: the dressings had to be unwrapped, things sorted out, chemicals prepared, and the scissors held out for Oudot to start work the second the carriage was at rest.

'Come on, your turn, Biscante!' said Oudot hurriedly. 'Sarki . . . '

He made a vague gesture that meant: 'Clean up all the muck round the Bara Sahib.'

With foresight Lachenal had removed his dressings himself and presented his first foot to the executioner ready for the sacrifice. At the station before Gorakhpur two toes from his right foot went. The three others would have to be done at Gorakhpur itself.

'Gently, Oudot, please, gently!'

'I swear I'm doing everything I can, Biscante. I can't do more. Come on, quick!'

Lachenal held his foot with both hands. With his eyes starting from his head, he pleaded with Oudot.

'Gorakhpur,' said Schatz, 'we're there!'

The train slowed up. Couzy, Rébuffat, Schatz and some of the Sherpas got ready to jump on to the goods wagon. All the equipment had to be rapidly loaded into other trucks which were coupled to the Lucknow train, due to leave in an hour.

Great beads of sweat were pouring off Oudot. He trimmed and trimmed again without paying much attention to poor Biscante's cries: there was only half an hour and he still had another toe to cut. Altogether it made a considerable number since he started. This time the scissors were too big.

'Quick, Matha, the little scissors.'

The train stopped at this moment with considerable jolting. 'Damn!' The scissors had fallen down inside the window-slot! Oudot was at his wits' end.

'While I go on, try to get them.'

'It can't be done. You can't take a great door like this off it's hinges all in a minute!'

This was not at all to Lachenal's liking; but that big toe had to be done.

'But I don't want you to do it! Gently, gently . . . ' he said between sobs.

Natives appeared at the doors.

'Get the hell out of here!' roared Oudot.

They did not understand what he said, but they obeyed, which was the main thing.

'No, Oudot, please!'

This time Oudot was at the end of his patience. He stopped and looked at Lachenal:

'Really, it's a bit much! You might be a little more obliging.'

This left Lachenal speechless. If it is a matter of being obliging, he said to himself, he can cut off both arms and both legs!

The train was due to leave in a few seconds. Crowds were moving about all the time on the platforms, and getting in our way. The moment the bandages were on, Terray seized Lachenal and carried him off. We just had time to call:

'Goodbye, Biscante! Cheer up! See you in Delhi!'

Things had to be cleaned up now; the nauseating smell drove even the natives away. Sarki and Phutharkay set to: they opened the door wide and with a sort of old broom made of twigs they pushed everything on to the floor. In the midst of a whole heap of rubbish rolled an amazing number of toes of all sizes which were then swept on to the platform before the startled eyes of the natives. Whistles blew, the carriages jolted, and amid cries and shouts the train started. We drew out alongside a mass of humanity. I just had time to spot Terray, who waved us goodbye with a pair of boots.

Lulled by the rhythmical song of wheels on rails, my thoughts turned to that remote capital whither we were bound, a city indeed of the Thousand and One Nights.

## *There are Other Annapurnas*

In our compartment of the Indian O.T.R. Company train Ichac, Noyelle, Oudot and I lay silently on the long seats, refreshed by the cool breeze blown on us by the fan. Our thoughts wandered and gradually darkness fell.

After a twenty-four hours' journey across the plain of the Ganges, in what for us was unheard-of-comfort, we arrived at Raxaul, on the frontier between India and Nepal. The transfer of our baggage at the Nepalese station was quickly effected under the supervision of Sarki and Pansy, who were accompanying us to Katmandu. Sarki had not left me for an instant since Annapurna, though it had not been an easy job for him. I often thought of his great thirty-six, hour march to establish the liason upon which the whole fate of the Expedition depended. Katmandu was for him a dream city of which he scarcely dared to think; he had earned this reward a hundred times over, and so indeed had Pansy, a Himalayan veteran whose devotion and quiet good-nature made him a most lovable character. Our Sirdar, Angtharkay, had not been able to come with us: huge floods in his home district had made him very anxious, for he had a large family, so he had asked us to let him go direct to Darjeeling. The farewell scene at Gorakhpur had been most touching, when the Sherpas received, in addition to their pay, generous baksheesh as well as their personal equipment, a matter of considerable value—even by European standards it was the very latest thing. Each in turn had come to salute me, with hands joined together, Indian fashion. Some of them, like Phutharkay, bowed slowly with a gesture of respect, then, touching me with one hand, they placed their foreheads against my clothes. For all their satisfaction at being through with this expedition which would remain for them, as for us, a great memory, they looked sad, and their regret seemed quite genuine.

The Maharajah had detailed an officer to look after our comfort and bring us to Katmandu. But there was bad news: the train would not leave till the next day. We were disappointed, but not surprised: the Nepalese rolling-stock consisted of only three engines! Happily the delay was cut short, thanks to the initiative of our three liaison officers—Noyelle, G. B. and this Nepalese officer. General Bijaya, Minister of Foreign Affairs, and son of the Maharajah, had telegraphed for a *wagon-de-luxe* to be put at our disposal, and this would be coupled to a goods train, which was due to leave at 3 A.M. next morning.

In the middle of the night and to the accompaniment of the piercing noise of crickets, insects and other creatures, we settled ourselves as well as we could in the luxurious compartments. The others were already sound asleep when the train drew out; there was such a jolting that I was afraid of being shot out of my bedding. The track had a gauge of two feet! The tiny coach balanced precariously, pitching and rolling enough to make one sick, and I could not sleep a wink.

We crossed a particularly dense and unhealthy jungle, and in the morning reached the terminus where the Maharajah's officer ordered a really nourishing breakfast for us. Outside, a Chevrolet lorry was waiting for the baggage, and an American station-wagon for ourselves. I was put in the front of the car. It was the first time I had sat up for a month, but I was so thin that I could not appreciate the comfort as much as I should have hoped. It should only have taken a few minutes to travel the nineteen miles to Bhimphedi; actually it took over two hours. The road was narrow, but good, and we crossed numbers of rivers by prefabricated bridges. This is the only road in Nepal and the inhabitants are extremely proud of it; it is, in fact, an important arterial route and the only means of reaching Katmandu. We climbed up gradually, followed by the lorry with the delighted Sherpas perched on top; here and there the road ascended in zigzags. Many of the houses had corrugated iron roofs—the ugliest boon that western industrialism has conferred on these remote people. At 11 o'clock we reached Bhimphedi where horses and 'dandies'—a sort of sedan-chair—were awaiting us. The road went no further. To get to Katmandu, where we were due to arrive in the evening, we had to follow a mountain path unfit for cars. Oudot was tired out and suffering from some very painful boils, so he chose a 'dandy' rather than a horse, and so did I.

The path zigzagged up a steep slope, but the coolies were wonderfully skilful and adjusted their steps so that we felt not the slightest jolt, and the bearers changed over without slowing down the pace. All day long we continued. The 'dandy' was too small for me and I was obliged to curl myself up while trying to protect my bandages. I could not remain seated for long, and Oudot gave me injections of solucamphor to help me bear up. Rest-houses, at the disposal of the guests of the Maharajah, were spaced out along the route. At 1 o'clock we came to a fort manned by Gurkhas, a Vauban-style building of which the Nepalese were very proud. After a quick lunch in the rest-houses, situated in the top of the fort, we set out again; we still had a long way to go, and two passes to cross, to reach Katmandu.

My position became unbearable; the only thing was to do what I had already tried during the dark days at Lete—to sink into a kind of stupor and try to forget my present suffering. There was a pass at about 6500 feet which would take us over the hills that blocked our view. Looking up I saw huge cables going right across the valley and wondered if it could be a cable railway. So indeed it was, the longest in the world, I learned, measuring nearly nineteen miles. It provisioned Katmandu and the surrounding neighbourhood, a population of some hundred and fifty thousand people.

The others, who had good mounts, had ridden on ahead. They would wait for us at the beginning of a carriage road. A carriage road? I showed surprise when I was told that a car would take us to Katmandu. How had a car got there? It certainly could not have come along the rough track which we ourselves had had such difficulty in following. I gathered some scraps of information:

'Cars are brought by coolies.'

Turning towards Oudot, I said:

'Then they must be manhandled along these paths. But it isn't possible, just look at the angle!'

In some places they could not have walked two abreast. And the metal bridge we had just crossed was barely five feet wide.

'They're not *pushed*, they're *carried*.'

It was incredible. There were lorries, too, it seemed. But what about those two passes, over 6000 feet high? Then it was explained to me. The cars, without their wheels, are lashed on to huge platforms carried by anything from fifty to seventy coolies. They avoided the greater part of our route by following the river beds, where the coolies walk barefoot. They cross the two passes in the same manner: at such points the track was wider and the zigzags less acute. Marching in step, bent under their yoke, the coolies sing rhythmical chants to help them along. It has thus been possible to construct a network of roads for about twelve miles round Katmandu; and about a hundred cars are in circulation.

It grew dark and the coolies laboured as we neared the pass, for they had had a hard day. From this point, they said, there is a splendid view of the Himalaya. Below, at the opening of this celebrated valley of Nepal, lies the plain where Katmandu, historic bulwark of the country, displays its hundreds of temples, shrines and palaces. It must be a wonderful view; unfortunately it was dark when we arrived at the pass, the sky was overcast, and I did not know how the porters could see their way. There was no question of making a halt, even though I was so utterly fatigued that I was ready to give up the ghost. My situation reminded me forcibly of the cages in which Louis XI kept his prisoners.

But there, in the distance, were electric lights! Next day I learned there was a power station on the banks of the Bragmati. The hours went by and the lights were long in drawing nearer. It was pitch dark as we passed through the sleeping villages. I had not even the strength to groan audibly.

Some time about midnight a small village loomed up. Shadows flitted about, and I felt that this was the end, and so indeed it was: a little further on an old American car stood waiting. The coolies had to be paid, and the baggage loaded on to a lorry, while I took my place beside Oudot in the car. At this precise moment, a puncture was discovered and it took a quarter of an hour to change the wheel before we could be off. A frightful storm caught us en route: torrential rain drummed on the bodywork of the car. It was a bad road, and the springs of our car were broken.

We went up a drive, passed a Gurkha presenting arms, and at one o'clock in the morning came to the Maharajah's rest-house. There were shouts of welcome from the others who were waiting for us: Ichac, Noyelle, and G.B. came out to meet us, and I was delighted to see our Minister to India, Monsieur Christian Belle. He was in charge of Nepalese affairs, and, in spite of the absence in France of our Ambassador, Monsieur Daniel Levi, had immediately decided to come and present the members of the Expedition personally to the Maharajah. This very good friend of ours, who already knew all about our adventures, was shocked by my condition.

Here, at last, the first time for months, I should be able to enjoy a few days' rest. There was furniture—tables—a refrigerator! There was even a bathroom. But all this counted for nothing beside what awaited us on the table: a bottle of Alsatian wine! I felt quite giddy and was all set for an orgy—but the dignified turbaned butler dispensed the precious liquid with so much ceremony that I remembered my manners. It was a welcome surprise to hear that I would have a bed. The plan was that we should remain here until July 11th, inclusive: for me this meant three days of rest and good food; for the others, three days of visiting the fascinating capital. All the life of Nepal centres on Katmandu.

The others got ready to see the sights of the town, but before setting off Oudot trimmed my four wounds, and told me to keep the bandages off my feet and hands for most of the day. This was rather a problem: I must not touch anything, I must keep my four limbs in the air, and be on the look-out for flies and mosquitoes. Time, I feared, would drag while I lay like this, and I had a horror of all these insects that carry every imaginable germ. When flies settle—they are much larger than the European kind and have red bellies—they stick like leeches. My fears were only too well justified: when, later, at Delhi, Oudot took off my dressings he found that my foot was harbouring a lot of wriggling maggots. At the approach of the surgeon's tweezers, they withdrew into their holes. By the time we reached Paris these maggots had grown huge, and there was quite half a pound of them. At first I was horrified—I was being spared nothing! I never got over my horror, in spite of Oudot's paternal explanations that maggots would clean wounds more effectually than any modern product. They were even, he said, deliberately introduced into certain wounds.

The others came back delighted with their sightseeing. They had visited a number of temples decorated with designs of carved wood and some extremely original statuettes. Nepal had once known a period when the arts had flourished greatly.

Next day preparations were made for the *durbar*—the audience with the sovereign. Noyelle told us that the ceremony would be held in the late afternoon and would be divided into two distinct parts: the first would be the official ceremony, the second a reception of a far more personal character. We were all most excited at the thought of the durbar—we had heard so much about it. Exact punctuality was called for; we must be not a minute early, nor a minute late; the protocol was very strict. Apart from Monsieur Christian Belle, who would be in the uniform of a Minister Plenipotentiary, we should all be wearing the precious white dinner jackets we had lugged all the way from Paris. We now had to transform ourselves from mountaineers and explorers into men of fashion, courtiers even!

At the appointed hour, our two large cars entered the palace grounds. At the gates Gurkha sentries presented arms. There was a magnificent approach through a formal French garden, laid out with a lake, round which we drove slowly. Soldiers of a complete mounted unit rode towards us, dressed in red, with long drooping moustaches, and carrying tall spears. We came out on to a concrete square in front of the Maharajah's palace, and the others quickly got out and ordered me to be carried in on a chair. Soldiers ran up and helped me to take my seat. Mounting the steps of the palace, we were received by His Highness, Mohun Shumsher Jung Bahadur Rana, Maharajah of Nepal. He came forward to meet us dressed in a white uniform glittering with amazing decorations and jewels of inestimable value. His headgear alone was made up of outsize precious stones; there was one diamond in the centre about four inches across. A moustache in the style of the Emperor Franz-Josef added greatly to his dignity.

He came towards me with a kind and fatherly look, and I greeted him respectfully, Indian fashion, holding my bandaged hands together. He said he was happy to welcome me to his palace and to congratulate me and my friends. We went up the rest of the steps together and entered the great hall ablaze with light where the nobles of the kingdom were assembled in hundreds, and their ranks fell back to make way for us. We went right across the hall to the far end, where seats had been reserved for us near the throne. The Maharajah himself arranged the carrying-chair so that I could follow the ceremony properly. I looked round me in amazement; everyone wore the same uniform as the Maharajah, though of course theirs were not so splendid; diamonds, emeralds and rubies glittered and sparkled. It is astonishing that there still exist such fabulous treasures and courts so out of keeping with our times.

As we were, after all, a few minutes in advance of the officially appointed time, I had leisure to gaze on the princes of the line placed in order of succession: Baber, Kaiser . . . these names were always completed by Shumsher Jung Bahadur Rana. About fifteen of them were sitting silent and still. The Maharajah's official function is that of Prime Minister, an hereditary post that descends, according to well-defined rules and regulations, to his brothers or his sons. The King of Nepal, Tribhuvana Shumsher Jung Bahadur Rana, who is practically never seen, even by his subjects, represents the spiritual powers. On the right were further rows of princes, dressed in the same glittering uniforms, and sitting in an exactly defined order of precedence. Then came the ministers, the chiefs of the army, and all the high dignitaries and notables of Nepal.

'How's it going?' whispered Ichac, who was sitting next to me.

'Pretty awful. I don't think I can hold out much longer'

In fact, while I kept this upright position my wounds began to suppurate through the bandages. Ichac, too, was embarrassed: the etiquette here was extremely strict—as strict as anywhere in the world. It was not proper for a guest to take photographs. But photography was highly appreciated in this country, and the assembly shut its eyes to slight lapses of etiquette. From time to time there was a flash as Ichac rose discreetly to take a picture. Then he resumed his role of guest. The official court photographers had enormous cameras on tripods which they adjusted with meticulous care, as if they were afraid of losing their heads should the picture turn out unsuccessfully. They watched Ichac condescendingly, no doubt writing him off as an amateur—photographs could not be taken casually like that!

Monsieur Christian Belle got up and addressed a speech in English to the Maharajah. He thanked him in the name of France for the special permission granted to us to penetrate into the interior kingdom; Nepal now could claim the highest mountain that man had climbed. As a mark of gratitude he presented the Maharajah, on behalf of the President of the French Republic, with a modern Aubusson tapestry. The art is unknown in Nepal, and there was general astonishment when we explained that it was not a carpet to be laid on the floor, but a sort of embroidery meant to be hung on the walls like a picture. The silence which up till then had been absolute was broken by murmurs of admiration.

Order was restored when the Maharajah rose in his turn and replied to our Minister. He said he was happy to have given us permission, and it could not have been used to greater advantage. This permission, which indeed was something quite exceptional, showed how favourably disposed he was to further the good relations between France and Nepal, which had once bound together his father and Silvain Lévi, the great French scholar and expert on Sanskrit.

While he was speaking the hereditary princes looked furtively at each other and consulted their watches. Only a few seconds to go, according to schedule: was etiquette going to be transgressed? No! The Maharajah wound up, and after a few courteous words the ceremony came to an end and the dignitaries disappeared as if by magic.

In a few minutes the unofficial ceremony would begin. Already a number of people had appeared in undress uniform; black suits, hats of trimmed fur, and a single badge—the Gurkhas'—consisting of two gold kukris intertwined. The Maharajah reappeared in the hall wearing a single decoration—the Grand Cross of the Legion of Honour. The general tone had changed: the rest of our party were talking with groups of ministers and hereditary princes who were admiring the tapestry on a large table. The Maharajah came towards me and for a few minutes we chatted together with great cordiality. I expressed my great liking for his country, so little known to the rest of the world, and told him what an excellent impression G.B. Rana had made upon me. Immediately he was promoted lieutenant and his pay doubled! G.B. was greatly moved: diffidently, and from a respectful distance, he made profuse signs of gratitude, and, bending double, saluted the Maharajah in the curious fashion with which we all were now familiar.

Behind the stiff exterior of these warriors, who, as their history shows, are assuredly not always very gentle, I was surprised to find such gentleness, such kindness towards myself. Suddenly, everyone stopped talking, and people came in respectfully bearing some little caskets. What was happening now! The Maharajah rose; I was carried to the centre of the great hall and the Court stood round us. The British Ambassador and the Indian Ambassador and his attachés, who had just arrived, were also present. Ceremoniously, and with great majesty, the Maharajah opened the caskets and explained to me that he had been instructed by the King, who was ill, to confer upon me the highest Gurkha order in the country, given only to troops in time of war—the Gurkha Right Hand, for valour.

With deep emotion he spoke these simple words:

'You are a brave man, and we welcome you here as a brave man.'

No other decoration could have touched me more deeply than that of these valorous Gurkha warriors. Although I was near to fainting in my chair I endeavored to say a few words. I expressed my thanks for this unexpected distinction, and said that I was but the intermediary and that it was the entire Expedition which had thus been honoured. Immediately the Maharajah congratulated me upon the decoration which I had been awarded. Then the princes of the line, the ministers and the diplomats filed past me with their congratulations. The party broke up into small groups. From time to time the Maharajah and his son, General Bijaya, came up to me to inquire if I was all right or to ask questions about the regions of eternal snow. This Annapurna venture had intrigued and disquieted them. We hoped that if national misfortunes followed, they would not attribute them to us for having infringed the divine law.

It was time to leave; I could not bear any more; my duty had been fully accomplished. The others realizing this, we said our farewells to our host. His Highness and his son, followed by the other personages, accompanied us with pomp to the great staircase. I was in a fever to lie down, but just as we were descending the steps I heard some brief orders being given, and the cars which were driving slowly up came to a halt. A tune rang out, a kind of waltz which had a familiar sound to French ears. Everyone stood to attention. When the tune came to an end I turned, rather astonished, towards the Minister of Foreign Affairs, and by way of comment, was about to say 'Nice of you to play us a French tune!' Lucky for me that I said nothing: the Minister leant towards me and asked in a low voice:

'What do you think of our national anthem?'

'Oh . . . magnificent, and very moving for us Frenchmen . . .'

At that moment the Marseillaise rang out. We were all surprised and deeply touched to hear it in a country so remote from our own. The performance must have involved laborious practice.

We all fell silent, and the Maharajah bade us a last farewell. We saluted him respectfully and entered our cars. The dignitaries were ranged on the steps on either side of the great staircase. Orders were given, and the cars moved slowly off, while the Marseillaise was played a second time.

That evening the others dined at the British Embassy and sent off a friendly message to Tilman, who was then in the Annapurna region. Next day after a well-earned rest we visited one of the ancient capitals, Bhadgaon, where we found some Hindu temples whose splendour never ceased to astonish us. In the centre of Katmandu, in the square beside the temple, we admired a statue of Kali the Goddess. The others went to see the renowned Buddhist *stupa*[1] at Swayambhonath, crowned with a tower made of concentric circles of metal.

The next day, July 12th, we left Katmandu, and according to custom, on leaving the rest-house we were each hung round with a magnificent garland of sweetly scented flowers. The Maharajah, who was full of thoughtful attentions, had ensured that my return should be effected without discomfort or fatigue, and I was borne on a very comfortable kind of litter carried by eight men. The all-too familiar jerky movement began again as we wound up towards the pass.

G.B. accompanied me as far as the first bend. He had served us most loyally and as an expression of my personal appreciation I made him a present of my revolver which, during all the war years,

---

[1]Monument to the dead, enclosing the ashes or relics of the Buddha, or else simply a memorial.

had never left my side. It is an unknown weapon in these parts and he deeply touched by this memento, which for the rest of his life would remind him of our joint adventure.

G. B. could not bring himself to leave me. He saluted me with great emotion, walked beside me for a time, and then gradually dropped behind. The path wound up towards the hill and was soon lost in the jungle. The garland of flowers spread its scent around me. G. B. wore an expression of infinite sadness and the tears ran down his brown face. I looked at the mountains in the blue distance. The great giants of the earth were there assembled in all their dazzling beauty, reaching up to heaven in supplication.

The others were far ahead. The jolting began again, bearing me away from what would soon be nothing but memories. In the gentle languor into which I let myself sink, I tried to envisage my first contact with the civilized world in the homeward-bound aeroplane, and the terrible shock of landing at Orly and meeting family and friends.

But I could never have imagined the violent emotional shock that I should in fact experience when it came to the point, nor the sudden nervous depression which would then take hold of me. Those surgical operations in the field, the sickening butchery that shook even the toughest of the natives, had gradually deadened our sensibilities, and we were no longer able to judge the horror of it all. A toe snapping off and chucked away as a useless accessory, blood flowing and spurting, the unbearable smell from suppurating wounds—all this left us unmoved.

In the aeroplane, before landing, Lachenal and I would be putting on fresh bandages for our arrival. But the minute we started down that iron ladder, all those friendly eyes looking at us with such pity, would at once tear aside the masks behind which we had sheltered. We were not to be pitied—and yet, the tears in those eyes and the expressions of distress, would suddenly bring me face to face with reality. A strange consolation indeed for my sufferings to have brought me!

Rocked in my stretcher, I meditated on our adventure now drawing to a close, and on our unexpected victory. One always talks of an ideal as a goal towards which one strives but which one never reaches. For every one of us, Annapurna was an ideal that had been realized. In our youth we had not been misled by fantasies, nor by the bloody battles of modern warfare which feed the imagination of the young. For us the mountains had been a natural field of activity where, playing on the frontiers of life and death, we had found the freedom for which we were blindly groping and which was as necessary to us as bread. The mountains had bestowed on us their beauties, and we adored them with a child's simplicity and revered them with a monk's veneration of the divine.

Annapurna, to which we had gone empty-handed, was a treasure on which we should live the rest of our days. With this realization we turn the page: a new life begins.

There are other Annapurnas in the lives of men.